"It's great when someone with 25 years' experience of successful sales and business shares their learning. Trevor has modelled top performers, combined it with his own skills and created a unique and universal approach. Successful selling is about helping buyers be successful. This book helps you and your buyers."

—MICHAEL BEALE
NLP TRAINER AND BUSINESS COACH | AUTHOR, COACHING PROGRAMME ESSENTIALS

"TSB is the manual that's missing from every MBA. It's also enjoyable and, more importantly, it works!"

—MIKE O'HARA
CEO, HIGH FREQUENCY TRADING REVIEW | OWNER, VOICES IN BUSINESS

"Clear English, a focussed approach, and lots of entertaining stories – a really great resource for any young Asian entrepreneur."

—MICHAEL SHER
HEAD OF CUSTOMER SUCCESS & SOLUTIONS GROUP, HP SOFTWARE, ASIA PACIFIC AND JAPAN

"I've believed for quite a while that 'selling' is an outdated concept. It's helping people to buy that matters. Turning Selling into Buying helps individuals and teams deliver real results. I've seen it work well for self-employed entrepreneurs and I'm now also seeing it work just as well for the 'intrapreneurs' who are employed by the best enterprises to lead their business units."

—PROFESSOR BRUCE M. FIRESTONE,
ENTREPRENEUR-IN-RESIDENCE, TELFER SCHOOL OF MANAGEMENT, UNIVERSITY OF OTTAWA
FOUNDER, OTTAWA SENATORS | DIRECTOR, EXPLORIEM.ORG
BROKER, CENTURY 21 REALTY INC. | AUTHOR, QUANTUM TRILOGY

"I've led several successful start-ups in my career and never seen a personal sales process as effective as this. I wish the front line sales that worked for me then had used this book. They'd have been more productive, and life would have been much easier without their guesses, assumptions and fabrications."

—RICHARD WOODFIELD BA, MA
CEO, PARALLAX GROUP PLC AND APAMA INC. UKMSL, WARWICK UNIVERSITY

"The 21st Century needs new business processes. TSB is independent of culture, is easily learned, and reliable. It's what every sales manager and CEO craves – repeatability, efficiency and productivity."

—FRANZ KÖPPER, CEO
SERIAL TECHNOLOGY ENTREPRENEUR, ZÜRICH, SWITZERLAND

See over for readers' videos...

Follow the QR code above
or go to *turningsellingintobuying.com/book-videos/*
to watch readers talking about this book

We all live by selling something...

It's all just common sense, but it's uncommon to do it consciously.

With thank to my late parents - Frank & Sheila Wilkins

Sorry I never stopped long enough to listen to your stories

Turning Selling *into* Buying

Skills, Words & Actions
that
Build a Willing Buyer
for your
Ideas, Products & Services

Trevor Græme Wilkins

Turning Selling into Buying

Copyright © 2013 Trevor Græme Wilkins of Principium Press

Turning Selling into Buying® is a Registered Canadian Copyright
Fearless Selling® is a Registered Canadian Copyright
TakeAway™, Convincer™, Commit Analysis™, ABC Analysis™
and T.I.R.E.S.™ are all Trademarks of Holis Associates Inc.

All illustrations are licenced to/the property of the author or from Wikimedia Commons

Printed Edition: 978-0-9917659-0-4
ePUB Edition: 978-0-9917659-1-1
ePDF Edition: 978-0-9917659-2-8

Book Design by wordzworth.com
Printed in Winnipeg, Manitoba 'by Kromar Printing - www.kromar.com
and by Lightning Source outside Canada

Published by Principium Press

Further copies of this book and linked training material
are available from: http://www.turningsellingintobuying.com/tsb_shop/

I am very grateful to all the people mentioned in the stories and examples in this book. They have generously contributed their success or failure to make Turning Selling into Buying so effective. Some are named and happy to be so, others have had their names changed as a matter of discretion …

Contents

Why you should be interested in this book	v
Who should be reading this book?	vi
Author's Preface	viii
How to Use This Book	xiii

PART ONE   "THE RIGHT STUFF" — 1

Chapter 1   Anyone can Sell - and Enjoy Doing It! — 3

From 'Old School' Sales Pressure to Sustainable Influence	5
Where it all began to Unravel	7
Where I Got It Right	9
In Summary: Turning Selling into Buying solves real life problems	13
Chapter 1: Review Questions & Self-Development Assignments	14

Chapter 2   How People Communicate & Influence — 17

How will this help me Build a Willing Buyer?	19
Foundations and Mindsets	19
Foundation One – The Human Communication Model	20
Foundation Two – The Filters We Apply	23
Foundation Three – The 'Frames' for our Model of the World	30
Foundation Four – The Fulcrum of Influence	32
The Four TSB Mindsets	36
In Summary: Brains are complex but can be influenced	45
Chapter 2: Review Questions & Self-Development Assignments	46

Chapter 3   How People Buy — 49

How will this help me Build a Willing Buyer?	51
How People Buy – Anything	57
So What Drives a Buying Decision?	59
Your Buyer's Actual TakeAways	62
Checking The TIRES with So What?	63
Compound and Potential TIRES	67
So What is an Offering?	69
So What's Included in Your Offering?	70

In Summary: People and companies buy for simple reasons	76
Chapter 3: Review Questions & Self-Development Assignments	77

Chapter 4   Four-See: The Buyer's Side of the Table — 81

How Does Four-See help me Build a Willing Buyer?	83
The Four-See Positions	85
Performing a Four-See Exercise	87
Detailed Instructions	90
Insights and uses of Four-See	93
Team Benefits	95
In Summary: Sit on the buyer's side of the table to influence them	97
Chapter 4: Review Questions & Self-Development Assignments	98

Chapter 5   Navigate Your Buyer's Mind — 101

How will this help me Build a Willing Buyer?	103
Element One – Chunking	104
Chunking in Real Life Influence Situations	111
Element Two – Frames and Reframes	124
Day-to-Day Reframes	128
Preframes	132
In Summary: You can 'Reach into your buyer's mind'	134
Chapter 5: Review Questions & Self-Development Assignments	135

PART TWO "READINESS" — 137

Chapter 6   Buyer Discovery — 139

How will this help me Build a Willing Buyer?	141
So For What Purpose Precisely do you need to Research Your Buyer?	142
Google Advanced Searches	146
LinkedIn	149
Building Your Network	153
Searching with Power – an Ethical Warning	156
Buyer's Staff & Colleagues	156
A Day in the Life of….	157
Periodicals/News Sites	158
Contacts	159
Other Sources	161
In Summary: Arm yourself well to maximise success	164
Chapter 6: Review Questions & Self-Development Assignments	166

Chapter 7   Build your 'Buying Drivers'   169

How will this help me Build a Willing Buyer?   171
What's a TakeAway Analysis all about?   173
Doing your own 'So What to TIRES' Analysis   174
The TakeAway Generator   187
Peak Power for your TakeAways   191
Same Product – Different Offering to Different Buyers   196
In Summary: Determine the few, simple reasons people truly buy from you   200
Chapter 7: Review Questions & Self-Development Assignments   204

Chapter 8   Using TakeAways to Influence   207

How will this help me Build a Willing Buyer?   209
TakeAway Quadrants   209
TakeAway Generation Exercise   219
Generating Value Statements   222
In Summary: Prepare Once, Use Many Times   226
Chapter 8: Review Questions & Self-Development Assignments   227

Chapter 9   Your Commit Analysis   229

How will a Commit Analysis help Build a Willing Buyer?   231
How People Become Convinced   233
Commit Key One – Potential TakeAways   241
Commit Key Two – Making the Decision Stick   241
Commit Key Three – The Delivery Narrative   248
Commit Key Four – Where's the money?   256
Non-Sales Variants   262
In Summary: Commit Keys turn desire to buy into a decision   264
Chapter 9: Review Questions & Self-Development Assignments   265

Chapter 10   The Best Elevator Pitch in the World   267

How will an Elevator Pitch help me Build a Willing Buyer?   269
What is an Elevator Pitch?   270
The 'Dragons' Den Effect'   271
The Call to Action   275
What an Elevator Pitch is NOT   277
Structure & Inputs   279
Your Pitch and some Examples   288
Why an Elevator Pitch 'Suite'?   291
In Summary: Elevator Pitches don't sell – they engage   295
Chapter 10: Review Questions & Self-Development Assignments   296

Afternote Making the Change Stick	**299**
Ensure your investment in this book stays effective	301
Moving the Furniture - a Personal Commitment	302
Joining the TSB Community	306
Extending your Model of the World	306
Commercial Activities	308
Opportunities for further development of TSB	311
If you found this book useful…	312
Annex A Index of Terms used in Turning Selling into Buying	**313**
Annex B Part One Answers	**319**
Annex C Part Two Answers	**333**
About the Author	342

Why you should be interested in this book

If you want to earn or influence more ... to do it more easily and predictably and to enjoy it more ...

If Influencing People to Buy is what you need to do ...
... then this is the book for you

The word **Selling** often raises strong emotions in people ...
... yet **Buying** is usually **so** much easier!

There's no such thing as a 'sales process' - only a Buying Process ...
... and every Buyer has their own motivation and process

Move to the Buyer's Side of the Table – You'll understand their REAL process ... and use it to Build a Willing Buyer
– rather than 'force' through a sale

Turning Selling into Buying answers the vital questions:
*"What would truly motivate someone to buy what I'm offering?
And keep them convinced enough to take action?"*

It doesn't matter whether you're influencing someone to buy your **Ideas**, your **Products**, your **Services** ... or even **Yourself.**

This book delivers totally new, but easily learned, techniques and insights that everyone can use - **at work or in life!**

Who should be reading this book?

Turning Selling into Buying (TSB) is for everyone who's determined to 'get on' – at work and in life – and is prepared to invest time and effort to improve their selling and influence skills.

If you want a book of hints and tips, there are plenty of other books. If you accept what fate throws at you, or never need to convince anyone, then this book isn't for you.

But if you want an enjoyable, compelling book that, with a little effort on your part, transforms the way you influence people to buy *ideas*, *products* **or** *services* **– then this book delivers it.**

Entrepreneurs and Intrapreneurs

If you're hunting your first reference sale – or seeking investors or partners – TSB is a game-changer that make things happen earlier, and more easily and predictably. When you stop leading every sale and need a sales team, you can safely grow it *from within* – built on solid experience – rather than the costly risk of bringing in the wrong sales leader.

Sales & Marketing Leaders, Business Development, Customer Service

If this describes you, TSB adds so many productive skills to your existing process:

- New insights and skills will make your results more predictable.
- You'll waste less time, eliminate costly assumptions, and bring in earlier results.
- Sales managers will waste less time and resources on wild goose chases.

Business and Technical Consulting

Are you great at what you do, but hate 'selling' yourself? Then TSB is for you. It suits a rational temperament and boosts anyone's self-confidence. You'll approach your clients positively, effectively and profitably once you know exactly what they'll gain from your work.

Project Director, Product Manager or Team Leader

This is at the heart of what you do every day – influencing others to buy into change. You need to sell ideas, plans, and the benefits of reaching an objective – TSB will save you and your company time and money. You'll also save energy and frustration along the way!

Personal Life

If you ever need to influence someone to buy into a decision, then these techniques and insights are for you. Maybe you have problems with your neighbour; perhaps you're a local charity fundraiser; maybe you just want to bridge the gap between you and your kids.

Small or Home Business

Do you need to sell a car, but you don't know how to turn a prospective buyer into cash? You're a painter who needs more work in a tough market, or a maybe a specialist with hard-to-sell technical services. You will benefit from TSB.

Job Seekers

Let's face it, when you're looking for a job or promotion, you're *selling yourself*. You need people to 'buy' you and what you deliver to their situation – maybe even more than in a commercial sale! With TSB, you can Turn Selling into Employing!

"Influence Skills for Life – Sales Tools for Work"

Author's Preface

My motivation for writing this book was a desire to share the very real pleasure that sales has become for me. It took me many hard – not always pleasurable – years in the business to recognize that on the few occasions I'd been able to build a "Willing Buyer", everything changed. Suddenly it was all so much easier and enjoyable than the 'old school' sales pressure I'd been taught. I used this new technique successfully in large and small deals in many different markets.

As colleagues noticed that I was getting good results and seemed much happier in general, they asked me to teach their teams. At first, it was an informal process. But I started out as a military engineer, so I inevitably documented a set of simple, structured modules to teach people how to *turn selling into buying*.

The Mystique
The word 'Sales' invokes an image of a fast talking, confident salesman (odd how it's usually a man) talking his prey into submission, selling hard, then 'closing the deal'. This is reinforced by stories of top salesmen selling sand to Berbers or ice cubes to Inuits.

Many of us in sales are guilty of encouraging this mystique – through attitude or actions. As a result, too many people are uneasy or have a mental block about selling and sales.

At worst, this discomfort becomes a terror of engaging in any situation where an idea or product must be 'sold' – and can hold a person back socially or professionally.

The Secret
So here's the thing ... the very best sales people *were never like that*. The best and most ethical influencers have always built a willing buyer.

They've all done the same things:

- Determined exactly "What's in it for this buyer to buy from me?"
- Recognised that the 'Buying Process' is shaped by the person buying – not by them, the seller.
- Drawn out and developed the buyer's needs, desires and financial drivers.
- Offered a relevant, cost-effective solution that is willingly bought – not 'sold'.

My Enthusiasm

As I used *Turning Selling into Buying* (TSB) - and then trained hundreds of people in it – I realised that it's *just as effective* for selling ideas, a vision, a proposal, or even getting a job. It delivers the confidence that frees 'non-sales' people to add their own special experience, creativity and enthusiasm to get that favourable decision. This confidence makes professional sales people happier and more productive.

I've taught classes and seminars for sales people, students, project managers, techies, customer service, CEOs, and many others. As well as the commercial benefits, they've also used it for so much else:

- Achieving the things they and their family deserved.
- Finding the right investors and partner for their ideas.
- Delivering their skills to society and business.
- Recruiting committed staff and distributors.

**Anyone can sell, can sell well and enjoy doing it!
Enjoy reading this book as much as I enjoyed writing it.**

This book is dedicated to the four most amazing women in my life -
My wonder-full daughters, *Sasha*, *Kayleigh* and *Jade*
for never stopping me wondering…

…but in particular to my amazing wife, *Jacqueline*, for proof-reading,
financial support, love, and dogged belief in this project –
way beyond the call of duty.

I also couldn't have done it without the (more masculine) support
of my great friends *Fred*, *Gary*, *Mike* and especially *Tim* and the
unswerving help and advice of *John*, *Glenn* and *Joe*

as for my 'Publishing Pros'…
Thanks for the all-nighters to *Karen* at Partner Publishing
the *hyper-efficient design team* at Wordzworth
and most of all the endless patience and coffee of Merge Design & Print

Thanks folks

How to Use This Book

If you make use of all the material in *Turning Selling into Buying* (TSB), the change in you can be dramatic. This introduction guides you through the process so that you can pick the route that suits you best.

It's important to make sure you understand each key issue in the book before diving into the exercises and web material. Without the full picture, much of their strength and value can be lost. Remember that:

> "The whole is greater than the sum of the parts"
> —ARISTOTLE

Web Resources

All chapters end with self-test and self-development assignments. Some have worked examples within them. For those using e-books, or to keep a printed book clean, the introduction to these chapters contains a web link to a downloadable worksheet. You can print this and keep it beside you while you read. There are also occasional direct links to other useful resources in the text.

In every case, the web link (url) is shown in a special, shortened form (e.g. goo.gl/3pAef) that's easier for you to type into a web browser. In e-books these are actually shown as a clickable live link: *goo.gl/3pAef*.

Every link in the book is also available from the TSB website. The title of the worksheet, image, or exercise is shown, along with its shortened and full url. Type in or click this web address: *goo.gl/p0Ajn* to get there. It can also be accessed from the website menus.

At the end of the book there are directions on how to access even more resources by joining the TSB Web Community. These will include videos and podcasts to support what you've learned in the book, as well as access to special discounts for other offerings.

Emphasis Conventions

To ensure you're in the right 'Frame of mind' to absorb them, some sections are highlighted in the book by shading:

Stories, Metaphors and Case Studies

> These are highlighted like this

Key Points that make TSB work

These are highlighted like this

Working Space

> These are illustrated by this Frame
> (and are also found on chapter's downloadable worksheet)

Your Individual Learning Process – from Technique to Skill

It's important to appreciate that most of us are good at one or more steps in the process of *Turning Selling into Buying*. I know people who are naturally great in discussions and can draw out exactly what a client's problems are - but those same people struggle to turn that need into an *order* or a *decision*. Others are great at theoretical analysis of what problems people *might* need to solve, but lose all confidence in front of a real buyer. Figuring out and then filling in the right gaps in your knowledge and skill can be tough.

For most of us, there's a standard way of learning new skills – as shown in the "Cycle of Competence" in Figure 1. As you learn each new group of techniques, you'll find that you're starting at different points along the journey. In a few areas, you may be an expert (see *Regular Use & Practice* at the top left). In others, you may have the embarrassing realisation that you've been doing something ineffectively *for years* – you'll be at the *Discovery* stage (on the right)

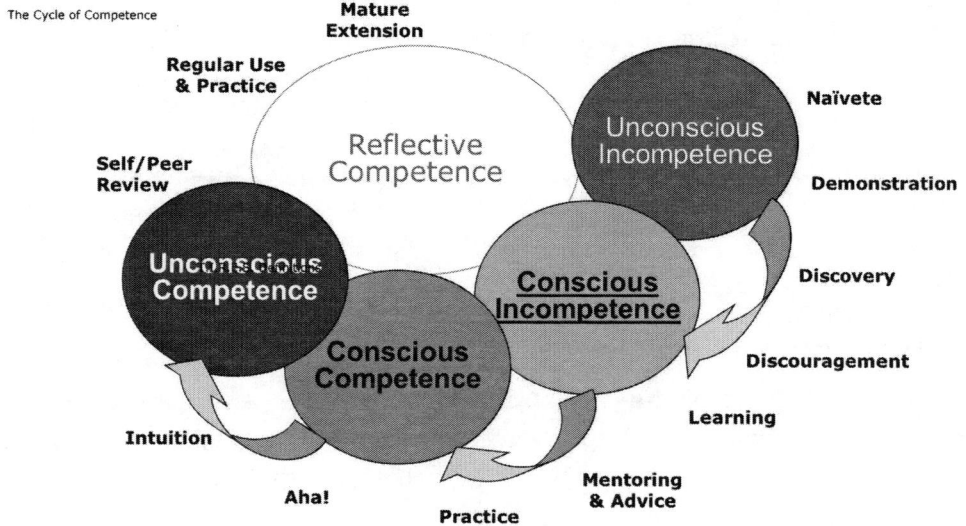

Figure 1

We all start with some naive level of competence, but usually don't understand the exact process – we're *Unconsciously Incompetent*.

Steering a bike is a great example of this principle. Do you know what countersteering is? It's the only way a two-wheeled vehicle can actually change direction – by pressing the handlebars – for a very short time – in the *opposite* direction to the way you'd intuitively turn. (Visit goo.gl/Fhd5i to find out more). If you ride a bicycle, scooter, or motorbike without falling off, you already do it unconsciously – but can you describe the process and use it to have more control and safety?

> A few years ago I took advanced motorcycle training and learned countersteering by sitting on a training rig that showed me how it worked. I was immediately discouraged at how little I knew – after all, I'd been riding motorbikes and bicycles for years! But then I learned more theory and put it into practice. The instructors even helped us by putting down sticky tape on the track that told us where to start the turn.
>
> The instructors recognised that most of us had gone from being a bit cocky to being nervously aware of our shortcomings – but at least we were being *Consciously Incompetent*!

The breakthrough came when I was mentored by an instructor who gave me the confidence to stop worrying about failing and just do it properly. As a result, I kept practicing until I had the *"Aha!"* moment. I had become *Consciously Competent* – I'd got it!

That evening, as I rode home from Silverstone, my buddy Neil and I stopped for a cup of tea, and I suddenly realised that I'd turned into the rest area with a completely intuitive countersteer!

I'd become *Unconsciously Competent* ... and so will you, as you use TSB techniques more and more.

Over the next few months, my training classmates and I kept comparing and discussing our experience (*Reflective Competence*). Now, years later, I countersteer all the time, without ever thinking about it – in fact, I think may have even invented some moves of my own!

If you like this model (and as I've just shown, it doesn't only apply to *Turning Selling into Buying*) go to goo.gl/dNTgF and download a picture of the Cycle of Competence to print out and put on the wall – then as you work through TSB, you can see where you are in the cycle.

As you move from *Unconscious Incompetence* to *Reflective Competence*, you'll learn new *techniques* and associated insights. Using them regularly will turn them into *skills*. As well as a Self-Test section (with answers at the back of the book), each chapter includes a number of Self Development Assignments that will give you a framework to build new skills.

This same approach of *problem – technique – practice – skill* is taken in all the TSB training material that's available on the web and in our seminars and workshops.

Index of Terms

I've done my best to avoid jargon in the book. But, to be able to use one or two words instead of a couple of paragraphs, I've had to create some TSB shorthand. You'll find the main ones used throughout the book at Annex A. Full definitions are given, as well as a cross-reference to the chapter you should go to for even more detail.

Four ways to read this book

- Cherry Pick

You can select only the chapters that focus on the challenges you have and simply learn new ways to fix what you find difficult – use the detailed Table of Contents to cherry pick. Each chapter opens with a list of new skills you'll learn and how they help you build a Willing Buyer.

- Select As You Read

Just work your way through the whole book, picking out fresh ideas that you can add to what you're already good at and learning new ways to do the things you find difficult.

- Step by Step

Take one chapter at a time – read and understand each section within it. Then go out turn your newly learned techniques into real-life skills, using the Personal Development Assignments to help with this. Then move on to the next chapter, firmly founded on the new skills you're developing.

- Focussed Study

If you want to make big changes, I recommend you read the book all the way through once, skipping the exercises, to 'get' the full picture. Then go back (perhaps having gathered information about your own situation) and work through the examples and exercises.

Navigation

Every chapter starts with the same graphic showing your journey towards *Turning Selling into Buying* (as in Figure 2). But the section associated with that chapter is highlighted to allow you to:

- Understand how each chapter logically build on the previous one.
- Monitor your progress throughout the book.
- Understand intuitively where you are within Part One or Part Two.
- Look forward to what's coming next.

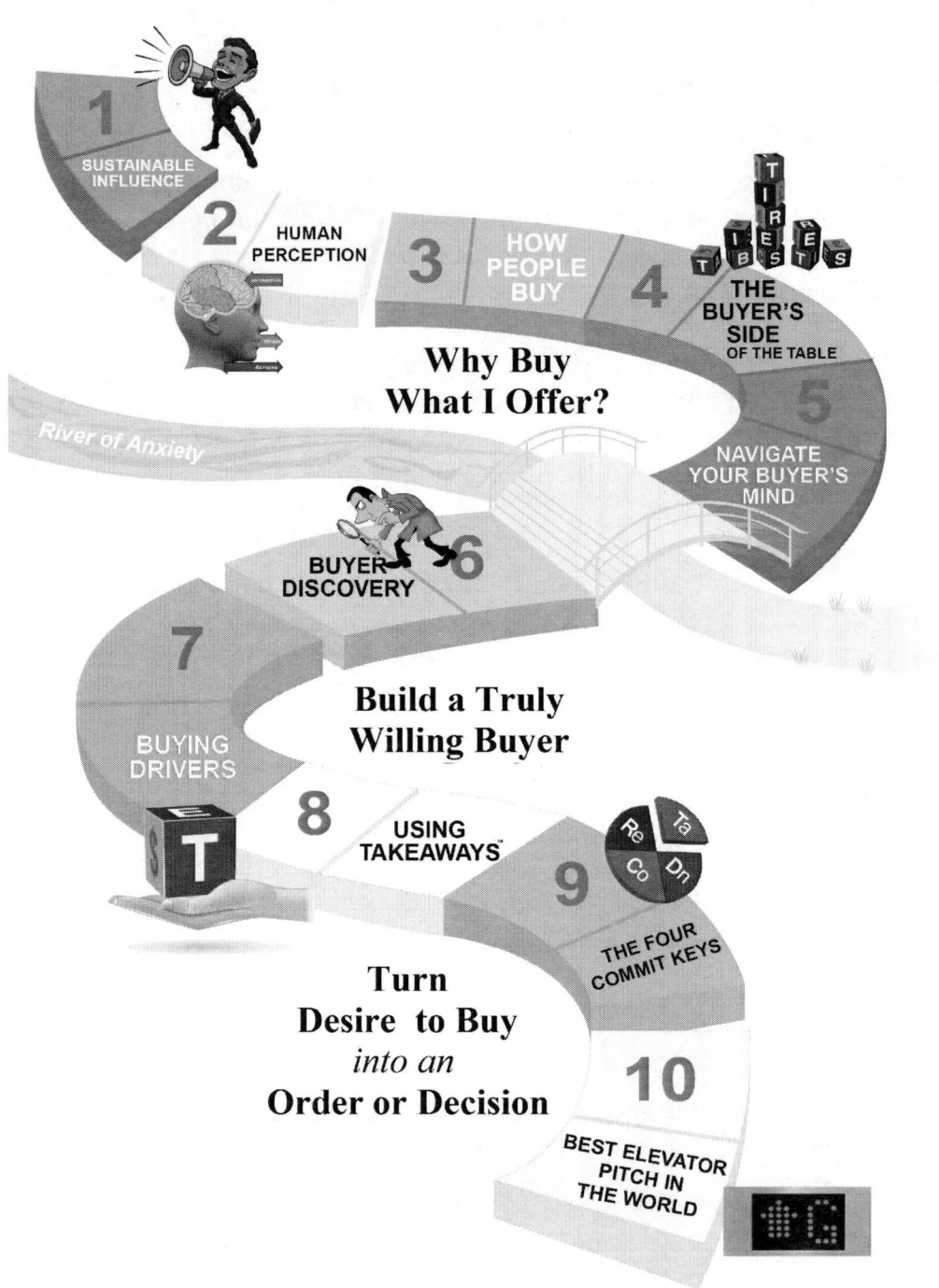

Figure 2

PART ONE

Chapter One: Anyone can 'sell'
Understand where TSB came from and the problems it solves. Starting a journey knowing where you're going to end up – and why you're travelling there – seems wise!

Chapter Two: How People Communicate and Influence
Acquire the Mindsets and Foundation skills that you'll use to improve any communication or influence. These simple, easy-to-learn concepts are the platform for the rest of the book and you'll keep re-using them.

Chapter Three: How People Buy
Learn the 5 reasons that anyone buys or 'buys into' something, and how your offering can be made to satisfy those needs. These are the biggest yet most obvious secrets in the book. Once you've got your head around them, you'll never see the world the same way again.

Chapter Four: The Buyer's Side of the Table
Discover through simple, practical exercises how productive it is to see the situation from the buyer's side of the table. What you learn and practice in this chapter is not just useful for work, it's also valuable tools for dealing with life.

Chapter Five: Navigate Your Buyer's Mind
Learn the two key skills needed to change your buyer's mind from 'no Desire to Buy' to 'wanting to buy'. They're things we do and say every day – but what changes is that you'll be aware of their power, and consciously use them to create a specific change.

PART TWO

Chapter Six: Buyer Discovery

Gather a wide range of techniques for finding information that will help you get inside your buyer's mind. This is very practical chapter helps you to find out about people, their motivations, their organisations, and the industries and sectors where you'll work.

Chapter Seven: Build Your Buying Drivers – the 'TakeAway Analysis'

You'll create, enrich, and develop every single Buying Driver for your offering that might possibly be needed by a buyer. The list will include all the reasons your buyer might buy what you have to offer.

Chapter Eight: Using TakeAways for Influence – the 'ABC Analysis'

You'll now extend the Buying Drivers (TakeAways) you've created in chapter 7. You'll learn how to document and use them to help you draw out which of them is actually needed by your buyer. You'll also create simple but powerful value statements about each of them.

Chapter Nine: Commit Analysis – the 'Action Drivers'

You'll add the three final Commit Keys to chapter 8's work. These are what motivate a commercial buyer into action – to turn a Desire to Buy into an Order or Decision. The most powerful of these is a financial justification that buyers can powerfully relate to.

Chapter Ten: The Best Elevator Pitch in the World

You'll pull everything together to build the best set of 'Elevator Pitches' in the world. These will be effective in both a formal gathering and a casual meeting.

Afternote: Making the Change Stick

This is where you'll find out how you can make your new learning even more effective and maintain the momentum of change. The *Turning Selling into Buying* community has great tools to support you.

PART ONE

"The Right Stuff"

Master the right tools, to influence the right people, the right way

How to Use Part One of Turning Selling into Buying

In this first half of the book, you'll learn a range of new techniques and insights that will "Build a Willing Buyer." In the second half, you'll apply them to your own specific situation.

To help you integrate these new ideas fully, each chapter ends with self-tests and real-life assignments.

**Enjoy learning how to convert wary prospects into satisfied Buyers...
...of your ideas, products and services...**

CHAPTER 1
Anyone can Sell
- and Enjoy Doing It!

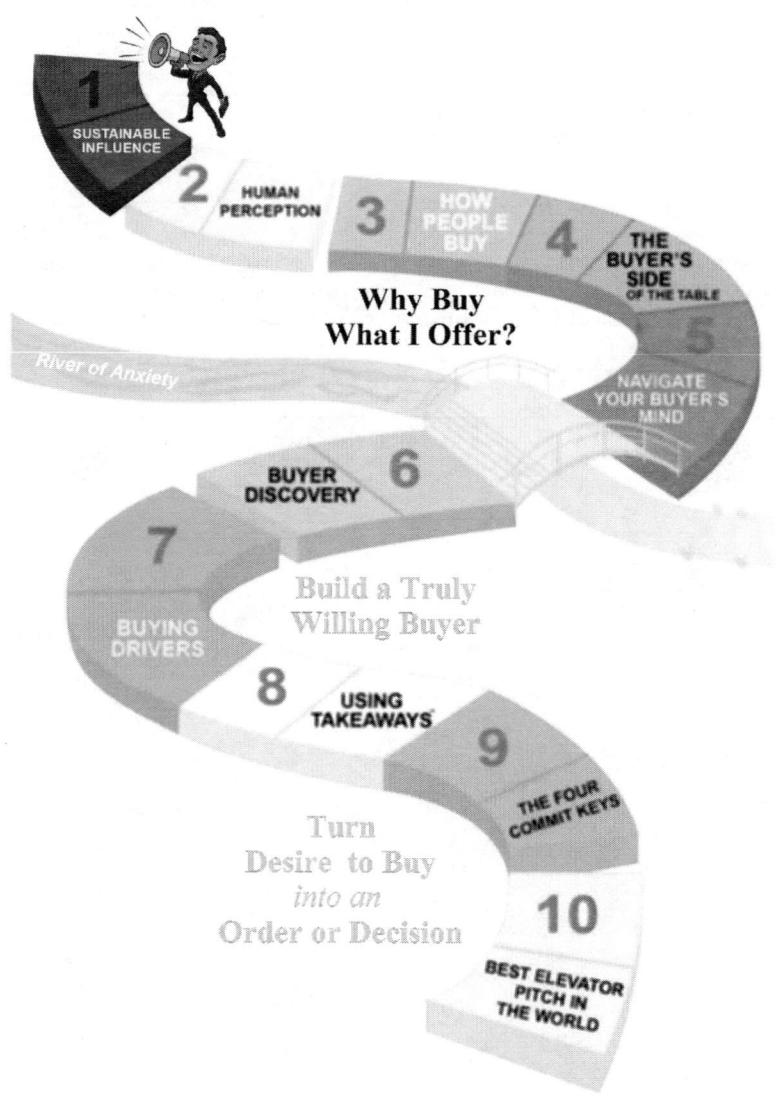

BY THE END OF THIS CHAPTER, YOU'LL UNDERSTAND …

- The practical, proven origins of *Turning Selling into Buying* (TSB)
- Business and personal challenges *sustainably* overcome by TSB
- Why TSB beats 'Old School' sales – every time and in every way
- What you'll personally TakeAway from this tool set

FROM 'OLD SCHOOL' SALES PRESSURE TO SUSTAINABLE INFLUENCE

It's been nearly thirty years since I was influenced to 'buy into' the idea of becoming a salesman. At the time, I was a good engineer, an ex-British Army officer, and also an entrepreneur – I'd set up a successful business building navigation systems for racing yachts. The last thing on my mind was becoming a professional salesman.

My first experience of how someone could successfully *Turn Selling into Buying* totally changed my career path. The person who won me over to the idea of joining his sales team was a manager at the London Stock Exchange called Roger Faulkes – and he did so without doing any 'selling' at all!

He was part of the interview process for the job of managing the City of London's new electronic trading systems. I didn't really see why I needed an interview with a sales manager, but I wanted the techie job, so I went along with it. He started by relaxing me very agreeably. He asked me about my life, what I wanted out of civilian life, how much money I needed to earn, and much more. The key moment came after a pleasant 10 minutes of questions and answers. Roger paused, looked me in the eye and said:

"Your talents are wasted in Operations – you should join us here in Sales & Marketing. From what I'm hearing, you can learn and earn a heck of a lot more – and have a lot of fun doing it."

Boy, was I hooked – he had spotted my 'Buying Drivers' perfectly!

He hadn't hooked me with a fancy job title. He didn't tell me about the fascinating work I'd do. Not once did he pitch the quality of the training or the people I'd be working with.

But he absolutely read me right. He recognised and developed exactly what made me tick (my Buying Drivers) and he reeled me in. Once he'd described the job fully and convinced me it would deliver what I was looking for, I took it … and my life was never the same again (for the good, I might add).

> It's important to note that if Roger had tried a conventional 'pitch' – how great the job was, the salary, what it involved, etc. – I probably would have said no as I was so set on being the Operations Manager. But he didn't – he influenced me by drilling down to the core of what I wanted to TakeAway – money, fun, and new experiences.
>
> **He gave me a 'Desire to Buy' – which is what this book's all about.**

I didn't realise it at the time, but Roger was the first person I ever met who truly turned me into a "Willing Buyer", rather than 'pitching' what he wanted to sell to me.

He was what I'd now call 'unconsciously competent' at what he was doing – he did it completely intuitively. He'd instinctively developed the questions that were so effective at influencing other people to do what was right for them and, at the same time, *satisfy his own needs*. I saw him at work many times afterwards, and he consistently did the same whenever he needed to influence someone.

I didn't do anything about it at the time, but my brain filed away the experience and indexed it as 'really interesting stuff I should use some day'.

So what were my lessons that day? Well in short:

- Before he saw me, Roger took the time to weigh up what someone joining his new organisation might gain personally from working in such an exciting job. He worked out the possible answers to the question SO WHAT'S IN IT FOR ME?
- He made the effort to research the interview notes and résumé of every potential candidate – always doing his best to *see the opportunity from our point of view*. This also gave him an indication of who would be likely to do the job well.
- As he interviewed each candidate, he was *genuinely interested* in each one of us – and it showed. In my case, he'd even taken the trouble to research a little about what my army regiment did.
- He put us at ease, and then asked open but *carefully navigated* questions about our lives and interests, and how we viewed work – visiting each aspect in turn.

- If he saw a match between our needs and what he could offer, he drilled down further – casually and conversationally. If he learned how important money was to us, now he wanted detail. If he saw we were sociable, he dug down further to see how much we wanted to 'live with our clients' and their difficult situations. He knew we were all good under pressure, but how much of it did we actually want in our next job? His aim was *always to match our Buying Drivers with what he could offer us.*

- Once he saw we wanted to take away what he could truly supply, he *offered it, clearly and confidently* – the job description was secondary.

- He waited till he'd made us Willing Buyers before he actually explained what we'd be doing if we took the job and *used detailed facts to convince us* the opportunity was real.

In my case, I was hooked. It was the right decision. I still have strong friendships with the great people I worked with. One was even Best Woman at my wedding!

WHERE IT ALL BEGAN TO UNRAVEL

So I worked well and happily for a couple of years and enjoyed being successful at what I did. But then things started to go wrong, and that's where I hope this book will make your life so much easier than mine.

I forgot what I'd learned from Roger. I got sucked into the *Sales Delusion* – thinking we were something special, manipulative, cleverer, and tougher than everyone else who wasn't in sales.

Worst of all I worked and 'pitched' so hard that my work/life balance went off the scale. I actually ended up making myself very ill (as did others) – a lesson I carry with me to this day.

I was (and am still) a perfectionist who prepared for every sales opportunity, small or large, with the same degree of rigour and determination. But I was so busy doing it right that I didn't have time to recognize the *repetitiveness of so much of what I did*. It was effective, successful, and profitable – but also very stressful and horribly time consuming.

When a 'date night' was called for, or my kids needed me, or I was invited to a party, I went – but it became a gritty and determined duty, not the pleasure it should have been.

This book is designed to help you free up your time for better things, yet still be magnificently effective at what you do – to *build your influence toolkit once, then use it many times*.

My colleague Dave Perfect and I became experts at using this 'build once, use many times' technique when we created expensive software. But it took me a long time to spot the benefit of taking the same approach to sales influence – more's the pity!

Old School Sales – Manipulation or Influence?

This attitude wasn't good for me or my colleagues. But it was even worse for the view of 'Sales' held by the outside world. I've lost count of how often I've asked my students which of them *"Got up each morning, eager and excited to sell?"* Too often, the result has been a few, hesitant hands, and even those people admit to anxiety – and prefer to put the problem into a box marked 'Later – much later.''

Society, media, films and now even video games all perpetuate this *sales delusion* – of how tough and manipulative sales and selling has to be, and how unique those of us in that business need to be to succeed.

This is rubbish! It might have been true in the past, but in the 21st Century our buyers are much smarter and better educated – and so are we. The web has made them far more knowledgeable and has given us both equal access to accurate information. More buyers demand a better balance from a deal, with long term trust – not the unprincipled 'smash and grab' sales approach of the past.

Turning Selling into Buying is the 'New Ethics'
of today's Sales, Influence and Leadership.....

WHERE I GOT IT RIGHT

Roll forward 20 years of hard work – success and failure; fun and heartache; pain and pleasure. I worked in financial and commercial markets, led sales and partner teams, travelled all over Europe, the Middle and Far East, and South Africa. I was lucky enough to work with companies large and small, based in North America, Europe, and the UK.

I sold solutions to my customers' toughest business problems. These involved a complex mix of hardware, services, software, development, consultancy, finance – and a lot of partnering. I was also a project manager for several multi-million dollar projects. I did the rounds seeking venture capital for our start-up – at meeting after meeting.

Probably the most satisfying of all my experiences was setting up and running a really successful channel operation with companies such as IBM and Oracle. This generated more revenue than the rest of the company put together – both satisfying and lucrative!

The 'Best of the Best'

All this time, I was fortunate to have colleagues, staff, and bosses around me who were talented and experienced. Many of the people who needed influence skills *didn't even have the word 'sales' anywhere on their business card*. They were product managers or developers; they were the presales specialists and project managers who are the lifeblood of tech companies; they were the customer service and account managers who interact with and influence real customers – with real-life problems – every single day.

But most of all, they were just regular people like you and me who needed to balance their personal and professional life – the pressures of home, kids, relationships, friends, and their own needs with the time and financial pressures of business.

> After a time, I saw that a few, just a very few, of the people that I worked with, stood out as relaxed, happy, and amazingly successful. They had a confident ability to cope with pressure and most stayed happy and healthy. These ***Best of the Best*** were also uncannily accurate in forecasting sales, or predicting which way a decision or meeting would go.

> When the rest of us were getting irritable or grumpy because things were going badly – these people seemed unflappable. When time was short, not only did they know where best to focus *their* efforts but they'd even find time to give helpful advice *to us* as well!

I was driven to learn what made these people tick – what made them stand out from the rest of us – and especially, whether it was actually repeatable.

I wanted the extra free time they had. I wanted the extra money they earned. I wanted to be more in control of my results. But most of all, I wanted to feel as relaxed and fearless as they clearly were!

The Model

So I began to study them. I modelled how they acted, how they thought, the words they used, and their strategies and actions before, during, and after every meeting. I also interviewed them – my bosses, peers, business partners, and even a few customers and suppliers.

Very quickly, a **Universal Process** began to emerge. It had no *pitch*, no *close*, and no *misdirection*. In fact, these rare people didn't seem to use many of the old school sales techniques at all! Not only that, but it seemed to apply no matter what was being sold. It worked as well selling an idea as getting someone to buy a commodity. It worked as effectively for selling consulting as it did in a complex technology solution.

As I continued, I used the model in more and more varied situations. When we were looking for investors for our start-up, rather than just looking for the most money available, we used the ideas to find ourselves a partner who was *actually right for us*. When I was building a distribution channel, it created skilled partnerships – not just a bulk price discount. In the last few years, as I've worked with newly qualified students and people who've lost their jobs in the downturn, I've even watched it used successfully in job hunting and negotiating pay raises!

The key is **Building a Willing Buyer** – not Forcing a Sale

The death of 'Spray & Pray' Selling

The Best of the Best never lazily spray and pray a list of product features and functions at their buyer in the hope that something sticks long enough to make a sale. They don't leave the buyer to work out what's useful and what's not. They recognise each buyer's motivations to buy by seeing it from the Buyer's Side of the Table. Then they make use of that knowledge to facilitate a buying decision – just like Roger did with me. Not only is this less stressful for everyone, but it also builds a solid, sustainable relationship with your buyer – and generates enduring, sustainable business.

I was intrigued enough by what I discovered to continue adapting my old school sales techniques. I also began to add ideas from the fields of cognitive and behavioural psychology. My final step was to see that the key to easier success was to do as much preparation work as possible well in advance – not 'in the moment' with my buyer. I went into every meeting knowing exactly what would motivate someone to buy from me, and what would convince them to stay that way.

This preparation was a life-saver for me, and it may well be for you, too. This is especially true if you're a salesperson or have to regularly influence people to buy into your ideas. I saved so much time and effort by analysing only once but very effectively. It also allowed me to draw on specialists who could be wrung dry of useful information and experience that I could use in front of a buyer. The only time I needed to repeat that analysis was when there was a change in the buyer or what I was offering.

The success of this approach outside of business was unexpected. I used these ideas with my family and friends, in politics, and in day to day living. This showed me that they provided solid skills for life as well as productive tools for work. Feedback from my workshop students strengthened this.

As many students have said to me:
"Oh, how I wish I'd learned this stuff at school!"

Front Line Use

Using this approach with my own sales teams proved successful. I and my great friend and collaborator, Dave Perfect, then moved on to use it with ex-colleagues, friends and business partners who also found it productive. I then took it into the field in a series of public APEX seminars and Fearless Selling workshops for sales and marketing teams. Over the years, I've continued to refine it, using feedback from CEOs, entrepreneurs, sales teams and their managers, consultants, MBA students, and many others.

I was often pressed by students and colleagues to turn the seminar and workshop series into a book. So I spent a year converting my workshop material, exercises and workbooks into this book – *Turning Selling into Buying*.

> When I was 21, I took up free fall parachuting. I was young enough to do it with only few moments of anxiety, so I loved it. Being young, I also learned almost nothing from the experience at the time!
>
> Many years later, a friend of mine decided that he wanted to try the exhilarating experience of free-fall parachuting. So he signed up for the classes needed to do a few jumps. He enjoyed them all and realised that, just as with the 'Best of the Best' in sales, free fall parachuting was another universal process that *absolutely anyone* could master.
>
> He learned the rules, practiced them intensively, and then followed them on the day – and of course, everything went brilliantly. In fact, he was concentrating so much on the process that he completely forgot to be scared when he stepped out of the door of the aircraft!
>
> *Turning Selling into Buying* can be your personal parachute training. There's some interesting theory, some demonstration, plenty of practice, and a solid chunk of preparation. By the time you step out and engage with your buyer, there will be no room left for Fear, Doubt or Anxiety.
>
> You'll know what you're doing, you'll do it well, and you'll enjoy doing it.

IN SUMMARY:
TURNING SELLING INTO BUYING SOLVES REAL LIFE PROBLEMS

I hope this first chapter gives you the motivation to invest a little time and effort in making TSB work for you – in work or life.

As I've used and taught TSB over the years, it's become clear that it fixes a universal list of problems that are relevant to selling ideas, products or services:

- **Improved Predictability** – of results; of revenue; of a buying plan's viability.
- **Less Wasted Time & Resources** – replacing assumptions with objective facts.
- **Earlier Results** – spotting and developing opportunities more easily and earlier.
- **Better Results** – through strong cost justification and greater buyer motivation.
- **Less Stress** – with an open, facilitative approach – centerd around your buyer.
- **Easier Management** –buying timescales and plans based on *objective* facts.
- **Better Partnerships** –building on what *your partner* needs – and supplying it.
- **Productive Teams** – where *everyone* contributes to influencing buyers to buy.

As you work your way through the book, make a note of the solutions to problems that you actually have at the moment, or you think may arise in the future.

As each chapter develops, apply your situation to all the examples and stories that are relevant, then go out and use your new skills and insights in real life.

I also urge you to join the *TSB* Community (see Afternote - Making the Changes Stick) where you can share *your* results and experiences and learn from the problems that others have solved.

CHAPTER 1:
REVIEW QUESTIONS & SELF-DEVELOPMENT ASSIGNMENTS

Anyone Can Sell, and Enjoy Doing It! – see Annex B for Answers

To print a copy of this section, download it directly from goo.gl/YBLRL or select it from the TSB Download Page at goo.gl/p0Ajn.

Self-Test Questions

1. What's the most important lesson you took away from the story about my interview at the Stock Exchange? How many of the seven steps used to 'make me a Willing Buyer' can you list?
2. What does *Turning Selling into Buying* do instead of 'pitching'?
3. What is a 'Willing Buyer'?
4. What have the 'Best of the Best' in sales and influence always done?
5. What was the big life-saver for everyone that could be for you too?
6. Name 4 of the 8 keys problems TSB solves. Which are most relevant to you?

Self-Development Assignments

Chapter 1, Assignment 1 – Listen and Watch

Seek out sales and marketing colleagues, customer service reps or engineers who are more than just techies. Ask to go on some customer calls with them – perhaps as a new colleague who wants to meet customers. Observe the person you're with. How much of their time is spent asking questions? How much listening? How much making statements? Watch the reaction of the buyer. When do they become interested? When do they stop listening? What works? What doesn't?

With a little imagination, you can also set this sort of experience up even in non-commercial situations.

Chapter 1, Assignment 2 – Buy and Listen

Go and buy something. If you can organise the equivalent at work, set that up, too. Then see how people sell to you. Do they engage with you? Are they helping you or selling to you? Do they sell you only what you ask for – or do they 'drill down' to something more strategic? Are they interested in more than just getting your agreement to the first thing they propose?

Most importantly of all … did you reach a point where you felt a Desire to Buy?

How easy was it then to take the final step from being a Willing Buyer to someone prepared to hand over money? What did the sales person do to help you with this process?

CHAPTER 2
How People Communicate & Influence

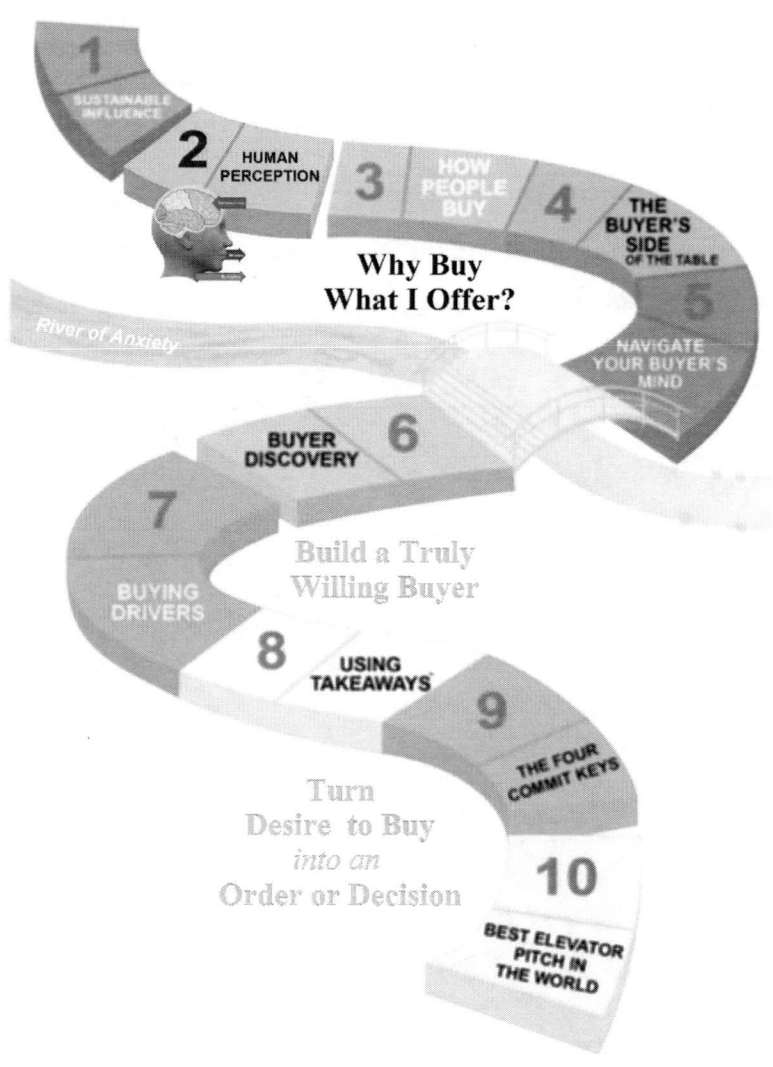

BY THE END OF THIS CHAPTER, YOU'LL UNDERSTAND ...

- Ways in which humans communicate with each other
- Different ways we each 'filter' our experience of the world
- Way we each set a 'Frame' for how we view different situations
- Best way to move your Buyer from 'being sold to' to 'wanting to buy'

HOW WILL THIS HELP ME BUILD A WILLING BUYER?

Building a "Willing Buyer" is all about *effective connection* with the other person and then *ethical engagement* with their problems, needs or desires. Once this is established and *sustainable*, you can work closely together to establish whether there's actually any business to be done together.

One of the things that sets *Turning Selling into Buying* apart is the extra verbal skills you'll learn to use – the ones necessary to change your buyer's mind from *"I haven't decided …"* to *"I want to …"*

FOUNDATIONS AND MINDSETS

This chapter introduces two topics that are at the heart of the TSB process. **Foundations** are the core *skills and insights* you'll use many times from now on.

They are how:

- We all react to the world of sensations around us.
- We make sense of this massive information assault.
- To change how the other person sees the world – and what you're offering them.
- To tip a buyer's balance from dubious to *convinced*.

Mindsets are the simple, ethical, but powerful *changes in attitude* that make the difference between 'selling something' and 'building a Willing Buyer'. They are:

- So What's In It For Me?
- Assumption is the mother of all screw-ups.
- The buyer is on the *Other Side of the Table* – seeing a different world from you.
- Question *Precisely* – Listen *Actively*.

If you momentarily forget a Foundation skill,
a Mindset will usually save the day!

FOUNDATION ONE – THE HUMAN COMMUNICATION MODEL

We each lead our life surrounded by sensations – the feel of the chair under me as I type this book; the ticking clock on the wall beside me; the brightness of the lights above my desk – even the faint smell of last night's rhubarb pie. We're bombarded by our five primary senses (sight, sound, touch, smell, and taste) as well as other even more subtle ones. See Figure 3.

But we're not usually *conscious* of any of these (except perhaps the smell of that pie). In fact, your brain would probably malfunction if it did try to consciously process everything. It's been calculated that our brain is besieged by around 4 billion bits of information per second. From this massive flow, we can actually process around 2,000 bits of information per second – still scarily high! The way we cope with even this small amount is to process it in several 'parallel paths' of information flow.

Large scale tests have shown that humans can *consciously* only handle between three and seven information flows in parallel at any one time – so thank goodness for filters! Do a simple test yourself – try simultaneously drawing a sketch, tapping a rhythm with your foot, remembering the plot of a recent film or book and humming a tune – and that's only four activities at once. If you can do all four effectively, you're in a minority! In a complex laboratory environment this has been proven many times and far more rigorously. See George Miller's significant research described at *goo.gl/sh4b*.

Much of our filtering is done *autonomically* by the deeper, older portions of our brain – the parts that keep us breathing, regulate temperature, respond to danger, and stop us wetting ourselves. A 'higher' region of the brain deals with the more complex (but still unconscious) filters that you'll learn to work with in order to understand how other people respond to you.

Once the stimulus has got through these filters, there will be a response. It might be a mental state – terror, excitement, boredom, etc. It might be a verbal response – an answer, a question, or a statement. It might generate a physical response – flight, leaning forward, flushing. Understanding these fully is a complex subject on its own, but simply understanding what's happening is a major step forward.

CHAPTER 2: HOW PEOPLE COMMUNICATE & INFLUENCE 21

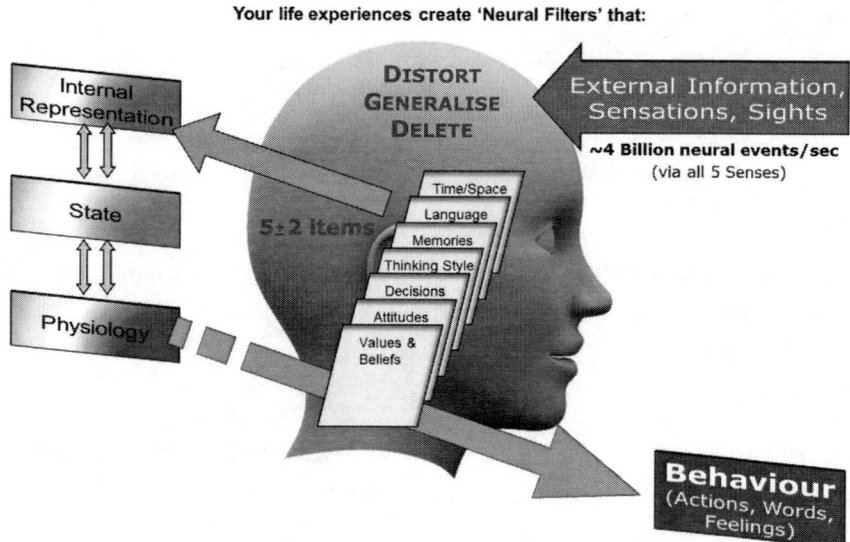

Figure 3

Figure 3 will help as you read through the next sections.

Filters

During our lives, we humans all build up our own individual set of higher level filters to protect us from the barrage of sensations we receive day and night. These filters can range from the mundane to the most complex. At a simple level, none of us notice the sound of our blood pumping (unless you consciously try to), or the temperature of the chair we're sitting on (until, of course, I mentioned it here). At the most complex level, individuals (and even groups with a common bond) can be completely blind to specific pieces of advice or information.

At a more day-to-day level, I'm sure you've personally encountered situations like this with individuals or groups. A more common example might be the completely genuine inability of a supporter of one sports team to see any good whatsoever in their opponents.

We all have everyday phrases that we use to describe these complex filters:

> "Bob looks at the world through rose-tinted glasses."
> "Sara only ever sees the down-side!"
> "Adnan is totally wrapped up in himself."

"Jasmine's background makes her biased."

"Jamal adds his own prejudices to everything!"

Human filters and their detailed operation is another big subject. But we can we usefully generalise their complexity by using the expression "Model of the World."

We all live the same physical world, but we each see and react to it differently – so our own Model of the World is what each of us effectively lives. It may not actually be reality – but it's *our perception of it*.

The most frequent mistake we make is to assume the other person is running the same model as us. This is probably the most frequent cause of disagreement. As you speak, the other person may be filtering something completely different to what you intended.

Recently I went with a friend to assess whether a vacant house was worth buying to refurbish – she had severe doubts about it, but the situation seemed perfect for her. The builder we took with us was filtering the quality of the structure, the cost of the paintwork and what services would need to be added. My friend was only filtering what terrible people the previous owners might have been, what stories each room had to tell, and whether there were hidden treasures beneath the floorboards.

The same house – totally different views. Mine was different again. We did, in the end, carefully influence her to change her Model of the World and it was a successful purchase for her.

To make this job even harder, we don't use the same set of filters all the time! We use different filters at different times, in different places and with different people. So when it comes to creating a Willing Buyer, you need to remember that *their* Model of the World may change significantly between meetings!

Information Flow

There are three types of neural filtration that we carry out. They are:

- Deletion
- Distortion
- Generalisation.

Understanding *deletion*, *distortion*, and *generalisation* is central to *Turning Selling into Buying*. We'll look at in greater detail in the section that follows.

The old-school method of selling is to spray and pray a long list of features and functions in the hope that something will stick long enough to create a sale. Because we have such a small degree of control over what's actually received by a buyer, this traditional method has a low chance of success.

If the buyer's Model of the World actually corresponds with ours, the chance of success is a little higher. If their model is very different (like my friend's view of that house) and *we can't adjust our model* to match theirs the chances of them seeing the benefits of buying are much lower.

Not only that, but spraying and praying can be annoying for the listener, who has to do all the work of picking out what might actually be useful for them. Its effects can therefore be very hard to predict (e.g. forecasting your results if you're in sales).

The final complexity that we need to acknowledge is that these filters operate at each of the 'mental processing' stages:

- On the way in – *"Yes, I hear what you say"*
  – deletion, distortion and generalisation of what's heard.
- As we think about something – *"Do I believe what I'm being told?"*
  – filtering the data as we analyse it.
- On the way out – *"So let me tell you what I reckon"*
  – unconsciously omitting something important or describing it inaccurately.

FOUNDATION TWO – THE FILTERS WE APPLY

Deletion

Deletion occurs when the other person selectively notices only *some aspects* of what you're doing or saying, and misses others. Without unconscious deletion, sitting on this chair writing all day would be exhausting – like ignoring the smell of that rhubarb pie!

Without aural deletion, noise would be unbearable. Remember the last time you were enthralled by a good book? Didn't the sound of the train you were travelling in, the people chatting loudly nearby and the rain beating on the windows all completely vanish?

> Without neural deletion we couldn't deal with
> the ocean of ideas that surge around us

As you listen, it's common to *not hear what you don't want to hear*. But the same applies when you speak – on the way out we often unconsciously omit information.

For instance, the statement

> *"The commitment you're asking for is difficult"*

omits key information, What aspect of the commitment makes it difficult? And what's the degree of difficulty? Later on you'll learn how you can improve your understanding of any situation – by challenging deletions and 'recovering' the missing information that the speaker's filter removed.

Distortion

This takes place when we interpret reality differently from those around us. Sometimes this is beneficial, sometimes less so. It's certainly not beneficial when, in the middle of the night, we distort the sound of a floorboard creaking into a burglar in our house. There are many more significant examples of this, and they're better known as *blame, presumption,* or *interpretation*.

One example might be a prospect who doesn't phone you back on the day they said they would. It's possible to *interpret* this as a rejection. But this is a self-made fantasy that completely hides the real situation – your buyer simply has a bad cold!

Another example might be to 'mind read' what your buyer really thinks of you or what you're offering. Whether the *presumption* you make is hugely optimistic or wildly paranoid, it's seldom helpful.

> Distortion is the major source of fear in sales, influence or persuasion…
> … we convince ourselves that failure will be catastrophic!

Generalisation

This filter does its work when we make an assumption or decision based on only a small number of events – or sometime even just one intense one! It's actually quite a good model of how our mind learns so well from real-life experiences. But it works really badly when we use incorrect or limited information.

Which of these is a useful generalisation?

> *"Oh, don't worry – she's just a young sales person from an internet start-up"*

or

> *"Be on your toes – she works for the largest consulting company in the world"*

In the first statement there's a clear 'putting down' of the person concerned. It may have occurred 'on the way in' as the speaker learned about the person they had encountered. It also appears to have happened 'on the way out' – *"don't worry"* and *"only"*. We usually call this 'jumping to conclusions'.

In the second example, the generalisation seems to be in the opposite direction. Because of what the business card says, the assumption is that the person is sharp and challenging. This might be an advantage or it might be a drawback.

Old school influence focuses on telling the buyer why they should buy from you. That approach will always leave you vulnerable to a lot of (possibly negative) generalisation – yet another reason why TSB teaches engagement, not bragging.

Advanced Filters

There are many more filters than the three you've just learned about. These advanced filters are also useful when it comes to creating a Willing Buyer. But, if you prefer, feel free to skip this section until you've got the big picture of *Turning Selling into Buying*.

If you're inspired to investigate filters more deeply, I suggest Roger Ellerton's excellent website at *goo.gl/pb4yN*.

Here, briefly, are the seven detailed filters that the full version of the Human Communication Model uses:

Values and Beliefs

These are the things we believe and value about ourselves, our actions, the people around us, world events and much else.

Values are typically things that we *move towards or away from*. They will often be an important part of your buyer's filter system.

Beliefs are our assumptions about how the world is, and can only be changed if the "Convincer Strategy" that we use is correctly executed (see chapter 9).

If your buyer believes that every sales person is a liar, then simply telling them how good your product, idea, or service really is unlikely to produce the result you want. TSB gives you the approach you need to deal with this in a different way.

If, however, your buyer believes anything they're told is true, that's almost as difficult. In a competitive situation, they're as likely to believe the competition's statements as yours!

Attitudes

These are a collection of *values and beliefs around a particular subject*. In commercial situations, they are often the soft information that we naturally draw out when we engage well with a buyer. They may have built up a set of values and beliefs about the wisdom of (for instance) using *financial advisers* or hiring *recent graduates*.

It's uncommon for a buyer to reveal or share the deeper parts of their attitudes in a commercial situation. But if you see that your buyer has a rather relaxed attitude to detail and timekeeping, you're not going to rely on them much when planning the 'route to a purchase order'!

Decisions

These are *generalisations that we've sealed in to our Model of the World*, to save us having to re-interpret and re-learn them – over and over again.

I, for instance, made the decision long ago to never hit the Send Button on an email when I'm under pressure or tired. It's proven to be a useful strategy. I could work out all the reasons why I shouldn't hit the send button every time – but it's far more effective as a decision that I *always* act on.

If you discover that the person you're influencing to invest in your company has decided they're not going to invest in a green tech company – and that's what you do – you have a problem to overcome. A useful way might be to gently investigate the motivation for that decision. This may draw out values, beliefs or attitudes that can then be dealt with. This is called "Reframing", which we'll look at in much more detail later.

Memories

These are the experiences that we build up and store away in collections that reinforce each other. Our mind then automatically *matches the pattern of* everything we experience against these memories and checks for correlation, interpretation, and information that is useful to us. Does that shape look like a tiger? Have we met a con artist like this before?

If your buyer has had many, repeated experiences of being let down by promises, they're going to need a lot of convincing that what you say will actually happen – and in fact they might never be convinced. If however they have a positive memory of what's being discussed, then great – the tide is running your way!

Language

Our interpretation of the words we use, and the sentences we wrap around them, is very individual – regardless of the education we've had. Words are 'codes' and the same word or phrase can have a *dramatically different meaning to two apparently similar people* – which doesn't help communication much. These differences may not only be in the meaning – the same words can also create massively different emotions, too.

In North America, *pants* means what you wear on the outside – in England, where I was raised, *pants* describe what you wear *underneath* your trousers. To young kids, *"pants"* might mean something is ridiculous!

Affection is a word that can mean a dozen different things to as many different people. The words *Business Development* are used in many different ways in a commercial situation. And of course, even the word *Sales* differs wildly in its interpretation and the feelings it creates in the person who hears it.

Time & Space

This is probably our simplest filter and one with which we're most familiar. We change our Time and Space filter significantly depending on where we are – at the office or at home; with friends or with employees; on holiday or at a funeral. We all adapt and 'reload' our filters, almost as often as we *change environments*.

You may, for example, know your buyer from playing sports together, but you know very well that they are likely to be a 'different person' that you meet in a sales call with them.

Thinking Style

Last, but not least, we all develop *habitual patterns of thinking and filtering*. These may include a preference for *detail* or an *overview*, or a tendency to move *towards a solution* rather than *away from a problem*.

One buyer might say that they want to move towards an objective - perhaps *"a happier and more profitable retail team"*. Another person may describe exactly the same problem as *"needing to get away from the costly effort of managing our retail team"*. Each will want to hear about how you can solve 'their version' of the problem – in a way that matches their Thinking Style.

Filter Creation

So where do these highly individual filters come from? Well they're what make you 'you' and me 'me'. They're what makes the nice old lady at the fruit shop give you an extra portion of grapes; what makes your bank manager so easy to talk to; and what makes my crazy but wonderful teenage daughter appear to live on another planet.

The influences on us throughout our lives build up our individual filters and thus, ultimately, our *Model of the World*. These influences include:

- Our family and our close friends.
- Schools and associations.
- Our religion and community.
- Books we read, films we watch, the media in general.
- Significant emotional experiences we experience.

But the good news is that these filters can be changed. That's what's at the heart of influence.

The Effect of Filters

Take another look at the Human Communication Model image in Figure 3. You can see that your filters are what build up an *internal representation* of what you are experiencing. Your depiction may hardly be filtered at all, or it may be heavily Distorted, Deleted and Generalised. Either way, your internal representation is what creates feelings of happiness, relief, anger, elation, and so much else.

We call this "State" and it's how your mind 'makes you feel' as a result of the physical and neurochemical changes your mind creates in your body. Like so much else to do with a Model of the World, we all have our own highly individual definition of State – elated, relaxed, powerful, satisfied, exhausted – all of these are different for you than they are for me. But they each describe a different State.

Our internal representation is also what creates our *behaviour*. In most cases our reaction is likely to be verbal (or perhaps an email). But reactions are not always words or an email. The result might be the buyer clamming up because you've hit a subject they don't want to talk about, or one they've been forbidden to discuss.

On the other hand, your words could be a hot button for your buyer – and the information flood gates open. This is where the "Active Listening" that you'll learn later becomes so important.

Last but not least, the Human Communication Model applies to us *all*. The reactions that *you have*, the words *you* use, the things *you* do – are all determined by *your* internal model. The more familiar, honest and comfortable you can become with your own model, the better your results will be – in both your professional and personal life.

To learn much more about the developing science of the unconscious mind, listen to or read the transcript of a great interview with Leonard Mlodinow at *goo.gl/nDRPC* or read his book *Subliminal*.

FOUNDATION THREE – THE 'FRAMES' FOR OUR MODEL OF THE WORLD

A "*Frame*" is the overall context within which your buyer observes the world. They are still using the filters described in Foundations One and Two, but the Frame decides what's important *after the filter* and what's not. It tells them what they should focus on and what they should ignore. The Frame 'tells' your buyer what's significant *in that context*. This is vitally important because, as the context (and thus the Frame) changes, *we experience different results.*

A finance director may look at a new piece of recruitment software and perceive the cost savings and reduced legal risks. A union leader might look at the same piece of software and perceive only the staff reductions and risk of lower skills it brings. The same product – but each individual has a very different Frame.

At the office, I may evaluate a new video card for hi-res medical imaging and the money that will be saved by remote diagnosis. When I'm with my baby daughter, my Frame changes, and that same video card's ability to create bright colours that keep her stimulated is much important.

This change of Frame can be hugely valuable to you when you influence someone. Imagine the effect of asking a question such as:

> *"What would happen if everyone in your team could get answers that fast?"*

The answer to your question generated by a buyer and the *change of context* it creates for them can be one of your most powerful influence tools.

In creating the answer, they may have *new* experiences, or make a *new* decision or bring forward *forgotten* memories. This may very slightly change their Model of the World as a result of your question. When your buyer accepts this change of Frame that you create (we call this a re-frame), the result is dramatic, even with a small change.

Another way to give your buyer these experiences may be to tell them a story, to describe a case study, or use a metaphor that puts them into a different place or time. In this case 'living the story' (as all humans do) will change their model. We'll look at this later in your "Delivery Narrative" in chapter 9.

Let's look at two simple examples. The first is commercial, the second is more personal.

Example One

Your buyer (a municipal government department) is not excited by what they've read about the new solar power generating panels you offer. In fact, they're unable to recognise one of the key Buying Drivers that you know applies to them – that the panels can reduce their maintenance costs. This is because their view (their Frame) is too limited. They're only looking at their local district area, and, to make matters worse, only for the present financial year.

You could just *tell them* that over more time and over a wider geography, the financial benefit will be greater. But how much more effective would it be if they worked it out for themselves, by answering a good reframe question?

(In fact, asking you that is a good example of a reframe question in itself!)

A good 'time reframe' question you might ask your government buyer is

> *"So what are your maintenance costs over a long period – say five years?"*

This may reveal the fact that an expensive maintenance team shuts down the generator for a rebuild every three years. Follow this up with a 'geographical reframe' question which asks

> *"How many maintenance teams there are in the whole region?"*

and you may uncover that every district funds its own maintenance team.

Taken together (with data you've prepared well beforehand), the costs are much higher than they first appear. Once the context is changed (reframed), more information is considered, and their Model of the World is altered. At this point, the business case for your solar panels is seen to be stronger – *and they've worked it out for themselves.*

Example Two

Here is a classic reframe. At a parent-teacher interview, the parents are concerned about a behavioural problem they see in their son. They explain that he never stops talking, is very strong willed and won't stop giving his opinions on anything and everything. They're concerned that he's hard to cope with and they want to change the way he behaves.

The teacher pauses, reflects, then says:

> *"Well congratulations, you must be so pleased. He's clearly going to be self-reliant, confident and sure of himself all his life. Won't that be such a great relief when he goes out into the world and you don't worry about looking after him? Let's see how we can work together to give him some tools to communicate even better."*

The Frame of reference of the parents is widened and lengthened to include the distant future and how they will feel once their son has left home. They are able to look at far more information, and are able to feel much more comfortable with their child's behaviour.

There are some people who are completely natural reframers. They do it highly effectively – and usually without conscious thought. We may never get to be as good as them, but you can get very close. It just takes conscious practice – like learning to countersteer a bike!

FOUNDATION FOUR – THE FULCRUM OF INFLUENCE

All of us, since we were children, have tried to influence other people to change their minds – whether it's letting you join their team, share their sweets, or play with a new toy. But of course, most of us started at the wrong end of the problem and our attempt to change people's minds ended in a playground fight, or a disagreement.

The very simple "Fulcrum of Influence" model that we use in TSB highlights what we've all experienced unconsciously throughout our lives. We've all had variable results in changing minds, but could never really work out why – here's the answer!

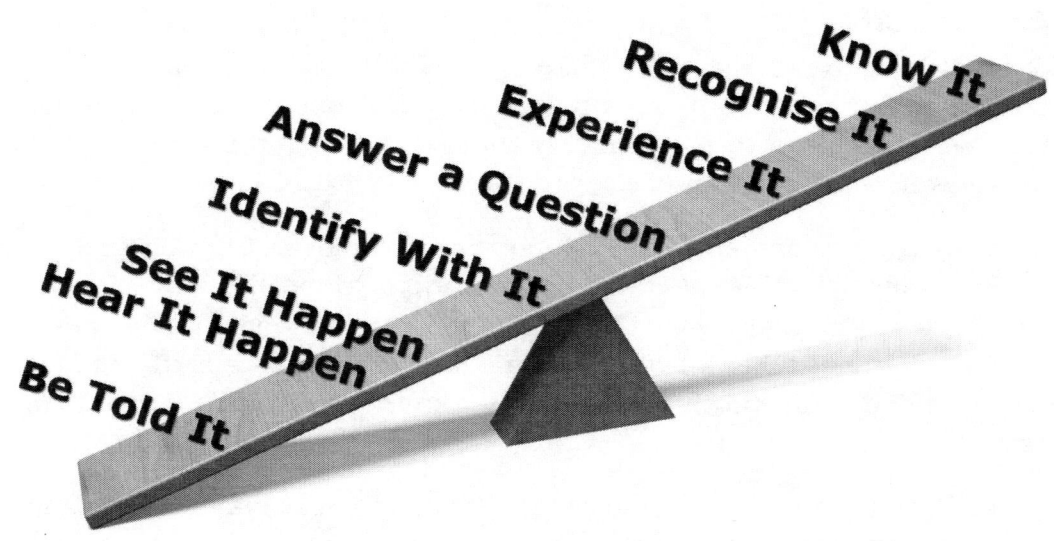

Figure 4

The best way to appreciate this is by looking at Figure 4. Not all situations require you to take every step. You may start in the middle, maybe go back a step, and then forward. But the aim is to end up at the right hand end, with a Willing Buyer.

Be Told Something

This is the least effective way of influencing someone. To influence people, you need to *change their Model of the World* to include what you've just told them *as a truth*. If you're influencing people to buy, you need them to incorporate the new truth – *"Doing this is useful."*

Simply telling them that it's a great idea or would be good for them has a very low success rate, even with constant (and annoying) repetition. There are a few people who are convinced on first hearing, and with no further proof – but they're rare.

Hear It or See It

Observing something happen from an outside position is more effective. Buyers can believe more in the information, since they're not simply 'being told'. For most people, seeing something happening is a more effective agent of change than just hearing about it.

Hearing a Story

All of us identify with a compelling story – we're almost hard-wired to listen. Not only that, but our unconscious will usually *put us inside* a story we can relate to – whenever there's the slightest ability to see ourselves in that scene.

Every good story has an arc in which the hero moves from one point to another, solving problems and slaying dragons along the way. Your aim is to have your buyer walk that same arc. At the end of a successful story, your buyer's Model of the World is changed to include the new ideas, services, and products that they experienced while slaying *their dragons* along their path.

Stories have great value in two places. They're great ways of creating a Frame or creating a different one (reframing). But they're also useful further down the influence road. Once you've built a Willing Buyer, you can use a detailed "Delivery Narrative" to help them experience the journey from making the decision to receiving the Buying Drivers. This also helps turn their 'Desire to Buy' into an order or decision. You'll learn how to do this in chapter 9.

Answer a Question

This is where you cross the pivot point. Once your buyer has 'worked it out', you're in a good position to influence them strongly. It's the point at which Precision Questioning and Active Listening become so powerful. Here are a couple of examples:

> "What if everyone got their rebate this quickly – not just a few customers?"
>
> "How many extra phone calls could you make if someone else was making your travel bookings?"

To answer either of these, your buyer will need to go inside their head and run a complex set of thoughts. But the answer is likely to be very convincing because *they* had worked it out. You will have 'swung the bar' strongly in favour of a permanent change.

Experience It

This is the next step along the bar. Even stronger than a story or working it out is to engage with the experience itself – to actually have the experience of being a passenger in a car with a flat tire and help fix it with a can of spray repair foam. This is a much more convincing than imagining how easily a can of spray foam might fix a roadside puncture.

The ultimate convincing experience would be if your buyer was not only the person who fixed the flat tire, but also gained some financial benefit from their investment in the spray can (which you sell). Maybe they arrived at a profitable sales meeting on time or didn't have to pay for roadside assistance.

Recognise It

This is the final step along the influence bar. At this point, your buyer understands the whole issue and has incorporated the new model into theirs. The change is made and it'll usually remain unless another 'convincing experience' comes along to alter it.

Most importantly of all (as you'll learn in chapter 9) your buyer has almost certainly moved from a Desire to Buy to a decision to act – whether that's to spend money with you or to make a decision.

You also now have a great testimonial for what you offer – and a far more effective Convincer than you telling someone!

If you want to become better at influencing people, then become conscious of the *Fulcrum of Influence*. Make the effort to move any discussion further towards the right hand end of it and it will pay off quickly.

If you remain at the left hand end of the fulcrum and just pile on assertions for your case, your results will be unpredictable, slow, and laborious – if you get a result at all.

The center point of the seesaw is where you should usually start. This is where your precision questioning, story-telling and active listening combine together to move your buyer to recognising the need to buy – the most convincing thing by far that they can experience.

Ask the *right* question – get the *right* answer –
tell the *right* story – drive the *right* change

THE FOUR TSB MINDSETS

Introduction

The TSB Mindsets are simple and nearly as powerful as the Foundations. If you take nothing else away from this book, they'll improve your communication for the rest of your life – add the Foundations, and the world will never be quite the same.

Each Mindset is simply a different approach to seeing the world around you – they are reframes in *your* model. You can integrate them into your approach to life and work until they are not simply techniques, but *permanent* skills.

Mindset One – So What's Actually In It For Them?

People aren't motivated to buy by features, functions, promises or potential. There are only five reasons that any individual, group or organisation is ever motivated to buy or to 'buy into' something:

- **Time** – achieving a goal sooner or more regularly.
- **Income** – increasing revenue.
- **Risk** – reducing the risk of an undesirable event.
- **Expense** – reducing current or future costs.
- **State** – simply feeling happier, more satisfied or less stressed.

These are the five TSB Buying Drivers and we'll look at them in much more detail in chapter 3. If you can *accurately* elicit what your buyer wants to take away from working with you, then great. If you can cost-effectively supply it as well, then you're well on the way to a favourable decision.

Whether your buyer is a Wall Street trader or a charity worker who's digging a well in a drought-torn African State, their motivation for change and action will always be SO WHAT'S IN IT FOR ME? (SWIIFM for short).

In the case of the trader, the motivation may appear, from your side of the table, to be as simple as making money to spend on the high life or their child's college education. But what might *actually* be motivating them to work so hard could be something very different. For one trader it might simply be the thrill of the chase or a drive to be the seen as the best (**S**tate). For another it might be paying for their elderly parent's medical care (**E**xpense). You need to uncover this, if you can.

In the case of the charity worker, the main beneficiary would seem to be the people who now have easy access to water, instead of walking for three hours every day. But the aid workers who spend a year away from home are also enjoying a reward. There is 'Something In It For Them'. If I ran a charity and wanted to influence talented individuals to take a year out to work for me, it would be most productive to start out by *finding out about them*, not 'spraying' how much good they could do for the world.

We'll visit SWIIFM often during *Turning Selling into Buying*. But it's important to understand that, *even with the same offering*, the Buying Drivers can differ hugely. They can:

- Vary between different buyers.
- Vary in different situations.
- Vary as the components of your offering vary.

To continue the charity example, perhaps the volunteer's primary motivation is actually to take a break from a job managing transportation logistics – not the desire to make the world a better place. Pitching that particular volunteer a job organising transport in the charity's African HQ might not match their real Buying Drivers – so you probably wouldn't get your volunteer.

When *you* want to influence someone to buy your ideas, your products and services, or even to offer you a job, it's easy to fall into the trap of *selling to yourself* and your own Buying Drivers. It's all too easy to assume that your buyer thinks the same way as you and then project your own Buying Drivers onto them. Watch a good video example of this at *goo.gl/Um2V2*

MindSet Two – Assume Nothing, Investigate Everything

One of the greatest risks is assuming and guessing – especially in a familiar situation where you've had success before. At a personal level, incorrect assumptions can cause embarrassment, conflict and anxiety. In a sales situation, they can cause time and resources to be wasted on an 'opportunity' that's never going to close. At worst, they can lose you a customer or your whole business.

Start-ups and mid-level businesses often have to pitch to investors for funding. It's all too easy to assume that potential investors want a risk-free exit strategy and a quick return on their investment. But until you've *properly engaged with them* and asked some questions, you can't say for certain.

There may be several other possibilities. The investment company might be taking a more relaxed attitude – perhaps to diversify their portfolio, or perhaps to attract a new type of investor. They could have a quarterly bonus on the line, and signing you up (regardless of whether it is a good investment) will get them the bonus. Until you know this, assumptions about what parts of your offering attract them can be dangerous.

> Mike made a reasonable living as a consultant. He was an expert in the specialised field of Business Process Re-engineering. Over the years he'd learned who he should meet to get business and how much to charge.
>
> But he'd never quite made it big. He'd never won that major project where he could bring in other people. What he really wanted was to make money from subcontractors doing the work – this would give him much more time to find new business. He also wanted to break away from the government contracts that were the bulk of his business – they were profitable but repetitive.
>
> To improve his sales skills, he attended one of my *Fearless Selling* workshops where he learned how to ask great questions about a customer's problems – not make the assumptions he'd always made in the past. Initially, he was motivated by discovering a practical tool to increase the accuracy of his business analysis – but he soon realised it went further.
>
> A couple of months afterwards, we met for coffee. He told me that he'd found an unexpected and profitable benefit from his new questioning skills.
>
> In the past, he'd always assumed that clients just wanted to buy Business Process Re-engineering – so that's what he talked about.

Now he'd learned how to uncover what was in it for them instead of lecturing them on his specialist subject, life had changed. They now told him what lay behind the need for his services – and he'd uncovered profitable gems he might never otherwise have found.

He learned that he had capabilities that went well beyond Business Process Re-engineering. He also elicited needs that his associates could satisfy (for a nice percentage). Best of all, he won a contract with a growing company prepared to pay Mike generously to make them more efficient!

Needless to say, he paid for my coffee ... and the croissant!

MindSet Three – Sitting on the Buyer's Side of the Table

Mindset 3 is the logical and inevitable outcome of the first two. There is a famous expression:

"*Walk a mile in another person's shoes*"

meaning *"experience life exactly as I do, before judging me."*

When you're trying to build a Willing Buyer, this phrase is at the heart of the influence you're trying to achieve. If you want to understand what will truly motivate someone to buy from you – rather than simply guessing at it – you need to see the world to the very best of your ability from your buyer's point of view – from 'their side of the table'.

Imagine yourself being 'sold' to. Would you:

- Like to be 'pitched at' when you want to buy something?
- Want to make all the effort to work out your SWIIFM?
- Enjoy working out the financial case for placing an order?

If you truly sit on the Buyer's Side of the Table,
you'll answer *"No"* to all those questions.

You'd want the influencer you to see the problem through *your* eyes and act accordingly.

It's important to remember that when we try to sit on the buyer's side of the table, none of us truly leave ourselves behind.

When I think I'm experiencing the world through the eyes of my daughter's teacher, or feeling the pressures on my potential business partner – I'm not. It's very hard to be another person, with all the depth and complexities of belief and values they might have. But just trying *to the best of your ability* can make such a big difference:

- To your creativity.
- To your ability to connect with them.
- To your confidence to simply ask about their 'stuff'.
- To just being engaged and interested.

If you can develop the ability to do this at any meeting where you need to change someone's mind (we call this an influence meeting), you'll have a far better insight into how your buyer is interpreting your 'selling' conversation. We'll look at a powerful and easily learned way of doing this in chapter 4.

Mindset Four – Question Precisely, Listen Actively

Most of the day-to-day talking and listening that we do is *unconscious*. To protect ourselves from the huge amount of information that's thrown at us, we seldom use the *active* part of our brain to listen to the words we hear or to create the phrases we actually speak. All too often, our brain already knows the answer it's going to receive and 'knows' how it's going to react. *This applies equally to us and our buyers.*

As a result, we communicate poorly – usually driven by the assumptions, guesses, and omissions that our unconscious mind makes. Improving influence and communication means eliminating these errors through *Active Listening*. Once they've been eliminated, the uncertainty, anxiety and unnecessary activity around a sales effort disappear too. This is what Mindset Four is all about.

Precision Questioning

When we talk to other people, or even engage in a formal meeting, we're seldom aware of the precise structure, content, and applicability of the questions we ask. Precision Questioning is the art and science of *consciously* using specific words that *inevitably result in accurate, objective answers.*

Very often, people unconsciously make imprecise, generalised statements such as:

> "I want to make my staff happier."

Or they'll make assumptions about your knowledge:

> "My accounting process needs speeding up at the end of the quarter."

When they're under pressure they may even distort things:

> "My fuel consumption is truly appalling."

To reveal the *deeper meaning* hidden behind these statements, you need to use Precision Questioning. If you're actually *conscious* of the words you use, you'll get answers that will help you see if you have a solution to the buyer's needs.

Read the following three questions out loud while imagining that they're being asked by someone on the other side of your desk. Be *consciously honest* with yourself about how you feel as you hear each question:

> "So why did the cable break?"
> "So how did you make the cable break?"
> "So what caused the cable to break?"

The first question is open to a wide range of responses – and there may be nothing wrong with this. If you consciously choose to use an open question like this in an influence meeting, it might be good as a softening up question early on in a conversation – to test what style of an answer they'll give. But when you're looking for tough, objective answers, it doesn't deliver.

How did question two make you feel? It's the classic *presumptive* question that projects the answer within its own words – and is unlikely to get a useful response. In fact, it's most likely to generate a defensive cover-up response.

Question three is nice. It assumes that *something identifiable* caused the failure. But it didn't make any assumptions about what caused the problem. For example:

> "What failure in design caused it to break?"

would be a less useful question, It would assume that design is the problem (not maintenance or use). You may even be talking to the person who is responsible for the design – so you're back to the presumptive question and defensive response!

"*So what caused it to break?*" is pitched at the right level to get a useful response without annoying the responder. Depending on their answer, you can then drill down into the details or start looking at the big picture.

Active Listening

This is about consciously taking notice of and reacting to the *contents and structure* of the answer that your buyer gives.

- Is it another question?
- Is it a complete sentence?
- Is it a fact?
- What are they *not* saying?

Active Listening is key to gaining respect and effectiveness during an influence meeting. Your buyers will unconsciously put all of themselves into their response to your question – beliefs and value, past decisions, experience, and much else. There may be a lot of hidden information in the words they use, or there may be nothing. So at least give them the respect of Actively Listening to the contents and the structure of the answer your buyer gives you. It takes very little practice to become totally conscious and make yourself so much more effective!

Imagine now that you're a buyer getting this question from a potential vendor:

> "What's the biggest reporting problem in your working week?"

and the answer you give (as the buyer) is:

> "I guess it's the very great detail needed for the operations report – it takes up so much time."

Here are two possible responses you might hear back from the seller:

> "What do you hate most about it?"
> "Can I see an example of this very precise detail and the time it takes?"

Play them over in your mind to yourself, and imagine it's a real-life situation. I hope you'll see that the first response might annoy you a bit. You didn't actually say you hated doing the detailed operations report – the sales person has not shown they listened to your response. The second answer however, reassures you that they heard what you'd said, and you'll feel happier to give you more information.

Even if you can't spot anything that will help you influence your buyer, just playing back the words they use will build an improved level of rapport between the two of you – and tempt them to reveal more about the situation.

Active Listening is only what we *expect others to do* when we speak.

A few years ago, I was building a Framework to support patio lights and a canopy. Being a good engineer, I worked out exactly what I needed and went to a scaffolding company to buy some tubing.

At the customer service desk, after the usual pleasantries, I explained that I wanted *"6 metres of 48mm diameter 3mm wall thickness piping – preferably used and rusty"* – so that it wouldn't cost too much.

The guy on the front desk blew me away when he asked (apparently quite instinctively) *"For what purpose precisely do you want to buy it?"* I was so shocked that I must have looked at him a bit weirdly, but I answered him. He then followed up with *"Can you give me an example of how you're going to use it?"* Well, two precision questions in a row stopped the discussion and I asked him about how he'd been trained.

> It appears that he is very highly regarded in the company for his completely natural ability to drill down exactly to customers' problems and then influence them to buy the right solution (*whether it was more expensive or less*). As a result, many customers kept coming back for his practical pre-sales advice – which was simply based on him being genuinely interested, and asking very precise questions.
>
> As well as Active Questioning, he did plenty of Active Listening. So I went home with a much better solution than my own design – a 7 metre extruded aluminium girder with a cross-drilled flange! It cost a little more, but delivered so much more – and I've been back several times since.
>
> I later asked this excellent guy where he'd got his talent, and whether he'd ever done any training. He was very clear about it. It wasn't training – it was his grandmother. She'd always told him that his gift for questions was because *"he was the eighth son of the eighth son"* in their large family.
>
> Being born eighth is probably not a practical solution for most of us. But I guarantee that after chapter 5, asking precision questions as well as he did will become natural to you.

So what can we learn from my story? It's very simple and I've used it teaching retail salespeople and my students:

- Be genuinely interested in what your buyer is trying to achieve (or become so).
- Never make any assumptions about the purpose of their purchase.
- Similarly, never assume what they ask for is truly what they need.
- (Politely) challenge their decision to buy what they've asked for -
- especially if it's a ½ inch drill in the sketch at goo.gl/Um2V2!
- Help them to appreciate the real Buying Drivers behind their purchase.

At the very least, they'll come back again. At best you'll get a bigger sale. If they actually buy something cheaper, they'll be back again as well! It's as true in retail, as in B2B, partnership, and so much else.

IN SUMMARY:
BRAINS ARE COMPLEX BUT CAN BE INFLUENCED

When we communicate with someone, there's more going on than we're conscious of. Now you have a model to help you understand what's going on, I hope it's all a little clearer. Keep this picture (Figure 3) in your head from now on and every day consciously observe other people *deleting, distorting,* and *generalising*.

The next thing you learned is the unconscious structures we all use and change – our *frames of mind*. Watch out for these Frames in yourself and other people. You've also learnt that there *are* ways to change Frames. It takes effort to learn and practice these methods, but they're often your most reliable route to influencing a buyer.

Most importantly, you can now see that influencing someone to change their mind is most easily accomplished by getting them to *change it themselves*. One of the best ways to do this is to ask a question. In answering it, they will often change their Model of the World – *just enough to buy*. There are a lot more questions you will learn to use as you progress through the book.

If your buyer doesn't recognise that buying from you is beneficial, use these reframes and questions to *help them* discover the benefit of buying – and thus create a Willing Buyer – or save time for both of you by qualifying that there is no opportunity – and leave on good terms.

The Mindsets speak powerfully for themselves. If you go to goo.gl/HEvyA you can download a sheet, print it out, and put it on the wall to remind you of them every day, to help integrate them into your unconscious.

CHAPTER 2:
REVIEW QUESTIONS & SELF-DEVELOPMENT ASSIGNMENTS

How People Communicate & Influence – see Annex B for Answers

To print a copy of this section, download it directly from goo.gl/jouFq or select it from the TSB Download Page at goo.gl/p0Ajn.

Self-Test Questions

1 What new skills make TSB so different from old-school approaches to influence?
2 What's the difference between a TSB Foundation and a TSB Mindset?
3 List two of each (then go back and re-read the ones you couldn't list):

The Human Communication Model

4 List the five senses that constantly deliver information to you – both unconsciously and consciously:
5 How many parallel flows of that information can your mind *consciously* process at the same time?

Filters

6 Describe two types of people likely to run very different Models of the World and thus find it hard to communicate:
7 List the three types of filtration that our neurology carries out:
8 Give three examples of deleted information – each using a different sense:
9 Give two examples of a distortion filter in operation:
10 Give two examples of a generalisation:
11 What can you do to recover missing information when someone talks to you but it's clear to you that they're deleting, distorting or generalising?
12 List three of the seven *advanced filters* and give one example of each:
13 List three examples of the influences on each of us that create the filters we use:
14 What does State mean?

Frames

15 What is a Frame?

16 What is a Reframe?

17 Give one example each of a reframing question, and a reframing statement:

18 Describe a recent experience that you can now recognise was you being reframed by someone else – or you reframing them:

Influence

19 What is your understanding of the Fulcrum of Influence?

20 Name as many of the 6 steps on the Fulcrum of Influence as you can – from 'least effective change' to 'most effective change':

TSB Mindsets

21 What are the four TSB Mindsets?

22 What does SWIIFM stand for?

23 What is the Mother of all Screw-Ups?

24 In which situations is the ability to 'sit on the other side of the table' most useful?

25 What are the two components of Precision Listening?

26 What must you be *consciously* aware of in Active Listening?

Self-Development Assignments

Ch 2 Assignment 1 – Protecting yourself from overload

Practice being aware of how your mind filters everything you experience. As you go through your day, become *conscious* of the sounds that you weren't hearing before you started to focus. Then move onto seeing and the other three senses. If you cook some strong-smelling fish for dinner, be aware of how little you smell it once your mind 'becomes used to it'.

Ch 2 Assignment 2 – D, D, G Filters

Become aware of the next level of detail – how you delete, distort and generalise every day – when you think about things, when you speak to other people, when you write them down. Do you have any bad habits? Do have any good habits? Once you're comfortable, start to observe how other people use those same filters

Ch 2 Assignment 3 – Frames

During your day, you'll be in different situations – at home, at work, at play; with friends, with colleagues, with your boss; outdoors in the sun, indoors in the shade. Become aware of how you are setting a different Frame for your observation in each place. Does it vary? Is that difference useful? Are you conscious of any change of State? Is the different State obvious to those around you?

CHAPTER 3
How People Buy

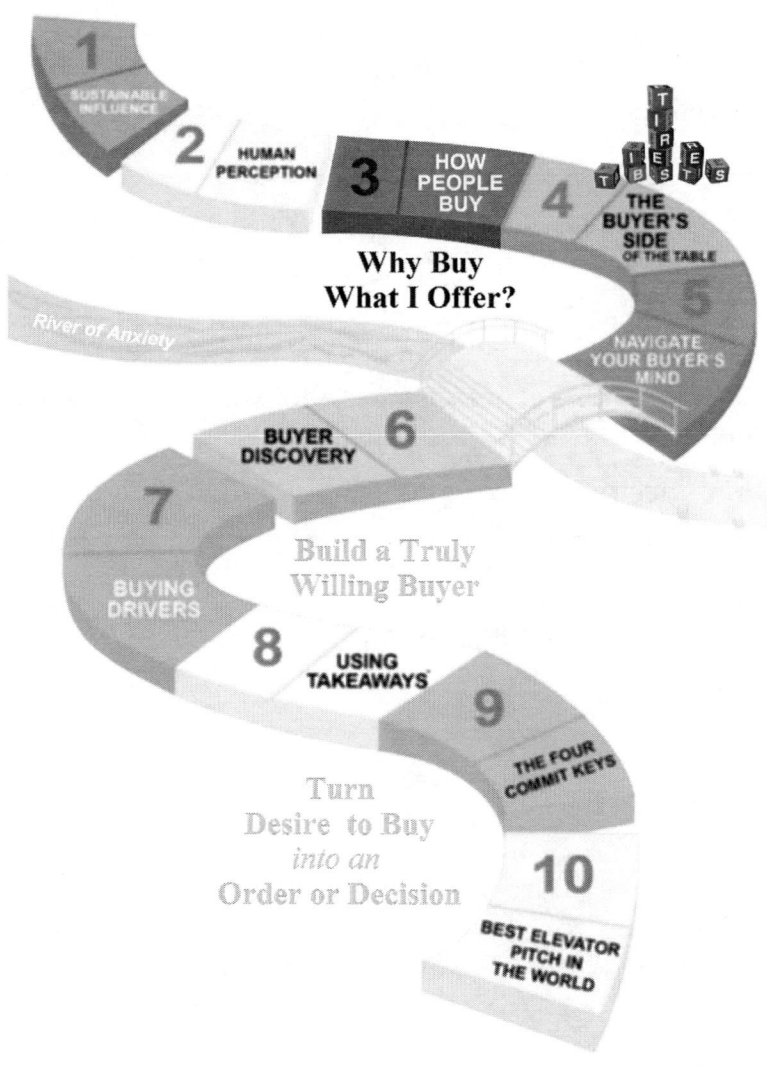

BY THE END OF THIS CHAPTER, YOU'LL UNDERSTAND ...

- How anyone decides to buy or 'buy into' something
- The only 5 ways people are influenced to buy from you
- Why "Buying Drivers" are better than Features, Advantages and Benefits
- The difference between an Offering, a Product and a Service

HOW WILL THIS HELP ME BUILD A WILLING BUYER?

This chapter is all about the practical psychology behind SWIIFM – *So What's In It For Me?* The same mechanism actually motivates us to make *all* buying decisions and this chapter teaches the insights and habits that you can use to:

- decide whether anyone would 'buy' your new idea, product or service.
- engage with anyone you need to influence.
- talk to any potential buyer and uncover their true Buying Drivers.
- help *them* justify a purchase, once they're ready to buy.

As you learned in chapter 2, even the most caring and considerate people are fundamentally motivated by SWIIFM. It's one of the human instincts that has evolved to make us as successful as we are. Even altruistic decisions (i.e. there doesn't appear to be anything in it for me) satisfy a need that can be as strong as greed – and more complex. Google 'Altruism Psychology' and you'll be amazed at what you find.

Errors that prevent you Building a Willing Buyer

Before we get into the details of SWIIFM, let's look at some of the classic selling mistakes that people make.

Selling to Yourself

This is at the heart of *Turning Selling into Buying*. Many people make the mistake of assuming that the person they're selling to has similar values, beliefs, priorities, etc. to them. Then they're shocked and feel rejected when the person they're trying to influence doesn't respond as they expect.

Leave YOUR Buying Drivers behind.

No Connection

There's an old sales expression – "*People buy from people*" and there are a lot of books and courses on how to be a 'friendly salesperson'. This is certainly important, but it's by no means the whole picture. If someone's done a bad job of influencing me, I probably still won't buy from them – no matter how much I like them.

The information I'm given may not be done in a way that convinces me. They may miss some steps that I need before making a decision. I may not understand what's in it for me. Either way, relying on old school schmooze doesn't work anymore.

So be alert – a good connection is no guarantee of a sale!

Before you can hope to change someone's Model of the World to include the new belief "*I want to buy from this person*", they have to believe what you say, and trust you as a person. There has to be some degree of rapport between the two of you before the buyer's Model of the World has any chance of changing. If they're not comfortable with the person helping them to make the change (you), belief will quickly revert back to "*I don't want to buy from this person.*"

Rapport is usually defined as 'a *relationship of trust in which both sides are open about the subjects they discuss, and respectfully enjoy the exchange of views*'. This directly implies a two way street with questions, answers and discussions – not simply being friendly and 'giving a pitch'.

Selling Features & Functions

Have you ever visited a specialist shop to find out whether they've got something that will solve your problem? But then, when you engage with a sales person, all they can talk about is the 'cool' features and functions of their products. You wanted to discuss *your problem* – they only wanted to discuss the products. This is frustrating for you – and unprofitable for the sales person.

This is a common problem even when technology is not involved. You may, for example, want to 'sell' the details of your great new organisation plan – the one you've proudly worked on for weeks. But your buyer (the Managing Director) is only interested in the bigger picture and the strategic effect of your changes.

Under pressure, many of us resort to our comfort zone of expertise and start spraying details in the hope that something will stick and our buyer will buy.

Selling on Price

> Kelly was channel manager for a large reseller of her company's technical solutions. She'd trained their sales people and equipped them with a set of great user stories and case studies that had always worked well for her company's own direct sales team. This included a very strong set of financial justifications to support the product's pricing. But she became increasingly concerned at how often the partner company's management asked for special price reductions to 'win a sale'.
>
> So she asked to go out with the reseller's sales people on a customer call. Within minutes it became clear what the problem was. Despite the great cost justifications, the reps still lacked the confidence to engage in pricing discussions. They were techies whose comfort zone was talking about the technology – not discussing money. As a result, they often dropped the price almost immediately when they were challenged. It got them a sale, but at what cost?
>
> So what was to be done? Kelly had no time to retrain the sales team. So she solved the problem by insisting that only senior account managers be assigned to selling her product line – not the less experienced ex-techie reps that made up much of the partner's sales force. These senior people had a proven track record of knowing a client's business and being able to discuss the numbers behind it. The idea worked. After a short workshop to walk them through her cost justification spreadsheets, prices stopped being discounted and revenue returned to where it should have been.

Selling what's Asked For, not what's Needed

This is the classic new sales person mistake (and plenty of experienced ones do it, too). You meet a buyer who says "*I want to buy 16 of your widgets*" and yippee – you're happy – you've made a sale! Well, there's a chance that by accepting that first sale *without any questions*, you may have lost out on something larger.

Because you didn't engage and determine the context of the purchase you may have missed out on more items, extra services, a more expensive version, or even a completely different purchase. (The Ted Levitt videos at *goo.gl/YrB7y* illustrate this particularly well.)

Only Selling to the person in front of you

Similar to the previous mistake, it's also too easy to only think of the person in front of you. On the buyer's side of the table there may be unseen beneficiaries and stakeholders that you don't know about. Some of them will need further convincing, some will want to buy more of what you offer, while others will want to buy something slightly different. Without engaging and broadening the need with your buyer, how will you ever know? There is a lot of power in the simple question:

"So besides you, who else would benefit from having this?"

Fearless Selling – Are you a Bulldog or a Collie?

So often, *poor performance* in business influence in general, and sales in particular, can be put down to fear. Just as often, *great success* can come from being fear-less and courageous. In my experience, there are two types of fearlessness – the courage and strength of the *Bulldog* and the intelligence and experience of the *Sheepdog*.

I've worked with many leaders and colleagues of both types – in business and in the military. Bulldogs have blind faith in their own ability. They're strong, tough and, like the dog, won't take no for an answer. Bulldogs have little time for planning, strategy, or analysis. They're totally determined – once they get their teeth into an opportunity, they just get on with it. They won't let go until they get the business (or are forced to give up through injury or exhaustion). They stay late at the office, get in earlier than everyone else and have a strong self-motivation. For many years my nickname was 'the Rottweiler' because of my determination. But as I described in the introduction, I've moved on to more enjoyable *and* productive places since then.

Turning Selling into Buying is about often operating more like a sheepdog, and less like a bulldog. Sheepdogs are a very different breed that's nowhere near as strong as a bulldog – but they can work just as hard. It has to use its brains, not its muscles, to achieve goals. It enjoys relaxing and playing; but it has the intelligence to quickly do whatever's necessary. A sheepdog is also very quick at recognising what's *not possible*. If you give it job that it's already worked out can't be done, it will refuse – unlike the bulldog, which will almost always 'give it a go'.

Both dogs can be successful – which is why we all need to develop the flexibility to dip into either way of attacking a problem depending upon the situation. But over time, a strong pattern of difference between the two breeds emerges.

Bulldogs spend less time with their families, their results are more unpredictable, and they're not always in the best of health. The effort of 'hanging on' can be very stressful! Sometimes their approach to a sale prevents them from engaging properly with their buyer – engagement that can often lead to spotting a different, easier route to success. That same, aggression can sometimes also get in the way of building a strong, sustainable customer/supplier partnership which delivers more revenue over the longer term.

The sheepdog, on the other hand, generally knows when to give up (or when not to start in the first place). Its likelihood of success is usually greater, and (equally important in sales) more predictable. It uses its intelligence to achieve what needs to be done and spends much more of its time happy at its job – herding sheep to the right place. It probably has a much better relationship with the sheep, too!

TSB delivers the skills to be as successful and predictable as a **Sheepdog**, whilst saving your strength for the few occasions when you need to be a **Bulldog**.

The causes of Sales Fear

There are consistently three reasons that people fear sales:

- Anxiety about lack of knowledge.
- Discomfort at being 'pushy'.
- Fear of rejection.

Anxiety

The first fear people admit to is being shown to have a lack of knowledge – they worry about looking stupid or appearing ignorant. Sometimes this fear is attached to the actual product, service, or idea that they sell. Sometimes it's caused by fear of not knowing enough about the buyer's situation or their need, or maybe their industry or company.

The hardest fear to shed is ignorance of the *business connection* between your buyer's need and what you offer. It's great to know exactly how your web application works; or even how it's used in the industry where you've sold it before. But what's more stressful is dealing with a buyer you know little about.

Perhaps you find an opportunity at an airline or a government department, but you've only sold to retailers before. Fortunately, chapters 8 and 9 step you through a process that will replace any fear of the unknown with confidence and creativity.

Discomfort

Many people see sales in the old school way – aggressively forcing a product or solution upon an unwilling prospect. Even the language of sales encourages this idea. Strong sales terms like *pitch, pressure,* and *close* abound. In TSB, the pitch is replaced by *engagement*, pressure by *development and agreement*, and the close by a *Buying Plan*.

If you're embarrassed to phone someone to push for a decision then, just reframe it as a continuation of last week's conversation. Your buyer said they were interested in solving a problem then – why would things have changed that much?

Because you've used your new TSB techniques, you'll also know exactly what personal, financial and corporate benefits they can TakeAway from doing business with you. Reframe the situation even further and you may see it as actually more embarrassing *not* to discuss the opportunity they have.

Rejection

This is at the heart of most sales people's anxiety. Eliminating the fear of rejection was a big motivation for me in developing the TSB techniques. I'd sometimes become stressed and nervous myself, but I'd seen far worse. I've seen mature, experienced operators become very different people when they actually had to ask for business. So much so, that they'd invent almost *any excuse* to avoid risking the chance of rejection.

The key transformation from old school sales to TSB is that you consider the whole decision 'from the buyer's side of the table'. You can see what drives the decision clearly enough to know that there's no rejection of you personally. If your buyer doesn't need what you're offering, you'll almost certainly have discussed it and agreed it with them. If there's no need for your product, that's OK – you didn't waste your buyer's time or your own. And the comfort you exhibit in dealing with the buyer's *"No"* may well produce a return call later when the buyer's need *does* fit your offering.

If your buyer needs what you offer, but is not responding to the Buying Drivers that you've jointly identified, something's gone wrong somewhere – and that means it can generally be fixed! A 'win back' opportunity from an unjustified *"No"* may be time for the bulldog and the sheepdog to join forces.

HOW PEOPLE BUY – ANYTHING

You saw in chapter 2 that your buyer's brain holds a complex model of their world. It doesn't matter whether it's a major purchase, or just a simple idea, or something in between. A buyer's decision to proceed will always be accompanied by a small change to their mental Model of the World.

Before the decision, their model doesn't include the new outcomes e.g. money saved, more happiness, etc. Once they've bought into your idea, and have been convinced to stay that way (more on that later) their model includes two new items – 'owning the decision' and 'benefitting from the outcomes'.

There are only five Buying Drivers strong enough to drive that change. We'll learn about them in great detail in the next section. But here's the problem – buyers usually don't consciously know which of the five is driving their decision. It's amazing how often buying decisions are made without any conscious or objective knowledge of the reason why. If you can make the process visible – for you and for your buyer – you can help them make the right decision – for them and you.

In a nutshell, that's the problem.
How can you expect to influence a process which
your buyer seldom understands?

SO WHAT?

It's 1990. It's the financial heart of the City of London and the pioneer days of banking software sales are in full swing. I'm working as a salesman for one of the biggest financial trading software houses – and there's a lot of money swilling around. There's also a lot of new technology being created – not all of it good, but all very 'cool'!

We were one of the first software houses to bring a hard edged approach to what had mostly been a cottage industry. One of the techniques from those days that I still use frequently became one of the first *Precision Questioning* skills used in this book.

Our division had a reputation for being tough and a bit crazy, but the whole operation was held together by our amazing Sales Director, Willy Ross, who had a reputation for always keeping us profitable. He had a lot of clever ways of doing this, but was famous for one in particular.

He'd say "*SO WHAT?*" to almost any statement made to him. If a person came to him with a sales problem, he'd say "*SO WHAT?*" until he reached the root of the problem or opportunity, be it business or personal. At board meetings, he'd challenge new proposals with the same question. If the head of Research & Development brought a new product idea to him, it would be "*SO WHAT?*" again. A salesman with a problem account – "*SO WHAT?*"

This was his shorthand for *"So what effect does that have on our business – in the longer term, looking at the bigger picture, and analysing the financial and personal effects?"* But that was a lot of words – and we were all in a hurry!

If he was feeling kind, he'd soften it:

"So what effect will that have on us?"

"So what will I get from spending all that money?"

"So what should we do?"

But mostly, it was just *"SO WHAT?"*

The effect was spectacular, not least because we soon all started thinking *"SO WHAT?" before* we brought him a problem. Just doing this often brought a solution to mind and saved Willy's time.

Not wanting to waste a good idea, I started using the SO WHAT technique myself – mostly within my team. But where I had a strong relationship, I'd use it with my partners and, *very* occasionally, with customers who knew me well. It was particularly useful to challenge a weak or bland statement made by my buyer. Sometimes, the only way to reveal what your buyer truly needs is to use a challenge or question like this.

SO WHAT DRIVES A BUYING DECISION?

Fast forward to the year 2000 and I'm with my good buddy Dave Perfect in yet another start-up. We're selling middleware – the boring but necessary transactional glue that business computers use to talk to each other. You couldn't see, feel or hear it work, and it was boring to demonstrate.

So, rather than focussing on the way it worked (which our competition favoured), Dave and I highlighted what the *business* could take away from using it. We often beat out our competitors for that one reason – our focus on how their business would change after the purchase, rather than what their techies liked.

In our discussions and proposals (and in the trainings that we later gave to our distributors) we started to use the phrase **"Cheaper, Faster, Safer"** to describe the business drivers for investing in this unseen but expensive software and services – which made life so much better for our clients.

Faster meant control over **Time.** Things could be done more rapidly. Time-critical transactions would complete more quickly. Maintenance time would be shorter. Testing time was less. Reporting deadlines could be achieved. *The ultimate outcome would always be financial, and this had to be addressed*, but **Time** was clearly a powerful driver for wanting to buy what we offered – not the 'cleverness' of our software.

Safer meant less **Risk**. Reduced risk of serious or expensive things happening. Risk was more visible or easier to deal with. Perhaps it moved elsewhere. Again, all good *Buying Drivers* – but needing financial analysis to turn a 'Desire to Buy safety' into a justification for spending money to achieve it.

But how about *Cheaper*? Well, some clients invested to save clerical costs. Others profited from increased market share. Others reduced the cost of late reporting penalties. In the finance markets, the variations are numerous and complex. So our *Cheaper* quickly became Improving **Income** or Reducing **Expense**.

We also soon realised that there was also often a fifth driver for buying from us. It was a softer, more human reason. The driver for buying what we offered was personal – to reduce anxiety or ease stress; to 'follow the crowd'; to feel good about doing it; to be happier; to be seen to be making good decisions. In a few cases, we found that vanity or stress was the *only* real Buying Driver.

We called this last Buying Driver **State**, a term we took from behavioural psychology. A State Buying Driver is the improvement in how you feel after the purchase is operational or decision made.

Figure 5

It soon became clear that the only truly universal motivators that changed a buyer's mind were these in Figure 5.

For obvious reasons, we collectively named our five Buying Drivers T.I.R.E.S!

SWIIFM seemed much harder to say (and much less descriptive), so TIRES is what they became. We soon found they motivated companies as much as they did individuals.

If we could make our buyer recognise that it was actually one or more of the TIRES that was being bought (and do it early) a Willing Buyer quickly emerged. In our discussions we'd always work hard to prove a link between *our underlying offering and the desired TIRES*. Once this tipping point was reached, then we'd start to create a Desire to Buy.

But of course, that was seldom the end point. More often than not, money came into the final act. That's the point at which we needed to turn this Desire to Buy into an order or a decision. Every Buying Driver can usually be turned into a financial return of some sort, and you'll learn how to do this in chapter 9.

YOUR BUYER'S ACTUAL TAKEAWAYS

I'm a fan of *Theodore (Ted) Levitt*, Economics Professor at Harvard Business School who died in 2006. He was world famous for one great marketing truism:

> *"People don't go to buy a ½ inch drill –
> they actually go to buy a ½ inch hole."*

The problem with this insight is that it didn't go far enough – simply taking home a ½ inch hole often isn't enough to solve the entire problem!

Running a pipe through that ½ inch hole may not to get you all the way, either. In fact, you sometimes have to work pretty hard to discover the real *root cause* of a purchase or an idea – but it's always there somewhere. You can see some great examples demonstrated at *goo.gl/IE6nD* on the *Turning Selling into Buying Channel* on YouTube.

> Your Buyer doesn't buy 'Stuff'…
> ….they buy **the effect** it has on them or their business –
> and perhaps not immediately.

If you and your team can analyse, accurately and objectively, how well you can deliver *that effect*, it's far more important than the 'stuff' itself. The output from your analysis will be far more useful to a sale than any detailed product knowledge ever will be. Your job will also become so much simpler – you'll need to connect only those few key functions of your offering to what the buyer desires. We named these key functions **TakeAways**. TakeAways are the last step in your 'delivery chain' – if they're needed, and you can prove they exist, you will always create a Willing Buyer. All you need to do then is turn that Desire to Buy into an Order or a Decision!

This therefore leads us to this definition of a TakeAway (which I'd seriously considered calling a Levitt):

A TakeAway is
the *desired effect or change* which will be in place
a *significant time after*
the delivery is complete or the work finished...
... and it should be *S*pecific, *M*easurable, *R*ealistic and *A*chievable!

The desired effect is not the 'stuff' they buy. It's not your great engineering – it's what the buyer takes away from using great engineering. It's not the power of the software or the processor – it's the effect of using it. It's not the stability of your firm – it's the effect of buying from a reliable supplier that they TakeAway. See Figure 6.

Figure 6

Unfortunately, this still doesn't get us all the way to where we want to be. What exactly is a *Desired Effect*? For one buyer a *Significant Time* might be minutes – for another it might be 10 years! How will it be paid for? Is it worth them paying that much? There's no point in achieving a great result if they go bankrupt doing it.

So how *do* we ensure that a TakeAway is a real, commercially useful point to discuss? It's those TIRES! It's the *Buying Drivers* that Dave Perfect and I had used so successfully for so many years!

CHECKING THE TIRES WITH SO WHAT?

You now have two great tools to analyse your offering and truly understand what would motivate someone to buy from you. It makes no difference whether you have a product, service, some third party products, or a complex mix of these. It even works with an idea or a vision.

Before you even meet your buyer, use SO WHAT to analyse a list of the features and functions of your offering. Just keep asking the question until you reach a statement which improves **T**ime, **I**ncome, **R**isk, **Ex**pense or **S**tate. See Figure 7. You'll learn in great detail how to do this in chapter 7.

The strongest rule in *Turning Selling into Buying* is shown in Figure 7.

A TakeAway is not a TakeAway unless it passes the TIRES check:

T.I.R.E.S. Definitions

TIME: Does the Buyer need the TakeAway to deliver an event ...

... earlier; later; under more control; more predictably; more regularly?

INCOME: Does the TakeAway make their income ...

... larger; more predictable; better 'shaped' over time; certain; delimited?

RISK: Does it alter the threat of an event occurring – making the risk ...

... decrease; more understood; visible; assigned elsewhere; mitigatable?

EXPENSE: Does the TakeAway make the expense...

... reduce, better controlled; better 'shaped' over time; sent elsewhere?

STATE: Does the final result of the TakeAway make someone...

... smile more; less stressed; more content; in a better light; more attractive?

Figure 7

Time is Money – Right?

That's true, of course, but the *desire for time improvements* is usually what first creates a Desire to Buy. Your buyer is not usually at first thinking about money arriving earlier or reduced costs. It's been our experience that it's useful to keep these time benefits at the forefront of your buyer's mind, rather than jump straight to the monetary benefits.

But it gets interesting once the Desire to Buy begins to firm up and is closer to becoming a purchase order or decision. That's the time to help your buyer monetise the time benefits that kept them interested. You'll learn how to do this in chapter 8.

Exercise – Can you recognise a TakeAway?

Try the tests that follow. Which of these **Statements** describes a TakeAway?

(**HINT**: Use *SO WHAT TO TIRES* to help you)

(Before starting, cover up the answers – then reveal them and the commentary *after* you've done a TIRES check on each statement)

OUR MACHINE TOOLS DELIVER GREATER EFFICIENCY
No.

It doesn't pass the TIRES check. Efficiency is *never* a TakeAway – which is odd considering how often it's used to sell things. How is the efficiency measured? How much greater? More efficient than what, specifically? Is it described with a **T**, an **I**, an **R**, an **E** or an **S**? Since you don't know yet, the statement does not describe a TakeAway.

OUR DELIVERY SERVICE IS 15% CHEAPER TO RUN THAN YOUR CURRENT SYSTEM
Yes.

This is a nice clean description of a TakeAway that's clear, measured and includes a comparison. The TakeAway is the reduction in cost ('cheaper') – clearly an **E**!

DOES CALCULATIONS FASTER
Maybe

This is not a black or white answer. It's our first demonstration of the importance of 'Frame of reference' when deciding if something is a TakeAway and which TIRES it delivers.

In a financial trading environment, this feature might be a long way from the TakeAway – which might be several steps on – the increased profit (**I**) made by being able to quote a better stock price, for a more complex deal – and faster (**T**).

In a classroom, however, it might be just one step away from the students' need to finish their math test within the time allotted (**T**).

For someone who just gets pleasure (**S**) playing with numbers on a calculator (they do exist!), it could actually be a TakeAway as it stands.

COOLER LOOKING
Maybe

Once again, this depends on the Frame. If my sole purpose is the pleasure of wearing a nice jacket, this is definitely a (**S**)tate TakeAway. If I want the jacket for a job interview, then it's one *So What* step away from an (**I**) TakeAway. It may be, that, as I dig deeper, the Cooler Looking jacket is well made, which might save me the (**E**)xpense of buying another one soon.

OUR SCREEN DELIVERS PIN SHARP 1080p HIGH DEFINITION IMAGES
Yes and No

If you're a remote surgeon controlling an online operation, the TakeAway is *not* the clearer image – it's the increased health of the patient which may be a couple of *So What* steps away. If you're the hospital administrator, it's also the reduced cost (**E**) of bad patient outcomes from poor surgery. It's also the (**T**)ime saved in getting the operation done. If you just want to watch movies, then this is an (**S**) TakeAway – directly.

THIS PROCESSOR HAS A 6 GHz PROCESSOR SPEED
Probably No

You're probably getting this by now. This is not an obvious TakeAway and it's probably quite a few *So Whats* away from one. Processors are used in so many ways nowadays that you'd need to drill down properly to draw out exactly what the buyer would TakeAway from using a higher speed processor.

The only, slightly obscure situation where it might be an **(I)** TakeAway is when I'm a retail supplier and can make a profit by selling high speed processors. In that case, it's the TakeAway that my *wholesaler* is supplying to me – not an end user.

Frame of Reference

I hope these exercises have made it clear why this is so important. As the Frame varies, so does what the buyer takes away from their decision. A change in Frame can involve many things, including:

- The circumstances of a specific buyer.
- The timescales in operation.
- Everyone affected by the buying decision.
- The precise make-up of your offering.
- And much more.

You must always take the Frame of reference into consideration when deciding if a TakeAway is a TakeAway – or simply a feature.

COMPOUND AND POTENTIAL TIRES

In real life, the most powerful TakeAways are often supported by a combination of several T.I.R.E.S. We call these "TIRE Compounds". Here are a few examples:

- **T/I – Time to Income**. *"These bonds have an earlier maturity date. The income is the same as the ones you invest in right now, but you get the income earlier."*
- **R/S – Risk of Stress**. *"Our virtual office services greatly reduce the stress caused by admin problems."*
- **S/I – Income from State**. *"Our chauffeur service means that in the first hour of the day, you're making good, profitable decisions, not wrestling with traffic."*

Think up other combinations of TIRE Compounds. See Figure 8 for a fuller list.

Practice by keeping your eyes peeled for advertising that passes the TIRES check – good ads will always do so. Some of the most effective ones (Apple is good at doing this) create a State-driven Desire to Buy that is so strong that cost benefit information is often completely ignored.

T.I.R.E.S. Detail & Compounds

TIME
Earlier/Control/Reassign/Predict/Repeatable
- Does something happen earlier and thus more usefully?
- Is the time more under their control?
- Is that time period re-assigned elsewhere?
- Can you predict the length or start point more accurately?
- Does the frequency or period of an event improve?

INCOME
Increase/Predict/Shape/Guarantee/Cap/Floor
- Is their income increased?
- Is the size or timing of income more predictable?
- Is the shape of the income curve more beneficial?
- Is the income more likely to occur?
- Is there a lower/higher value beyond which it will not go?

RISK
Decrease/Understand/Predict/Reassign/Mitigate
- Is the risk of something bad happening decreased?
- Is their risk better understood or monitored?
- Does the predictability of an event improve?
- Has the result of that risk been reassigned elsewhere?
- Can the risk be mitigated more effectively?

EXPENSE
Reduce/Manage/Reshape/Reassign
- Is their expenditure reduced?
- Is the rate of expense more controllable?
- Is the shape of the expense curve more beneficial?
- Is the expense reassigned elsewhere?

STATE
Smile, Satisfy, Stress, Shine, Seen
- Are they happier?
- Are they more fulfilled?
- Are they more content?
- Is their stress (however they define it) reduced?
- Do others see them in a better light?
- Is their pleasure increased?

TIRE COMPOUNDS - EXAMPLES:
T/R - is the risk of delay reduced?
T/I - is the time income arrives reduced or more predictable?
R/S - is the risk of feeling uncomfortable reduced?
E/S - are they more comfortable with less money going out?
(probably needs chunking)

Figure 8

But there are still too many ads out there that present features and functions, then leave it up to the buyer to work out what they'd TakeAway from a purchase. Most people are not particularly good at figuring this out – so they don't buy. That's the most common reason why ads fail – there are no clear TakeAways.

NOTE: It's important to emphasise that any analysis you carry out at this stage will only identify *potential TakeAways*. Each combination of buyer, situation, and offering only creates a well-documented shortlist of what *might motivate* a buyer. This process is called an ABC Analysis.

In an ideal engagement with a buyer you would move the conversation around the complete 'landscape' of potential TakeAways. You'd visit each potential TakeAway and *check whether it is needed*. If it is – then develop and explore it; if it's not, then you can move the conversation to the next one.

SO WHAT IS AN OFFERING?

We're surrounded by people and organisations working hard to sell us products and services. In most cases, the TakeAway from doing business with them is not actually driven by the core product or service. It's driven by their complete "offering" – as is our decision to buy from them. When you do your own ABC Analysis in chapter 7, the first thing you'll do is define exactly what's included in your offering. I'll illustrate the importance of this concept with a story.

I teach an entrepreneurship class close to Preston Hardware – a wonderful retailer. Their prices are not high, but they're not rock bottom, either. If price was truly your only consideration, you'd go to a 'big box' hardware store. But Preston's offer extends far beyond the sticker price. Here are some of the reasons that buying from them is such an easy decision:

Purchasing

I know that, when I buy from Preston, the purchasers working behind the scenes on my behalf are second to none. If I buy a galvanised fitting, the plating will be thicker than average, an electric switch will take longer to wear out than normal, and varnish will give a better sheen than most. The purchasing department's work is very much what I'm buying at Preston Hardware.

Returns

Their offering includes the ability to return something – but not the normal 'no questions asked' way. They'll always (politely but firmly) question my reason for making the return. If the real problem is my skill or knowledge, they'll always help me decide whether I really should be returning it – or perhaps be doing the job in a different way.

Stability

Preston Hardware has been at the heart of Ottawa's Little Italy for 70 years and has a long-serving, loyal staff. They're not about to go out of business – just as I need to return the toilet seat I bought two weeks before! I see the same staff every time I visit and they know my strengths and weaknesses.

The Staff

I go to Preston because most of their staff are both knowledgeable and friendly. At the end of a hard day's writing, the guy on the 'fixings counter' always puts a smile on my face. I know that he's truly concerned that I get the right nail for the job and will challenge what I say. When I go in a big box store, maybe 1 in 50 retail staff engages with me and drills down to my real TakeAways.

The Preston Hardware offering combines so many things. Quality goods, knowledgeable staff, a stable business with pride in looking after its customers, and even the fact that I can engage with their staff and buy nails individually or by the kilo (much cheaper than the packs at other stores). This creates a complex offering that easily beats the lure of lower priced warehouse stores.

Your Offering can be just as well thought out, described,
and implemented as Preston's...
...they're not as successful as they are simply by luck!
Craft and expose your Offering well –
then differentiate yourself as well as they do!

SO WHAT'S INCLUDED IN *YOUR* OFFERING?

Because buyers purchase your complete offering, not your product or service, this is an important section to understand *and implement*. Buyers won't always appreciate everything that's included in your product or service unless you tell them. The wider your offering, and the better exposed it is in your marketing and then in your sales activity, the stronger the case will be for buying from you.

It's become popular to call everything a 'solution'. Beds are described as sleep solutions and sugar and caffeine mixtures are energy solutions! Neither is a TakeAway... This trend started in the software industry, and it's certainly an improvement on just selling a product. But today's buyers have become much more sophisticated. They use online crowd-sourced reviews, consumer blog reviews, print and electronic articles – even specialty TV shows – when they're deciding whether to make a purchase.

If you want to become *the thing to buy*, (as we were lucky to be in the software industry in the '90s) you need to completely understand what you can offer to every combination of Buyer, Market, and Geography that you're targeting. Once that's done, you can tune your messaging and engagement for each combination.

It makes no difference whether you want your buyer to support your ideas, to offer you a position, or to invest in the expansion of your business – you need to understand *the full extent* of what they can TakeAway from doing business with you.

Here's a list of some of the many things that I've seen included in an offering. Take a look at them, and see which could apply to you. If something *doesn't* apply, can you take action to *make it so*? Is there something in the makeup of your offering that makes it unique? Can you prove it?

The following worksheet can be printed at goo.gl/i0oaX.

Licence Terms

Is there something in your product licence that makes it attractive?

> Write your answers here:

Payment Terms

Do you have particularly desirable terms and conditions?
Do you offer financing?

> Write your answers here:

Training

Do you offer it? What makes it so attractive?
In-house or outsourced?

> Write your answers here:

Durability

Does your product last longer? Than what, specifically?

> Write your answers here:

Stability

Are you demonstrably unlikely to go bust?
How important is that to a Buyer?

> Write your answers here:

Partners

Do you have added value partners?
What might buyers TakeAway from using them?

> Write your answers here:

Support

How vital is support? What's special about yours?
Do you offer optional levels?

> Write your answers here:

Management

Is a potential partner going to be attracted to your team's experience? Why?

> Write your answers here:

Reputation

Is the buyer interested? How might it affect them?
What do they get from it?

> Write your answers here:

Professional Services

Do you specify, install, and test – or is that the buyer's responsibility? Why?

> Write your answers here:

Integrity

Are you attractive as a supplier/employee/partner because your integrity is proven?

```
Write your answers here:
```

Experience

How important is this? So what do they get from it?
How provable an asset is your experience?

```
Write your answers here:
```

You can, of course, also package up different offerings from exactly the same product or services. This is particularly important with different target buyers. There is a good example later in chapter 7.7.

The worksheet is comprehensive, but you'll doubtless find more extensions to what you offer as time goes on. Please share your creativity with us on the TSB Community Board.

The 'Green Jelly' TakeAway Story

> When Freda first started selling her message oriented middleware, there was a strong financial case for buying it. The problem was that techies traditionally made decisions about purchasing complex infrastructure products like hers – because they understood how it worked nearly as well as Freda (who is very smart indeed). Unfortunately, they understood very little of the detailed business model behind its use. Worse still, they completely missed the most important factor – the financial return from such an investment. The result was huge amounts of time discussing and haggling over price.

So she decided to engage directly with the 'C' Level Executives (CTO, CEO, CFO, etc.) – the people whose lives *did* center around the money. The executives quickly recognised, with the help of her spread sheets, that time would be saved, that there were cost savings, and reduced contingent risk (the possible costs associated with failure).

But there was a problem. The good thing about middleware is that it's almost completely invisible. Freda's favourite expression was *"you only know it's there when it goes wrong"*. Because they couldn't see it, her buyers often asked her how it worked – their "Convincer Channel" often needed more data (see chapter 9). Despite her best efforts, most of the decision-making executives struggled to understand a product that just didn't overlap with their Model of the World – the software was truly clever and too complex for most people

To solve the problem, Freda invented the 'Green Jelly' metaphor for non-techies!

This wonderful stuff solved a lot of problems for many years. She asked her 'C' level decision makers to simply imagine they could just plug their computers into a bowl of green jelly that would do all the business routing, authentication, and secure transformation needed to run the business.

She 'Framed' the Green Jelly in their minds by asking:

*"Do you **really** need to know how it works?"*

*"Don't you just want to know **what** it will do for your business?"*

*"If I **prove** my 'Green Jelly' performs as promised, and saves money, will you invest in it?"*

And, you know what? It worked. It worked every time (as long as she could supply the proof – which she always could). She and I probably made as many Green Jelly sales as conventional ones.

The most important people are influenced by proof of what they can TakeAway – *not by knowing how something works*.

Sales people often forget this key point in their eagerness to show how clever their offering can be.

IN SUMMARY:
PEOPLE AND COMPANIES BUY FOR SIMPLE REASONS

This chapter is the book's down-to-earth foundation – yet will produce the most change. See the TIRES that drive decisions all around you and see them *as a buyer* – not as yourself. Make yourself a powerful influencer by knowing what it feels like to be influenced.

Keep your buyer's TakeAways in your head – not just yours – whenever you want to create a change. Remember a buyer is driven by a fundamental human trait – SWIIFM!

Finally, people buy your *complete offering*. So make sure you fully understand what you are offering. Ensure that it's broad, rich in TakeAways, and as well exposed as you can make it.

CHAPTER 3:
REVIEW QUESTIONS & SELF-DEVELOPMENT ASSIGNMENTS

How People Buy – see Annex B for Answers

To print a copy of this section, download it directly from goo.gl/jNZh0 or select it from the TSB Download Page at goo.gl/p0Ajn.

Self-Test Questions

1. What is the fundamental motivation behind any decision that a person or organisation takes to buy something or to 'buy into' an idea?
2. Name as many of the 6 classic mistakes people make when they sell to or influence anyone else:
3. Which is the mistake you make least? Which is the one do you do most?
4. Are you a bulldog or a sheepdog? When is each best employed?
5. What are the three main causes of fear, doubt or anxiety in sales or influence?
6. Which one affects *you* most? Which one affects you *least*?

Buying Drivers

7. What (in full) are the only five reasons that anyone is motivated to buy?
8. Give one good example of each type and then check that what you've written passes the test.
9. What phrase was Ted Levitt famous for at the Harvard Business School?
10. What is the (full) definition of a TakeAway?
11. Is each of these a TakeAway? If not why not? What changes would make it a TakeAway?

    "Training costs reduced by 25%"
    "Has a harder surface than a regular driveshaft"
    "Supported by live call center staff 98% of the time"
    "A low void ratio and high aspect ratio that reduce fuel consumption by 20%"
    "Your consultant will have an MBA and 20 years' experience"

12. What are TIRE Compounds? Give three examples (with letters and description)

Your Offering

13   Define an Offering:

14   Develop *your* Offering by using the Offering Worksheet downloadable from goo.gl/i0oaX or at: http://turningsellingintobuying.com/tsb-book-links/

15   Create a metaphor similar to 'Green Jelly' – but for your Offering. Make it easy for your buyer to see the TakeAways separately from the features and functions.

Self-Development Assignments

Ch 3 Assignment 1 – TakeAways or Features?

Look at product advertisements around you and check whether the company concerned is offering 'Features and Functions' or actual Take-Aways. If you're attracted to buy a particular offering, which TIRES are motivating you? If you can't see what Buying Driver are being presented by the image, story, or statement, how would you improve the ad? If you're not attracted, could the Offering be extended to attract you? Could you apply any of these lessons to *your* Offering?

Ch 3 Assignment 2 – Being Sold To

When you're being sold to, you're *truly* on the buyer's side of the table. So next time you're being sold to (and it could be an idea, or a service just as much as being in a shop), observe the other person doing the selling. Whether it's face to face, or over the phone, check which of the six classic selling errors they're guilty of. Do they search for or explore your TIRES/TakeAways?

Ch 3 Assignment 3 – Fear, Doubt & Anxiety

Next time you have an opportunity to sell an idea, product or service, and you're not instantly motivated to engage (or maybe even actually fear it) – stop.

Use it as an opportunity to find out about yourself. You don't need to tell anyone else, so ask yourself:

> "What's going on here? What specific outcome is holding me back?"

Be completely honest with yourself in your answer. Which of the three classic fears is the underlying one? If there are several, what's the order of their power? Is it the same on each occasion? If not, what's the pattern? What can you do to improve your confidence, knowledge, or fluency and thus reduce the problem?

CHAPTER 4
Four-See: The Buyer's Side of the Table

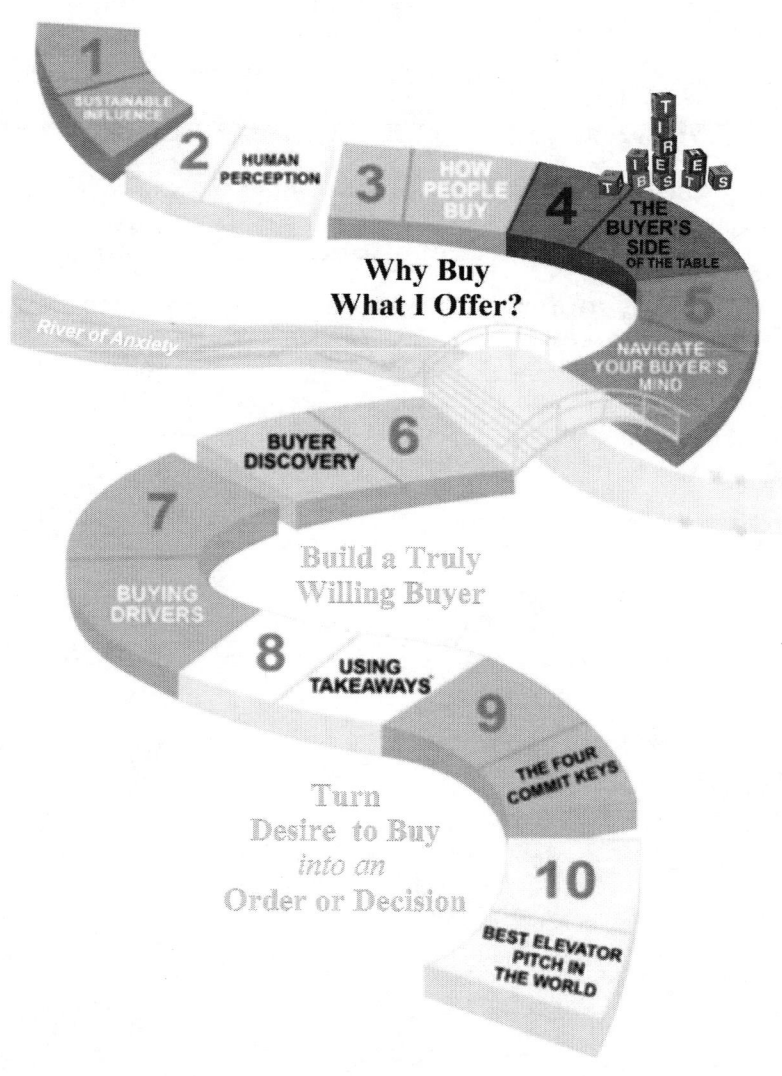

BY THE END OF THIS CHAPTER, YOU'LL UNDERSTAND ...

- Why the Buying Process is more important than your Sales Process
- How to drive out productive insights with the Four-See Exercise
- How these will support you, before, during and after a meeting
- Practical tips on using Four-See at work and play

HOW DOES FOUR-SEE HELP ME BUILD A WILLING BUYER?

Four-See is a unique exercise or dry-run that delivers useful insights into any decision making or influence process. It allows you, with the right preparation and research, to get as 'inside the head of your buyer' as it's feasible to be. It places the people who use it strongly into the position of each of the parties involved in a decision, a buying process or a dispute and allows them to experience several unique views of the situation from the other sides of the table.

This can do a great deal to break down any communication divide that exists between seller and buyer. In particular it is useful for making the pressures on your buyer very visible – with all the benefits that brings to the influencer (you). In short, it allows you into your buyer's world in a limited but useful way.

The tight structure of this exercise is necessary because most of us find it difficult to fully set aside our own Model of the World and see the situation openly from another person's view. It's always been my experience that the insights delivered are much more powerful than those created by simply 'thinking' about it. Investing a little time and effort in the Four-See exercise can deliver great benefits to you and your buyer – while still protecting your own position and goals.

I've seen Four-See used productively in:

- Preparation for a specific sales call or presentation.
- 'Becoming the buyer' who responds to *So What* in an ABC Analysis.
- Project management situations where a change is being resisted.
- Selling, setting up or managing a 3rd party distribution agreement.
- Assisting in mediating disputes.

Overview

This exercise is named Four-See because it's proven to be a useful tool for helping to *foresee* so many of the problems and outcomes of an influence meeting. Originally developed by psychotherapist *Virginia Satir*, it was an effective part of her therapeutic approach in improving communication between people.

I've adapted and extended it for commercial and personal use and my students have always found it not only enjoyable but also valuable for improving confidence, effectiveness, and team building.

Here's a list of some of the things you may get from the exercise:

- Useful insights into the *commercial pressures* on your buyer.
- Some view of the likely *filters* in their Model of the World.
- Partial view of the *pressures* and *motivations* in their life situation.
- A stronger view of *constraints* and *incentives* imposed on the buyer.
- A more confident *personal State* for engaging with your buyer.
- Great deduction of the TakeAways your buyer is likely to be seeking.
- Valuable understanding of the 3rd parties and stakeholders involved.

Once Four-See is integrated into your thinking you'll find it becomes a frequent, almost automatic, tool. I use it before any important meeting, sometimes alone, sometimes with my team. I have my own short form which I use in the reception area while I'm waiting (I always try to arrive early), in the airport lounge, or even in the taxi. I would encourage you to create one for yourself.

When you're under pressure, tired, upset or simply 'not on it',
a quick mental Four-See is a sure way of grounding
yourself back in reality just before a call.

Occasionally I'll do a much more extensive Four-See exercise with my team as a warm up for a key sales call. It's also a useful team building exercise when a number of people are going to be involved with a big sale over a significant time.

THE FOUR-SEE POSITIONS

FIRST POSITION – THE INFLUENCER

This is your own, completely candid view of what you're offering, and the way you're offering it. You'll take quality time to become (privately) more conscious of how you truly see, hear, and feel the situation through your own filters. It includes (re)awakening your awareness of the personal beliefs, abilities, behaviours, motivations, and goals that you bring to *your* side of the table.

It's also a good time to let go of self-delusion, anxiety and poor decisions about the opportunity – indeed *anything that might affect a good outcome*. It also gives you an opportunity to disclose (privately or publicly – your choice) the true facts, strengths, and shortcomings about you and your offering. Doing this will either give you either increased confidence or the opportunity to take action to gain it.

SECOND POSITION – THE BUYER

This is the perceptual position of your buyer. You must put yourself, to the very *best of your ability*, into their position. Then experience and see, hear, understand and feel the situation *as if you were them*. You must be non-judgemental about the person involved and drop your own beliefs and values – don't *drag them along with you*. If you know, or have some insight into what your buyer's mental filters might be (beliefs, experiences, decisions, values, etc.) let them operate inside you.

Most important of all, allow you buyer's SWIIFM – S0 WHAT'S IN IT FOR ME – to completely replace yours. The expression "*Before judging someone, walk a mile in their shoes*" is much overused. SECOND POSITION puts some real muscle into it!

The "Buyer Discovery" skills you'll learn in chapter 6 are an absolute goldmine when preparing for SECOND POSITION. There's a good list there of many ways to expose yourself to the same pressures as your buyer. If you find some others that you are productive, please share them at the TSB forum.

THIRD POSITION – THE IMPARTIAL ADVISER

The 3rd perceptual position is that of a real or imaginary observer who's totally independent – someone with no axe to grind. It's a person (or sometimes a group, or an institution) that has absolutely nothing to gain or lose from the meeting outcomes – and is keen for it to be successful for all parties.

You'll step strongly away from the two previous roles and their situations and experience. Become a detached, uninvolved witness. See and hear the two people in FIRST and SECOND POSITION with fresh eyes, as if you were seeing them interacting for the first time. In the exercise detail later, you'll discover that you also 'magically' know all of the filters being used by the FIRST and SECOND POSITION people. This powerful inside knowledge will allow you to give useful advice to both parties.

FOURTH POSITION – AN AFFECTED PARTY or STAKEHOLDER

This is the only position in Four-See where you can choose to be several different people (but one at a time). Each of them actually exists somewhere in the 'larger system' (the company, the region, the family, or the world) and is likely to *be affected* by or to *have an opinion on* the outcomes of the decision.

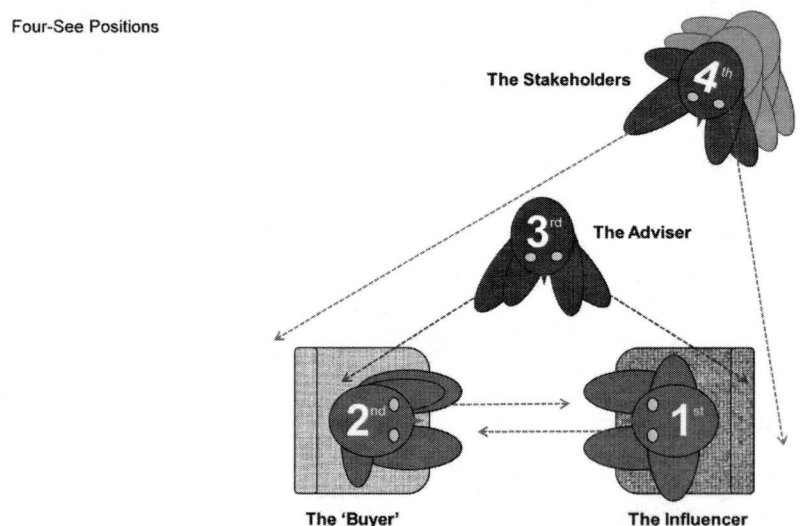

Figure 9

The number of people and whom you choose is totally dependent upon the real situation. I've know it to include as diverse figures as a customer, a supplier, a citizen, an investor, an institution, the government, nature, god, the law, etc. People generally find 2 or 3 to be sufficient, but there's no set number. See Figure 9.

PERFORMING A FOUR-SEE EXERCISE

First Run Through

This exercise is best practiced the first time with two or three friends or close colleagues who are supportive and *want it to work*. Ideally, they're actually in your team if it's a work problem. Each person should go through all four positions in the exercise at least once – but only using *personal situations* the first time though.

They should pick straightforward communication problems at work, minor disputes with siblings or children, decisions to be made at clubs or associations. They key thing is to keep the problem uncomplicated – don't jump in at the deep end by trying to solve the problem of world peace or your brother's divorce on your first run through!

As insights occur, or mistakes are made, the group can then share and learn very effectively. The finale is then to run a full Four-See on a *real* situation – a sale, problem, project, or decision – with *real* buyers. Although it's not absolutely necessary, I recommend everyone goes through this same 'live situation' once – again sharing their varying experience afterwards. This whole preliminary training exercise need take no more than an hour.

Once everyone has mastered the process, subsequent Four-Sees should average out at about 10 – 15 minutes, depending on their complexity, and whether the results are shared or 'internal'.

Setting Up

See Figure 9. To start, you'll need two chairs. They should face each other and ideally be chosen with different colours or styles to help the mind to lock in the very different experience you'll have in each position. Just occasionally, the real-life interaction takes place while standing, so it can be useful to reflect that with a standing Four-See exercise, too, but this is not common.

These two chairs will be FIRST POSITION and SECOND POSITION. Between them, but slightly to one side, create a clearly identified space for a person to stand and observe (it can even be marked with tape). This is the THIRD POSITION, from which the impartial onlooker can observe the interaction between FIRST AND SECOND POSITION.

FOURTH POSITION needs to be off at an angle; again just a clear standing space (or marked with tape) a short distance away from the FIRST and SECOND POSITION chairs.

NOTE: *Four-See is never carried out by four people at the same time.* It's always done by only one person moving between positions – usually the one most likely to directly benefit from the insights gained from moving through all four positions.

I've found that if several people involved in an account or a problem do the exercise, one after another, their comparisons at the end can build an even stronger insight into how to create a positive outcome. The team can decide whether to compare notes after everyone has been through, or after each person's circuit – it's your choice.

I sometimes use a 'trusted companion' to sit in while I do the exercise. We can then discuss and document the results at the end – but they take no actual part in the exercise itself.

Remembered, Constructed, Enriched

There are two routes into the Four-See exercise. The first is if you've actually met with the person involved and have real memories to draw on. The second is where you've not met, and only have your own research and imagination. In both cases, I'll use the word *visualise* throughout the instructions, but what you actually do will depend on you and the exact circumstances.

You may actually be *visual*ising a picture, or running a movie. You may be experiencing the feelings, remembering the sounds and words you heard, maybe even smelling or tasting something. You'll also be recalling the thoughts, reflection, and analysis you did as you experienced all this. If you can do it, it can also be useful to be aware of any assumptions, guesses, and decisions that you took with you into the meeting. In the absence of a better word, I will call doing this 'visualisation'.

If you've already met the person in SECOND, THIRD or FOURTH POSITION, you can access the memories of what actually happened. You can also enrich these memories with the research you've done, your imagination and real experiences that you've had.

If you've had no contact with the people involved, then the feelings, sounds, sights and actions will have to 'constructed' in your own head, again perhaps enriched by memories, imagination, and research.

EXAMPLE: You've met the buyer once at a hockey match and have a view of their character; but you've never met them at an influence meeting. You've researched their company and know there's a tight decision making process there, with little personal autonomy. You've phoned an ex-colleague who you've found out from LinkedIn now works in the same company and been told that the person is a bit of a maverick and likes to be independent. You've also found a link to their family blog on LinkedIn and seen they love outdoor activity. You know from a Google search that the company uses them a lot to talk to the press and to industry analysts. Now go visualise.

First Run Through

Like anything new, this exercise has a learning curve. You can shorten it with a practice script (downloadable at *goo.gl/qCCMR*). Find a trusted friend or colleague (+2 chairs) to help you through the exercise. After reading the script silently all the way through, they can gently and slowly read it aloud to you, cueing you as you go through each of the four positions.

No feedback or discussion should take place until the end – then go for it!

Finding the right helper the first time you practice will make Four-See so much easier – so take the time to find the right person.

Once you've discovered how easily you can access these insights yourself, you'll be able to do Four-See in the most extraordinary places – and without script or helper

---

DETAILED INSTRUCTIONS

FIRST POSITION

Sit in the first chair, and visualise yourself at a meeting similar to the one you're going to Four-See. If you've actually met with the specific person in SECOND POSITION, think back to that occasion; repeat if there have been several.

Visualise the way you felt, the things you heard, and what you saw. If it helps, close your eyes and let your mind travel back to that moment. Think about the Frame you used at that meeting. Are you intimidated? Do you feel confident? Are you enjoying being there? What are your most prominent beliefs during the meeting? Visualise what you know you can do, what worried you, the things you'd done well, and not so well.

Visualise the journey there, your State as you arrived. I always walk up to the chair, shake hands and sit down. Sit the way you sit with that person and visualise their office around you.

Get *into* State, that is feel as closely as possible to how you'll feel (or did feel) in the meeting, and with the same Frame around it. Once you're in that State, think about the factual matters that you'll be tackling – the specific issue, money, time, risk, etc. Think about the words you used and might use next time.

Do this for as long as is necessary to really know how it feels to be there.

SECOND POSITION

NOTE: Complete chapter 6 – Buyer Discovery before doing this

Before moving to SECOND POSITION, create a "Break State" to shake you out of your FIRST POSITION mindset. It's easy – open your eyes wide, go 'out of yourself' and focus on a mundane, specific task (e.g. counting the number of lights above you, the distance to the nearest door, four words beginning with 'K' or the month you started this job).

Then move to the SECOND POSITION chair. If, as suggested, it's different from the one in FIRST POSITION, focus consciously on the difference – reinforcing the Break State.

In SECOND POSITION, you become *to the best of your ability,* the person you wish to influence. You sit and act the way they do. Imagine, as best you can, the full range of influences and pressures on them, and the possible attitude they may have towards you and whatever you're offering – whether it's a sale, a project issue, an idea or a dispute.

The person in SECOND POSITION can also be imaginary (particularly if your offering is still being developed), which allows some useful scope for imagination. A little coaching from a person who's been close to (or even in) that situation, can be useful as well. I've even brought in someone who used to work in the same company to help with this.

Perhaps (for instance) you're a 23-year-old self-employed software designer who needs to influence a 50+ civil servant to pay for you to develop an application for a police service. Just being aware of a likely difference in motivation and worldview can help you to approach the conversation more confidently and effectively.

In Second Position, you're *doing your very best* to achieve an insight into the Model of the World used by your buyer. Although you're unlikely to gain any knowledge about that person's private life or upbringing, you should gain a lot of information about their current pressures and corporate priorities.

It's important to understand that you're *not guessing or making a firm assumption* about your buyer's motivations. You're simply creating sufficient insight to confidently engage with them without your own prejudices getting in the way.

THIRD POSITION

This is the position of an imaginary (or occasionally real) observer who wants to ensure success for both parties and has no personal interest or threat from any of the outcomes. This person is well-intentioned and can hear and see everything said, thought, and felt by the first two positions. You have complete and accurate knowledge of all the facts of the situation and your possible offering. You also have the 'magical power' to see exactly what filters and Frames are being run by the people in FIRST and SECOND POSITION.

After another Break State (count those ceiling lights again!) to get rid of both FIRST and SECOND POSITION States, move to that THIRD POSITION spot. Then run all of the imagined or remembered conversations that have just happened through your mind. Watch, hear, and feel how each party is reacting to the other.

Think in terms of what opinion, observations, or (most importantly of all) advice that you, the neutral observer can offer to improve communication between the parties. To get the best from this step of Four-See, you need to be in a strong, resourceful State so that you can take a completely objective view of (your own) behaviour that you observed, and look for opportunities to respond differently.

Sometimes picking different characters can help with this – a 'fly on the wall', a scientist, a lawyer, an ombudsman, a policeman – all may have different (but fair) advice to give. But generally it is only necessary to have a fair minded observer.

Don't forget your 'magic powers' – specifically consider the filters and Frames that you saw being used by FIRST and SECOND POSITION. What advice would you give to each person?

Carry out this exercise (perhaps watching different conversations) as many times as you need. At the end, you'll be in a good position to deliver objective, clear advice to both parties on their strengths and shortcomings in influence and communication. You'll be doing this at the end of the exercise.

FOURTH POSITION

This final position is that of anyone who *will* actually be affected by the outcome of the purchase, decision or vision. It's usually a multiple position. This means that you can select several different people, each of whom will be affected in different ways by the decision or purchase once it's been made. It's your choice as to who you select, and how many. I've found that by the time you are ready to model the FOURTH POSITION, it's fairly obvious who these individuals or institutions are, so don't work too hard at it before you start the exercise.

It's important each person or institution will be directly affected in some way by the final outcome of the buyer's decision. Think as laterally as you can. It works best if you try several positions that are as far from each other as possible. For example, an educational offering might impact teachers, children, parents, principals, custodians, school boards, education minister, school bus drivers, stationery suppliers, and staff.

When influencing someone to buy from you, the power of FOURTH POSITION comes mostly from the effect it will have on your buyer (in SECOND POSITION). If, for instance, your buyer is in the public sector, there will be a range of (FOURTH POSITION) legal, political, financial, and administrative constraints on them. If the decision being made has moral ramifications, this POSITION may be more spiritual. If, say, your buyer is considering creating a new call center, then FOURTH POSITION might include your buyer's customers and their experience as they call in. The scope is as wide as your imagination and experience.

As with THIRD POSITION, carry out a Break State (probably time to stop counting lights!) and run the different conversations, working out the advice you'll give.

INSIGHTS AND USES OF FOUR-SEE

Simply visiting each of the positions in the Four-See exercise is useful on its own. When you're in the waiting room doing this in your head, it's probably all you can manage! But a debrief at the end of doing the exercise in the office, whether with colleagues or just yourself, can boost the quality of output and help you approach the meeting much more relaxed.

The best way to start the debrief is to move the person doing it back to the comfort of FIRST POSITION. If it's a group exercise, a round of applause is usually supportive and appropriate – but probably not if you're alone or in an aircraft! Then take a few moments to reflect in silence about what you've learned at each POSITION.

First Position

What's changed in you, in your filters, the facts you know and your approach?

What will you change in what you do, think, say and act?

Second Position

What have you learned from truly seeing the situation from the other person's side of the table? From hearing them talk, and from understanding how your buyer was thinking and filtering? What knowledge has preparing for and doing this exercise given you?

Third Position

What role is each person taking? Dominant, supplicant? Parent, child? Clinical or passionate, etc.? Is one person long on information and short on enthusiasm – or vice versa? Is each person hearing as well as listening? What language patterns is each person using? What is the balance of telling, questioning and discussing (think of the Fulcrum of Influence)? What Filters did they use?

Fourth Position

What new outcomes have you discovered? How do the Fourth Position parties affect the actions of the people in First and Second Position? What do they think about it? Do you need to revisit Second Position because of new information from the Fourth Position? (There's no rule stopping you doing that!) Is the case for the decision you want to influence stronger or weaker? Can you see new solutions to the problem?

You can see a complete Four-See exercise and debrief in the video at *goo.gl/zULjS*

> Charlie was an old sales warrior. He'd successfully sold his company's project management software for years – all over Europe. But he was confronted with a new challenge. He'd been asked to raise his game at two levels. Firstly, he'd been asked to take the product to the USA, where he'd only had a little commercial experience. Secondly, his boss wanted him to focus on the defence sector over there – and he'd had almost zero exposure to that market.
>
> Luckily he had just been exposed to a TSB seminar. He'd enjoyed the Four-See exercise but hadn't yet used it outside the classroom.

It seemed like excellent opportunity to combine team building with a dose of new training – and generate a commercially useful result! Charlie liked the idea of bringing someone in from the outside so he brought in two other people for the morning – a presales engineer in his company who'd worked in the US market and a buddy from a defence supplier they were teaming up with.

The five of them went through the Four-See exercises together. Each one went through all positions. Some of them used the opportunity to research their character and arrived already *in role* with a host of background facts. Others used their imagination and (particularly in Third Position) identified potential conflicts between their present approach and what would be needed in the USA. They all became familiar with the very different pressures that a government buyer faces, rather than a commercial buyer.

A few days later, when Charlie and his team did their ABC Analysis, they found that the Buying Drivers they created were very different from those that worked with their existing customers.

The rest is history. They won a series of huge deals supplying solutions to one of the biggest defence contracts ever. Charlie's still over there – living in a very large, very nice house.

TEAM BENEFITS

Probably the most frequently used benefit from everyone doing the Four-See exercise is the wonderfully efficient verbal shorthand that it gives your team.

"Let's go to FOURTH on that one" or *"Are you truly seeing this decision from SECOND POSITION?"* means so much to a Four-See user – and takes up so little time. We even had a SECOND POSITION chair in the corner of our office that we used to *see a problem from the other side of the table*. A productive place to think before writing a proposal or phoning a customer!

So what's the most important thing Four-See delivers? Apart from the insights into how to positively influence your buyer, I think that one of the biggest benefits is to our own confidence and verbal fluency.

That's why I try to get *everyone* to do this exercise when I'm conducting a seminar or workshop.

I've never tested it in an MRI scanner, but the exercise also seems to work to loosen up the parts of the brain that you use for imagination, forward-thinking, communication, flexibility, clarity, alertness, awareness, etc. Your mind has been exercised while connecting with the issues and people in a way that doesn't happen if you go into your influence meeting 'cold'.

When you or your team meet your buyer, you'll feel much more confident and composed because you've *been over their ground already*.

IN SUMMARY:
SIT ON THE BUYER'S SIDE OF THE TABLE TO INFLUENCE THEM

Four-See gets you as close to what motivates a buying decision as imagination and research can generate. It's the closest you can get to actually sitting on the buyer's side of the table – especially with a good Buyer Discovery first.

Some people are naturally good coaches to lead the session. Others can be brought in who have personal experience and insights into your buyer's situation. Some people are great as facilitators. Use them all – they'll benefit as much as you.

Here are some of the 'added extras' I've seen delivered by Four-See:

- Real "Aha!" insights into how different SWIIFM is between different people.
- Better descriptions of your offering that make them more accessible to your buyer.
- A much wider range of TIRES-checked TakeAways.
- Practical awareness of how you come across to others.
- Unexpected buyer factors that can hugely strengthen your ROI.
- New questions, subjects, and reframes that will work well with your buyer.

Once you've done this a few times you'll be able to do it alone. Eventually, you won't just do it in the taxi or reception – a time may come when you'll actually find yourself unconsciously *doing it with the buyer* – while you're actually sitting in front of them. You'll be hearing, understanding, and influencing them better and better – and in real time.

CHAPTER 4:
REVIEW QUESTIONS & SELF-DEVELOPMENT ASSIGNMENTS

Chapter 4 – The Buyer's Side of the Table – see Annex B for Answers

To print a copy of this section, download it directly from goo.gl/mhVj6 or select it from the TSB Download Page at goo.gl/p0Ajn.

Self-Test Questions

1. What is the main benefit of using Four-See?
2. When and where can it be carried out?
3. Name the Four-See Positions – numbers *and* titles!
4. How many chairs, what should be distinctive about them – and why?
5. What (honestly) is the greatest benefit *you* are likely to get in FIRST POSITION?
6. Why should you always 'Break State' between positions? What are some ways to do this?
7. What should you try to complete *before* you go to SECOND POSITION?
8. What *must* you always leave behind when you move to SECOND POSITION?
9. What is the key quality of the individual in THIRD POSITION?
10. What 'magical capability' does THIRD POSITION have? How can they use it?
11. What communication attributes, faults, and successes should THIRD POSITION look for as they watch FIRST and SECOND position?
12. How many people in FOURTH POSITION? List characteristics each might have. List typical FOURTH POSITION people that might be useful in *your* situation.
13. Apart from an influence meeting, when else is Four-See effective?

Self-Development Assignments

Ch 4 Assignment 1 – Dummy Runs

Work with a group of trusted people using the script from goo.gl/3Gb2u or download it later at goo.gl/p0Ajn (password download999)

Pick some problems, influences, sales and practice. The same person *must always* sequence though all four positions. It's much less effective if everyone does THIRD POSITION or four different people sequentially do each position. Above all, have fun!

Ch 4 Assignment 2 – Personal Practice

Once you're familiar with the exercise and happy to get into each State, try it on your own – preferably with a real influence meeting afterwards. The first few times, don't do anything different at the meeting – but consider afterwards which parts of the meeting were helped by Four-See, and which weren't. Once you're confident, you can begin to use the outputs to change your approach to the meeting.

Ch 4 Assignment 3 – Team Building & Account Development

Does your team have a big opportunity? Are they going into a new market? Maybe they have a new offering? Often used as a lead in to a TakeAway Analysis or even a full commercial ABC Analysis, the Four-See exercise has great team-building opportunities as well as the more objective commercial outputs.

CHAPTER 5
Navigate Your Buyer's Mind

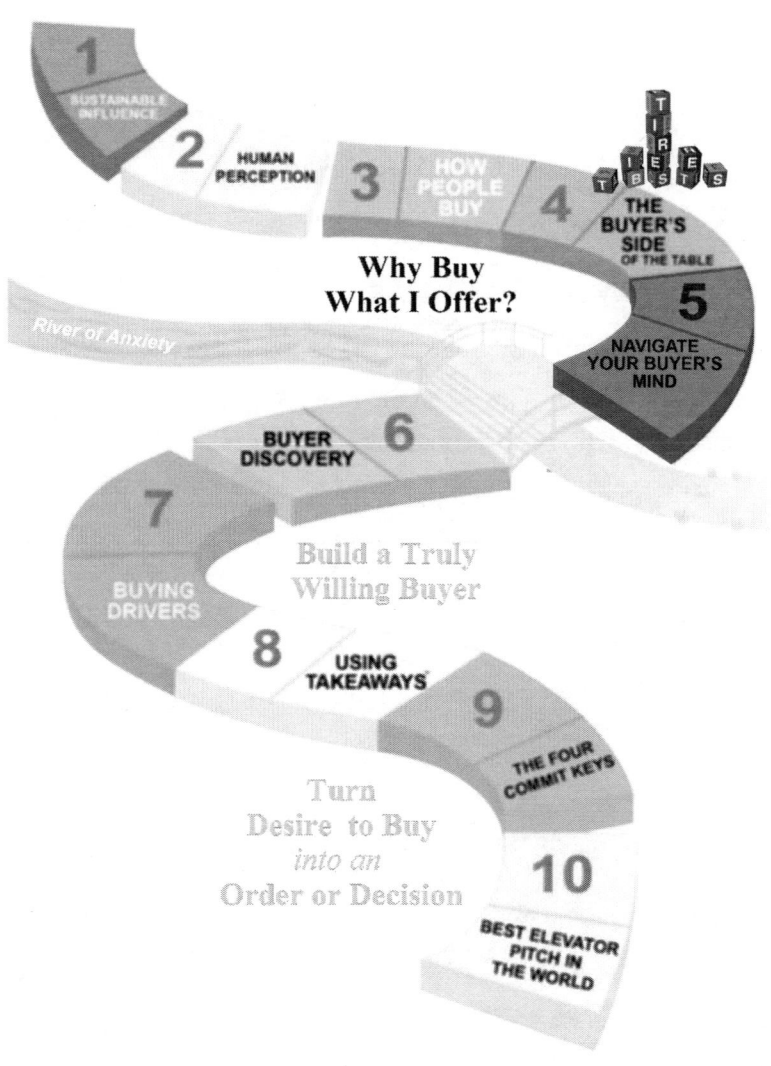

BY THE END OF THIS CHAPTER, YOU'LL UNDERSTAND …

- The ways in which we all use a "Hierarchy of Ideas" to think
- How to use "Chunking" to navigate your Buyer around *their* hierarchy
- Ways to draw out your buyer's real Buying Drivers
- The use of Reframing to alter a Buyer's view of your Offering

HOW WILL THIS HELP ME BUILD A WILLING BUYER?

This chapter contains some of the most powerful techniques in the book. Yet the language used is really simple – to learn and to use. That's why they're so useful for creating a Willing Buyer – you're not doing or saying anything weird or manipulative. What you're doing is *consciously* keeping control of the direction and ultimate target of the conversation. After all, you're only there for one reason (remember Willy Ross) – *"to have a good discussion and find out if there's anything we can help them with"*. Your buyer may be a lovely person, with some fascinating opinions or hobbies, but you're *there for a specific reason.*

You'll learn to move your buyer's ideas away from a declared need:
e.g. *"I need a new accountant"* to a TakeAway you can actually supply

"Our web accounts releases 3–5 profitable hours per week on average"

Now those are TakeAways someone will be motivated to buy!

And that's not all, you'll also be able expand the size and timescale of their needs and uncover other benefits that will help them to justify the decision. All the time you're doing this, you'll be increasing rapport with your buyer as they enjoy working with you in such a new and revelatory way.

Models of the World

We saw in chapter 2 how we each run a distinct Model of the World that helps us make sense of the world around us. In this chapter, we focus on how *everyone* (including your buyer) stores and accesses the ideas and facts held within their own model. There are four main benefits to understanding these connections.

They help us to:

- Gain an insight into the buyer's Model of the World and see their needs better.
- Understand how well (or not) our offering fits into the buyer's view of the world.
- Guide the buyer into new areas of consideration.

- Give the buyer a different view of their world model, and thus, of your offering.

When you perfect these techniques, you'll quickly see that not only do they influence others to buy ideas, products and services – they're also valuable life skills that you can use every day, with absolutely anyone in any situation!

ELEMENT ONE – CHUNKING

This is one of the most useful skills I've learned since leaving school. It's called the *Hierarchy of Ideas* and, by the end of this chapter, you'll be able to help your buyer plot a course through the mental structures that they unconsciously use.

Introduction

Suppose I was to show you a list of objects like this:

> NAILS : SCREWS : RIVETS : BOLTS : FASTENERS : STUDS

I think that everyone reading it would agree they all belong in the same list. We might also all agree that a higher level title for the list could be *Fasteners*. They're all made of metal, so we might even call the list *Metal Fasteners*. There might also be a *parallel* list of *Plastic Fasteners*.

Let's try another list:

> CAULIFLOWER : PORRIDGE : CHOCOLATE : CARROTS : SOUP

This looks like another list of similar items – foods. But if the reader is sensitive as to whether the items are legumes or cereals, processed or unprocessed, etc., they might not be so happy with grouping these items together.

They might feel that fresh cauliflower and carrots belong in their own list, or that porridge and soup should be at a lower level because they're processed items. But, to even have a chance to predict how someone else might order the list of food items, we'd need to ask some questions designed to reveal their Model of the World.

Here's the final list that we're going to spend some time on.

BUSES : BIKES : TRAINS : CARS : SUVS : TRUCKS : RVS

Let's ask some questions to find out more about our buyer's view of the list. The aim is as much to learn about the person responding as it is to discuss the items.

Here are some Precision Questions.

Navigation Questions – Going Up

Let's look at the fourth item:

"What is a Car an example of?"

When I ask this in seminars, the most frequent response is always:

"Transport"

But of course, there will almost always be some in the group whose model differs from average. They may answer:

"A status symbol"
"A danger to cyclists"
"A huge destroyer of this planet"

The very first answers we get are already giving us useful information about each individual's Model of the World.

Let's ask another question in response to the most common of those answers:

"For what purpose do you use transport?"

The majority answer might be *"movement"*, but variations include *"to get to work"*, *"as a taxi service for my kids"*, and even *"the sheer joy of driving fast!"*

So let's pursue the response *"the sheer joy of driving fast"* and ask that person another question:

"What is your intention in driving fast?"

NOTE: It's critical that you 'plug back in' the exact words the respondent used (in this example *"Driving fast"*). Of all the skills in Active Listening, this is one of the more important.

The answer to your new question might be:

"Happiness"
"Thrills"

The pattern here is that the answers to these particular questions are becoming more and more *abstract*, and less and less *specific*. They're becoming more *conceptual* and less *concrete*. This movement up the Hierarchy of Ideas is called "Chunking Up".

We can draw on a wide range of questions to 'navigate up' in this way:

"What is …… part of?"
"For what purpose do you/we ……?"
"What is ……part of?"
"What does ……mean?"
"What is ……a part of?"
"What is its/the/your intention in ……?"
"What is …… trying to achieve?"

The great thing about Chunking is how very predictable our brains are. It's almost impossible to not give Chunked Up information in response to one of these Chunking Up questions. You'll see how useful this is in a moment. It's also a great short hand for colleagues – *"Let's Chunk Up on that"* is a lot quicker and more specific than *"Why don't we look at some of the other, more strategic outcomes which that drives?"*

> There is NO correct answer to a Chunking question. Only the *direction* of questioning is under your control. The response is controlled by (and is a very powerful and accurate reflection of) your buyer's Model of the World.

Almost every response from your buyer teaches you more about them.

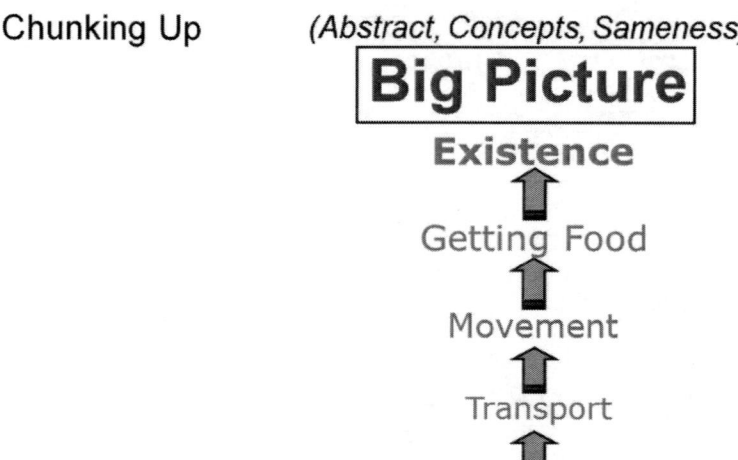

Figure 10

Figure 10 shows a possible sequence of responses to Chunking Up questions:

Notice how the responses 'taper in' – becoming similar, more abstract, and more conceptual – the higher you travel.

Navigation Questions – Going Down

So let's go back to that list again:

BUSES : BIKES : TRAINS : CARS : SUVS : TRUCKS : RVS

Now let's ask a different question
(you guessed right, it's a "Chunking Down" question this time):

"*What are cars composed of, specifically?*"

You might get answers such as:

"*Distinct parts and assemblies*"
"*Different models and manufacturers*"

Again, neither answer is right or wrong – they're driven by the responder's Model of the World. We can respond to each of these answers by drilling down even further with some other questions:

(Take care to use *exactly* the words given in the responses):

"What are examples of different models?" or maybe...
"What are examples of parts and assemblies?"

In reply, we'd begin to get some more lists:

"Kia, Ford, Volvo"

or maybe...

"Suspension, Engine, Transmission"

In this case, the questions evoke answers that become increasingly detailed. The answers are becoming more and more concrete, specific and detailed.

This mental movement into the *detail* is called ***Chunking Down***.

Here is a full set of *Chunking Down* questions.

"What precisely......?"
"Please give me specific examples (of) ......?"
"Give me more detail about"
"What is the root cause of ......?"
"How did it/you do that?"
Almost any "Who?/What?/When?/Where?" question

NOTE: Both the Chunking Down and Chunking Up questions are shown here in brutal simplicity. In real life you'd use softening phrases such as

"Please can you...", "OK then...", "So ...?"

Like Chunking Up, Chunking Down questions leave the brain with little room for manoeuvre – your buyer *has* to give you more detail. They have to go *down* the Hierarchy of Ideas. Once again, you're not just getting information, you're learning about the responder.

If you spot they're finding it hard to answer, then maybe they prefer Chunked Up concepts. If they are clearly *diving into* the detail you're asking for, maybe they relish being *down in the weeds* – they're naturally Chunked Down. It might be a good time to see what they're like in more *Chunked Up* areas of the situation.

Figure 11 shows a possible sequence of responses to Chunking Down questions.

Chunking Down

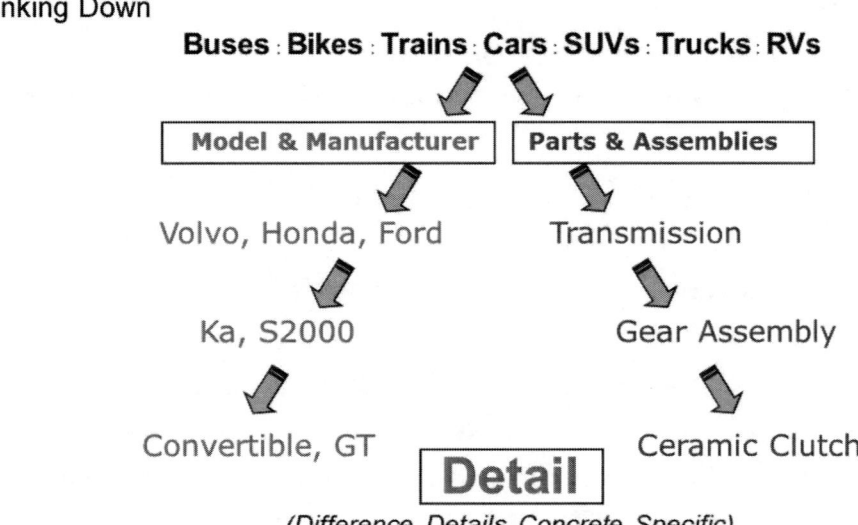

Figure 11

Notice how the responses have the opposite characteristic to Chunking Up. They 'spread out' as you go lower. The difference in content between individual answers (at the same level) can become very great.

For instance, 'Chiropractic Manipulation' and 'Keyhole Surgery' are both on the same level in response to the question *"How specifically can I fix my back?"* – but the difference between what happens is very great indeed.

Navigation Questions – Going Sideways

Horizontal Chunking is the third type. It stays at the same level of detail but extends the number and breadth of choices. It helps your buyer to present you with more options at *the same level*. Perhaps there are other users or stakeholders for your offering. Maybe your buyer has other, similar, problems that you can fix.

Here are the questions you can use to expand horizontally:

"What's another example of that?" "What else is like that? "
"Is there a similar instance (of that)? "Anything else?"

Softening phrases you can add include *"Ah! So…"*, *"Can you think of…"*, *"So …"*

Chunking Review

We all Chunk, all the time – but completely unconsciously. None of the words in these questions are uncommon. What makes the difference is that now you'll:

- Be *conscious* of the effect your words will have in controlling the discussion.

- Notice of the level and direction of the answers you get – if you listen.

- Control the direction of the answers – as you 'plug back in' your buyer's words.

At the end of this chapter are suggested assignments. These will be the easiest homework you do. But here's the hard part – try to keep the grin off your face when you ask a Chunking Up question and you actually get a Chunked Up answer! It really works. Figure 12 summarises all the Chunking questions.

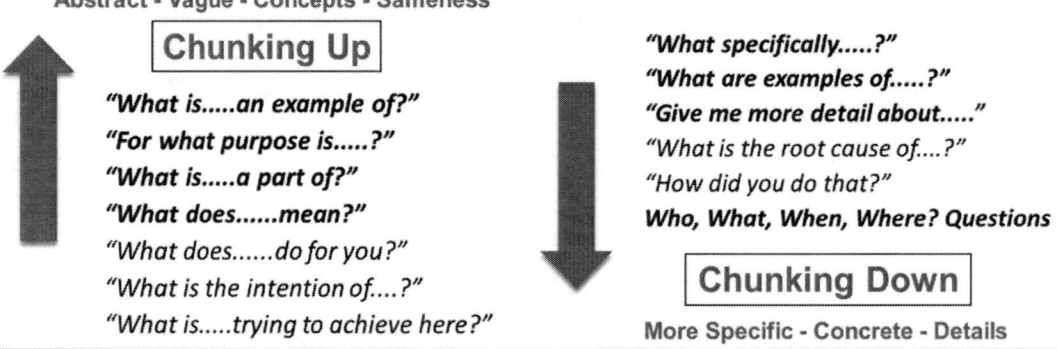

Figure 12

CHUNKING IN REAL LIFE INFLUENCE SITUATIONS

How do we use Chunking in real life influence situations such as a sales call, a contract negotiation, or even in personal relationships? Here are two examples.

Real Life Example One

You've gained your buyer's trust and they're beginning to talk to you about their situation. They mention the length of time it takes the company to prepare weekly financial reports for the central bank.

You'd like to move them to a point where they'll be able to consider your offering. So you ask a classic *Chunk Down* question to get at the detail:

"*Can you give me more details about how these problems happen?*"

Your buyer responds beautifully by going into great detail about the company's computer systems. Unfortunately, your offering is not related to computers. You offer outsourcing which is cheaper and faster than the buyer's staff it replaces.

However, you can easily get you buyer back on course. Don't develop the unproductive answer any further, simply ask:

"*That's useful to know – is there anything else that's a problem?*'

If you want to encourage them more towards your TakeAways, you can add a steering phrase "*...maybe on the staff side?*" The slight danger being that you may miss some gem of information that might make the need wider or longer lasting – it's your call!

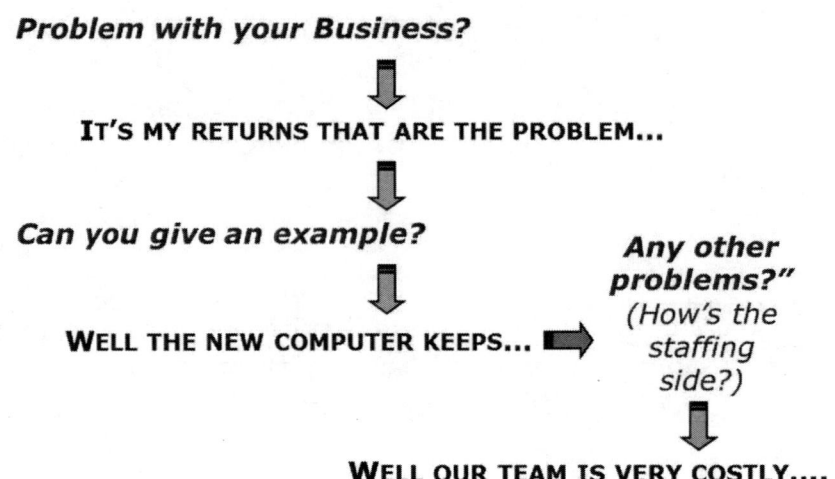

Figure 13

Figure 13 illustrates the process I've just described.

Real Life Example Two

In a tougher case, if your buyer goes down an unproductive line of thought (a 'Chunking Vector') you *can* direct them back to where you want them. You ask one or two Chunk Up questions to move them *back up* the vector; then a Horizontal Chunking questions (again perhaps with a steering phrase); then down another with some more Chunk Downs.

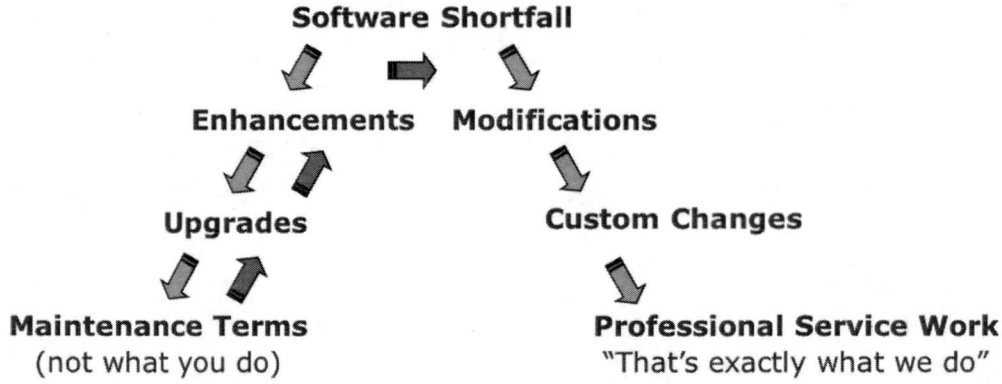

Figure 14

If they've gone *up* the wrong vector, then you do the opposite – one or two Chunk Downs and then a Horizontal Chunk. Work through Figure 14 on your own.

Like everything else in TSB, practice Chunking *consciously* for a time, but don't overthink it. Play about with Chunking with different people, in different situations, in different directions. Far better to get it wrong with friends or family than with an investor or your most important buyer!

You'll soon be wondering how you ever managed without the extra information and conscious control you now have.

Be Warned!
Just one word changes a Chunk Up to a Chunk Down:
"What is 'Perfection' an example of?"
is not the same as:
"What is an example of 'Perfection'?"
Try answering these for yourself – you'll see the difference immediately!

How Chunking lets you see into your Buyer's Model of the World

Preferred Level
Most people have a 'preferred level' in their Hierarchy of Ideas and it doesn't take too much acuity to spot it. Is their first reaction to an open question to give you a Chunked Up response? Do they tend to see the world's problems and opportunities in a strategic, 'big picture' way?

If your buyer's natural tendency is to take this long view and your offering is strongest when seen over a longer, strategic timescale, then you're in good shape. If their inclination is to first look at short term benefits, at the here and now detail, then you're going to have to Chunk Down further – to extend their timeline – at a pace they're comfortable with.

If your offering is strong in detailed and *very specific* aspects, and your buyer prefers to be involved with minutiae, then again, you're in a good position. If their natural position is the big picture, then again, you have to *Chunk them down* – but again, only at a pace that they find comfortable.

Mobility

There are a few people (I'm sure you can think of some) whose comfort zone is so strong that they're a real challenge to move to another level. Sometimes their desire to stay put is so strong that they'll actually reply to a Chunk Up questions with Chunked Down information!

Active Listening really helps here – you *must listen carefully and consciously* to what your buyer says – and notice the direction. All sorts of confusion can be created if you respond the wrong way.

There's no simple answer to this problem – except to be very determined. If they insist on giving illogical answers, there's often an underlying cause which might be useful to know. Sometimes there's an opportunity for a Reframe (see later in this chapter) to shake them up.

Maybe they just don't know the answer to your questions, but are afraid to admit it. Maybe they don't understand the problem or opportunity. Maybe they've been told not to discuss the matter at that level. All useful information to have.

Preferred Leap Size around the Hierarchy of Ideas

Take your mind back (or just turn back a few pages) to the original Chunking examples we looked at. Remember the woman who answered that a car was

> "The Destroyer of our planet"

Apart from gaining an insight into her ecological beliefs, there is another nugget of useful information there. She's likely to be a *big leaper*. That means that her mind is most comfortable making long conceptual jumps, not small ones. These people can be easy to work with, but the landing spot of their giant leaps can be hard to predict or control.

At the other extreme, a *small leaper* might give a series of answers:

> cake →birthday cake →child's birthday cake →cake in the shape of the child's age →sponge cake best for making sixes, etc.

You just need to be patient and stay at their pace.

Knowing whether a person is a big leaper or a small leaper is very important when we're influencing them to see an opportunity that's a long way away from their natural preferred level. You need to be patient with the small leaper – they'll get there in the end. The big leaper may reach the right level swiftly, but may not land in the right place! Time for that Horizontal Chunking.

The Key to Really Effective Chunking

I've coached many hundreds of student teams through Chunking exercises. I'm always surprised how much they vary. Some of them completely naturally take to it while others get bogged down and need a lot of coaching.

Observing them so often has taught me one key to success. It is (once again) *listening fully* to the reply given by the other person. The students who make it work are not only listening well – they're actively using the words they hear in the response – by plugging them back in to their very next question.

Let me illustrate this with two real examples that I observed recently in seminar exercises – both sets of questioners are trying to find out more information about why the buyer has to work late so often.

One went badly, one went well. Compare the usefulness of the information you get from Example 1 with Example 2's Active Listening. Can you work out which one had the most useful result?

Example One

> Q1: "Can you give me an example of working late?"

Response:

> "I'm sometimes asked to do totally unnecessary tasks by my unreasonable boss"

> Q2: "So why do you do all that extra work?"

Response:

> "I guess it's just because we're understaffed"

Example Two

> Q1: "Can you give me an example of working late?"

Response:

> "I'm sometimes asked to do totally unnecessary tasks by my unreasonable boss"

> Q2: *"So what's the root cause of your unreasonable boss asking you to do totally unnecessary tasks?"*

Response:

> *"I guess it's because he's been over-promoted and doesn't understand his job"*

Here's why active listening and then keeping the buyer's words as part of the next question is so important.

Whenever you ask you a question, your buyer's Model of the World is going to be the sole determinant of the reply… and you must *respect the words* in the answer.

If you choose to put your own interpretation on what is said (i.e. Delete, Distort or Generalise), a lot of information might be lost. As you ask more questions, your buyer may get lost in the conversation *very* quickly and, perhaps worst of all, they may even realise that you're **not listening**.

In the first example, the seller didn't quite listen to the buyer, so the second 'sloppy' question elicited the information that the company was understaffed. This answer was very different from the one received by seller who repeated back the exact words used by the buyer in the second question. That seller found out that the buyer considered the boss inexperienced and unable to do his job properly.

This sort of information might have a huge impact on how (or even if) you proceed! If you use *exactly the words* they use in your next question, they will give a much cleaner response *and* know unconsciously that *you're listening* – that's what active listening does for you!

I call all this approach 'having respect for your buyer' – it's important for gaining both information and rapport. The buyer may have spent many (sometimes hard) years getting to where they are, and developing their own unique Model of the World – often then modified by the Model their company uses. Everything they say is part of them and their situation – whether you agree with it or not – and they should be respected for it. If you disagree, there are better ways of changing them than not listening!

Lateral Thinking in Problem Solving

Sometimes just saying *"Anything Else?"* is not enough to find a solution. When this happens, use Lateral Chunking. Take the conversation two (or even three) levels up and then the same number down to land in a better place – exactly as before, when your buyer went down the wrong vector. Sometimes you'll be surprised by where you end up!

Now you see how it can work, give it a go yourself. Next time you're discussing options with a person or a group, ask a few Lateral Chunking questions and see where it gets you. This is actually one of the techniques used (consciously or unconsciously) by the best lateral thinkers.

Lateral Chunking Example

Joanne was a resident of Farnborough Park – a smart suburban neighbourhood having a major road system upgrade. She was in a meeting with the scheme architects about the final designs. The residents' committee had asked her to raise the issue of speed bumps. Many home owners were sure they were going to cause damage to the vehicles they drove over them every day.

Jo was fresh from an APEX seminar at her office and felt it was time to use some of her new linguistic skills. She decided to Chunk the architect up:

> (Q1) *"So for what purpose precisely are we building the speed bumps?"*

the reply she received was

> *"To slow down the cars of park visitors"*

This seemed like a good time for some Horizontal Chunking, so she asked

> (Assumptive Statement) *"Since the speed bumps damage cars so much, (Q2) what other ways are there of slowing cars down?"*

The reply came

> *"The only other option would be radar-operated 'You're Speeding' signs or complex 'Pinch points' on the road ... but they're 3-4 times the cost and way outside the budget"*

Joanne had a little sports car and was determined to push a little further to see if there was an alternative – so she decided to try a little Diagonal Chunking. So she Chunked Up one level further from her original question and asked

> (Q3) "So what are we going to achieve from slowing the traffic, then?"

After a bit of consultation, the answer came back

> "The Scheme Spec calls for protection for pedestrians to and from the shopping area on the North side of the park"

At this point Joanne saw a new option and Chunked Down one level

> (Q4) "So can you give me some examples of other ways of protecting pedestrians – that might dispense with speed bumps?"

The response came:

> "Well, the ideal would be to keep them off the roads in the first place"

To which Jo responded, completing the Lateral Chunking sequence (see below):

> (Q5) "...so could you build footpaths to do that?"

After further discussion, the reply came that there had originally been a plan for an access network through the center of the park, but it was dropped for some reason.

At this point Joanne felt she'd achieved enough and stopped. It was agreed that this idea would be included in the pricing options. Figure 15 illustrates what she did:

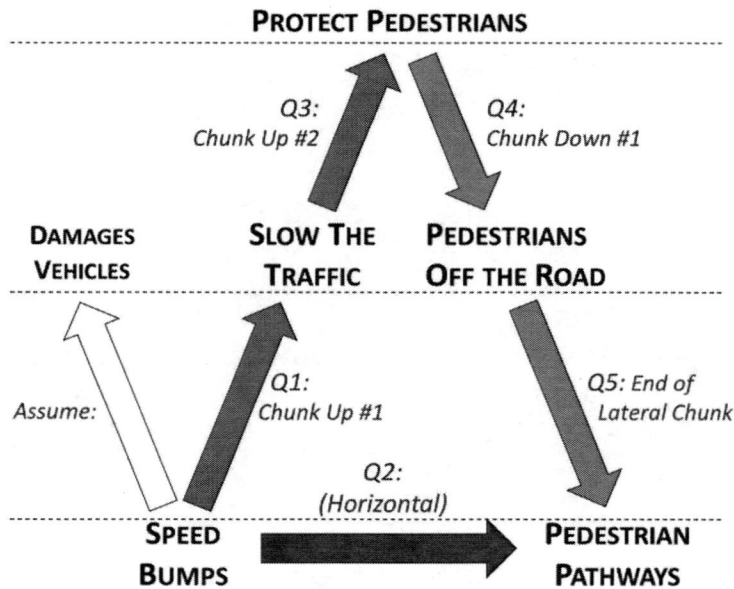

Figure 15

Other Really Useful Things to do with Chunking

Overwhelm

When someone is overwhelmed by the extent and complexity of a task, it can help them enormously to see the big picture and how they fit within it. This is where consciously Chunking Up can be very productive. It allows the overwhelmed person to see where they're heading and greatly reduces any tendency to panic. Often, by taking the biggest, scariest points of concern and Chunking Up from each of them, it's possible to see how they all lead to the same, positive outcome, easing anxiety and increasing understanding.

Sometimes a person is overwhelmed by the sheer size of a problem, rather than by its actual complexity. A fruitful approach here is to help them to Chunk Down to the detail and then tackle the immense problem one bite at a time – like eating an elephant (as we say in England). Many people find a series of small steps to their final destination much more motivating. Try it for yourself – the Chunking, not eating the elephant!

If you have a complex offering which will solve a big problem, sometimes Chunking it up or down is a good way of preventing your buyer becoming overwhelmed. Expose one problem, prove you can fix it, and then Chunk across, down or up to others you can address. Then, when the buyer is ready, reveal the full breadth of your offering!

Negotiation

Negotiating is a complex subject worth its own book, but Chunking is a good tool to possess even in a minor negotiation.

If you review the *Chunking Up* image at the beginning of the chapter you'll see that there's a tendency for 'sameness' and thus agreement as one Chunks Up. If you go high enough, it's pretty easy for two parties to agree with a Chunked Up statement such as *"Feeding one's family is important"* or *"Health is a good thing"*

It's getting to that the goal which may be the point of contention! Everyone may agree that *"Getting the Olympics started on time is important."* But the route to that outcome may cause disagreement.

Imagine if a city decided to run double shifts on the construction of the Olympic venues, but found the budget to do so by cutting rush hour public transit in half. The method would work, but the most people living in the city wouldn't agree with it!

When you're negotiating an agreement between two parties, the sequence below is a useful approach. It doesn't make much difference whether you're a mediator facilitating the process, or someone within who actually wants everyone to be happy with the result:

- Chunk them both up until there's clear agreement between the parties (Optionally Chunk Up one more to consolidate agreement and strengthen resolve).
- Chunk them both down very slowly (i.e. tiny leaps) until disagreement appears.
- Deal with/satisfy/create a plan to resolve that disagreement (Optionally Chunk Down to another point on the same level to gain more agreement).
- Once there's agreement, Chunk Down equally slowly until the next disagreement.
- Repeat the cycle until the situation is resolved.

- Document each stage of agreement as you go.
- Chunk Up together to the original agreement to consolidate commitment.
- Use reframes and challenges along the way.

Project Management

Project management is a great example of the day-to-day use of Chunking by people responsible for making scheduling and prioritisation decisions. They need to influence others to *buy in* to their plan or priorities. When project managers learn new TSB skills (or discover that they already use some of the skills intuitively), they really take them to the next level.

One of the biggest problems in any project, particularly one involving multiple people (staff, other area managers, sub-contractors, etc.), is the prioritisation of tasks and resources. The entire range of TSB questioning skills gives project managers effective tools to reach their desired outcome.

Here are a few useful questions a project manager can add to their collection:

> "Is this point actually relevant to this project?"
> (i.e. SO WHAT)
>
> "Give me a specific example?" "For what purpose, precisely?"
> (Chunking)
>
> "So, if that was dealt with over the whole life of the project....?"
> (Reframe)
>
> "What wouldn't be delivered if that didn't happen?"
> (Cartesian Challenge)
>
> "Huge? Compared with what?"
> (Challenge for missing information)

Chunking for Rapport

Rapport can be defined as "*A relationship of trust in which both sides are open about the subjects they discuss, and enjoy the exchange of views.*" Rapport needs to be earned respectfully and is vital in any influence situation where you're using Active Listening to draw out TakeAways.

One easy way to build rapport through Chunking is to consciously match the buyer's preferred Chunk level. Start your interaction at their level and move around only at the rate of their preferred leap size. Once they've become comfortable with you, then you can begin to challenge and change their Model of the World.

Maybe they deal with different issues at different levels. If they show that much flexibility – so should you. Match them again – then move them to the level that's best for the outcome you want.

> Mild-mannered Jenny is a good accountant, and an even better mum. She has to be – her son Tom has severe Down's syndrome and needs a lot of support.
>
> The transport company where she worked was running *Turning Selling into Buying* training. Even though Jenny had little to do with sales, the title of the workshop series intrigued her enough to sign up for it. That afternoon, she'd enthusiastically learned the Chunking challenges used in the Hierarchy of Ideas, and really enjoyed the energetic and sometimes tough exercises. At the end, she popped into her office to check that everything was OK before leaving to pick up her son.
>
> Unfortunately, her nemesis – the Finance Director – was waiting for her. This woman was long on financial expertise, but very, very short on human skills. Her ability to 'sit on the other side of the table' was close to zero – and she hadn't bothered to attend any of the TSB classes!
>
> *"Jenny, I need you to run the transactional analysis I've outlined on this sheet on the master ledger. Then feed the results into the new report writer and cross-reference them with the client address master file. Once that's done, run a full extract and email it to me as an Excel pivot table."*
>
> Oh dear! This was going to take at least 30 minutes and Jenny's son Tom became very upset when she was late picking him up from his day care center. Under normal circumstances, Jenny would have been tempted to ask *"Why?"* to see if there was any way out of the situation.

Bitter experience had taught her that the answer was likely to be *"Because I say so!"* which would not have helped. But she was so fired up by navigating the Hierarchy of Ideas that, without even thinking she responded *"So for what purpose precisely do you want these figures?"* – a Precision Question that came naturally after an afternoon of practice and discussion.

It was as if the Finance Director had walked into a brick wall. She was so used to steam-rolling Jenny into submission that she stood speechless for a moment. Then, unable to think of anything else, she described the final figures she needed, and what she'd use them for.

With a glow of delight (and perhaps just a little smugness) Jenny fired up her laptop – the figures were already there in another database! She printed them off, gave them to the amazed Finance Director and even picked Tom up early. She shared this story at the beginning of the next TSB class and we were all genuinely affected by both her joy and by how re-usable these skills were.

When I spoke to her about a year later, the whole relationship between her and the FD had shifted – and for the better – as a result of the new language Jenny had learned. She never did go into sales or marketing, but she'd learned how to eliminate assumptions and guesses!

Figure 16 is a graphic version of everything you've learned. You can download it as a reference sheet from *goo.gl/nd2M1* or select it at the TSB Book Downloads Page.

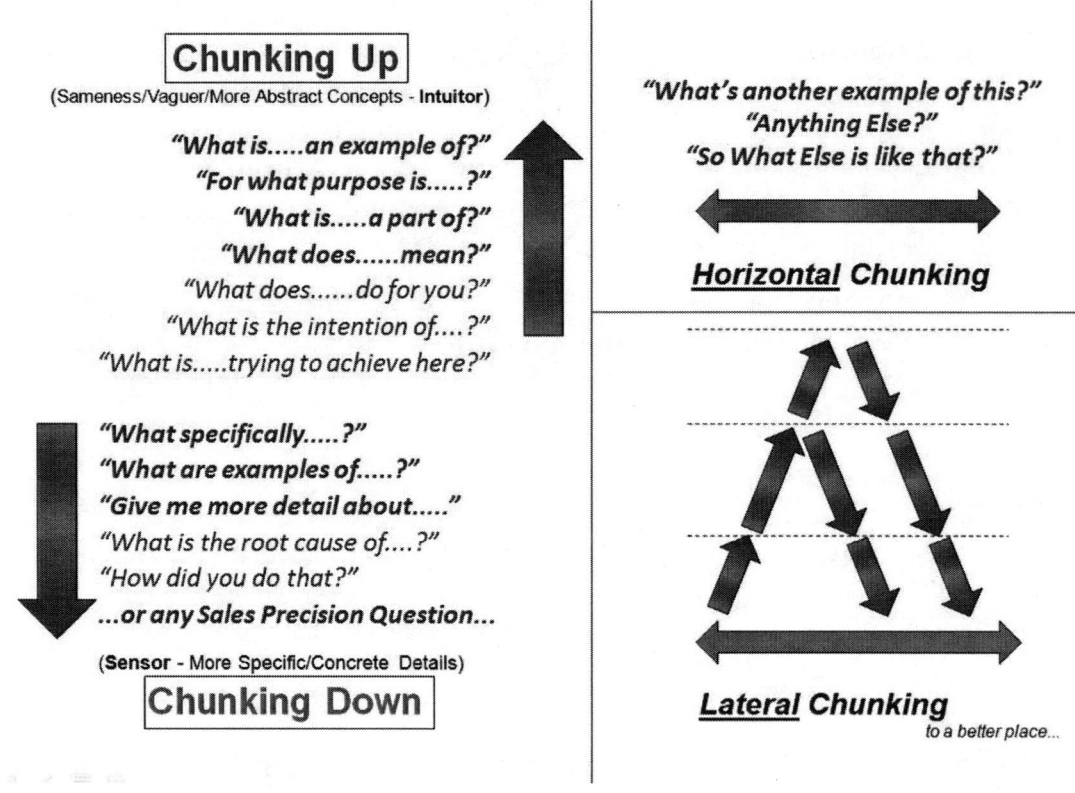

Figure 16

ELEMENT TWO – FRAMES AND REFRAMES

A few gifted people have a completely intuitive ability to calm down situations, change point-of-view, and create agreement – by using *reframing*.

The rest of this chapter is a practical guide to mastering this skill.

Frames – what are they?

You were introduced in chapter 2 to the idea that every one of us filters and processes our experience of the world in a completely different way. You can now add a *Frame of Reference* to those filters. The combination of filters and reference Frames is central to every decision we make. It is very much easier to change the Frame of reference than the core filters.

These (see chapter 2) are founded on beliefs, education, experience and much else, so they're much harder to shift.

A Frame of reference is really a vast, complex filter system. I may normally have a core preference for pictorial information over numeric information, but when I'm with my boss, (who's a numbers person) I'll make the effort to use her Frame. I see things in a different Frame again when I'm explaining something numeric to my daughter. Then I'll put myself into a different (equally complex) 'Father Frame'.

We Frame information in three places:

on the way in
An architect will see thing when looking at a building in a completely different way than a property developer or a performance artist. Those divergent impressions are determined by each person's years of different experience, decisions, training, culture, etc. – and are likely to be strongly rooted in them.

when we reflect
If a historian is reading a media story about political corruption, they may think about and evaluate it in a very different way to a local voter or politician. Of course, those two people can change State from one position to the other, and see different sides to the problem. The Four-See exercise in chapter 4 helps us to do this.

on the way out
We all Frame information whenever we make a statement or answer a question. A numbers-minded accountant might describe the motorbike she's decided to buy in terms of its power output and acceleration; a dancer may describe it in terms of her sensations and emotions, and a police traffic officer may talk about how it will help her to do her job. It's still the same bike.

Understanding that we Frame information in three different places and in several different ways is central to effective influence – particularly if you sell motorbikes!

So What is Reframing?

The filters that we use every day develop from just before birth, all through our lives – until the day we die. The basic ones (fight, flight, and feed) develop very quickly. Other filters, such as our character traits, take longer. The adult filters (like beliefs and values) develop as we interact more deeply with the world around us. The earlier the development of a particular filter, the harder it is to change. For example, we have an automatic need to flee at the sight of a tiger, but it's possible to reprogram even that deep seated reaction.

When it comes to TSB, we're not usually talking about making deep, therapeutic change. We're talking about influencing someone to change the beliefs in their Model of the World just enough to make a decision that didn't exist before; to buy something that didn't have a place in their world before; to do something they hadn't planned until you influenced them to do so.

Influencers face two sorts of challenge when they want to change another person's model. One is *factual*, the other *perceptual* (and the two are usually combined just to make our lives a little harder). Offering the buyer new, proven facts will distort their model in our favour. The statement:

> "Look at the results of this medical trial"

is unlikely to make a long-lasting change. But if you use a question to generate a perceptual change:

> "What difference will it make to your family if you live 10 years longer?"

and you're much more likely to create a durable and long lasting reframe. Combine the two and you have a powerful influence tool:

> "How will your kids feel if you benefit from the medical trial's results?"

Remember the Fulcrum of Influence in chapter 2 where you learned that 'being told' is the least effective method to influence someone? Answering a question or identifying with a story is the *most successful* way to create the change you want.

Sometimes, therefore, facts are not enough. If your buyer's filters are preventing them from seeing the monetary value, the time benefit, the risk, and the enjoyment in what's being offered, then you have a problem. There are really only two ways to deal with this.

Firstly, you could actually change the offering so that it fits your buyer's Frame. If it can be done without cost, delay or hassle, it may be an easier solution. Maybe my buyer wants team training. My sales training workshop are renowned for being high-energy team events. So why not reframe the offering if that's what the buyer wants? (That's how we created our 'Power Play Day' offering.)

The second approach is to keep the offer unchanged and attempt to change the way the buyer is using their filters (their Frame). Like so many linguistic skills, reframing is not an exact science. Our own skill is even affected by *our* Model of the World. I know a few people who reframe extraordinarily well, and completely unconsciously. The rest of us need to slowly and consciously build up the language skills to do the same thing. But do it enough and it can become fully integrated into your automatic way of influencing – with enormous benefits.

In both factual and perceptual change, the path we follow is to *help the buyer realise something for themselves*. As you saw in chapter 2, this is *always far more powerful* than simply telling them. A new, *self-generated* realisation that an investment is worth making, or an action is worth taking is far more powerful and long lasting than one that's imposed on us by simply being told.

You'll see in the following section that I always choose to make the reframe an offer or suggestion. Of course, there are situations – of urgency, of determination, or when the discussion has gone poorly, where you need to go back to a more assertive position. Sometimes very strong phrases such as:

> *"You know you're going to lose your job if we don't fix this problem?"*

have a place – but they can still be offered as questions!

So let's look at a few of the techniques that are most relevant to influence. You can practice using these *consciously* every day – right from the time you finish reading this chapter!

DAY-TO-DAY REFRAMES

Change Position

Change position is one of the most common reframes. The *Four-See exercise* creates a very different Frame of the world in each position. However, unless we have an exceptional rapport with our buyer, it's probably better not to suggest this exercise to them directly!

What you can do is verbally offer them the opportunity to see the problem they've raised *from a different point of view*. A simple example of this might be to counter the objection:

> "I'm not sure the Board will be comfortable spending so much money"

with:

> "How much money will they save using the service you've just seen?"

In a sales situation, these reframe questions can usefully be practiced alone or with a team before a call. In personal situations, a few minutes of quiet reflection doing a Four-See before the conversation can do wonders for mental preparedness and flexibility.

Change Frame Size

Sometimes your buyer's view of the world is limited in size. Perhaps they've become fixated by what's directly in front of them or don't even realise that there's another view of the problem or how to solve it. When you're approaching a TakeAway in the conversation, they may not even recognise their problem – or the value of fixing it – in the same terms as you.

For example, your buyer has just said:

> "Employing your consultants would take 25% of this year's budget"

This need not be a show stopper if we use a Change Frame Size counter such as:

> "What will the percentage benefit be to the company as a whole?"

Counter Example

This is one of the more powerful reframes and one that can be researched and practiced in advance. Sometimes brainstorming an upcoming influence meeting with colleagues can generate a useful set of these. Politicians do it all the time before debates.

This reframe example proposes another (generally factual) statement that moves or displaces the buyer's belief. Your assertion may be a rare or exceptional example, or it may be commonplace.

A good Counter Example to:

"I read on the Internet that your water pumps are unreliable"

might be:

*"Did you know they were used **without failure** by every emergency team in last month's floods?"*

Change Hierarchy

Now that you know about (and may have even already practiced) Chunking Up and down, you already have another great reframing tool. Chunking Up can move your buyer to a more strategic view of the problem or opportunity. Chunking Down can move them to a specific element that counters or changes their belief.

An example of a Chunk Down reframe might be to counter the statement:

"I'm not sure about a person who's only got experience in Europe"

with:

"What effect might those new skills have on your design team?"

A Chunk Up reframe to:

"We haven't invested in a microchip design company before"

might be:

"So what other plans do you have to diversify your portfolio?"

Change Hierarchy is a particularly powerful reframe as your movement up or down may take your buyer directly to a TakeAway and the opportunity to say:

"Well that's great – that's exactly what we do"

Basis Challenge

A basis challenge can be very powerful if prepared in advance. If it's done off the cuff you must be very confident of your facts. Quite simply, this reframe challenges the basis for the statement that the buyer has made. As usual, it's most effectively phrased as a question, but because of the need to maintain respect, it's usually best to back it up with some factual information.

Here is one example. The buyer's statement:

"Outsourcing always costs more than the original business process"

can be reframed with:

"Where did you get that from? Take a look at this Gartner Report..."

Intent v. Consequence

This reframe proposes a new, positive intention for an action or event. It should be used cautiously, and in good rapport, as it may generate a strong unforeseen reaction in your buyer.

An example objection might be:

"Your project manager has overwhelmed me with paperwork"

This might be reframed with:

"Did she say she'd keep you informed when the schedule was tight?"

or perhaps:

"Was that level of detail about the project status actually useful?"

An Early Example of Successful Reframing

It's 1979 and I'm a new Captain with my first Army Engineering command. Not only that, I was with a crack Cavalry Regiment – the 13/18th Royal Hussars. Unlike when they led the Charge of the Light Brigade in the Crimean War, we had Jaguar-powered aluminium tanks.

It was here that I had my first opportunity to use an influence reframe seriously – although I didn't know it was called that at the time.

The entire British Army was to drive to Germany to test our reaction to a Soviet invasion – and our regiment was to lead it. Lots of exposure and publicity; lots of reputations to be won or lost.

A few days before we left, we found a manufacturing defect in the armour of our brand new tanks – Stress Corrosion Cracking (SCC). This meant we had to take every single tank off the road, grind out the fault and re-weld the armour. We could do it in time – just – but only if we grounded all 60 vehicles just as their crews wanted to prepare them.

I was also horribly aware that my predecessor had been summarily sacked by the fiery Commanding Officer. Worse still, this was because of some unsubtle engineering rulings he'd made!

So I realised I had to use some finesse here! I knew that Colonel George's Model of the World didn't include much metallurgy, but I also knew he liked to feel himself master of every situation (we'd served in Northern Ireland together). So my reframe consisted of educating him – of Chunking him down into the detail of the problem and seeing it as an engineer – to become a real expert. But more importantly, to allow him to be seen (by the press, TV and his peers) as a modern CO who understood these new, high-tech tanks.

I prepared carefully, then sat him down and explained SCC to him – in huge detail. I showed him diagrams. I showed him timelines. I demonstrated that my aim was success for the regiment, not engineering excellence. I explained what would happen if we didn't fix it – the tracks would fall off – maybe in front of the TV cameras! I even compared it to having preventive maintenance work done on his beloved vintage Alvis – and it worked …. phew! It took a lot of reframes.

Not only did I get the permission I needed; not only were all his troopers told to get off their tanks; not only did he come round and talk to my guys as they worked through the night – but he became the star in Brigade HQ because of his ability to explain a complex engineering problem – attributes not usually associated with a Cavalry Officer!

So what did I learn from this (totally true) story that I can pass on to you? The sequence for a good reframe is:

1. Determine, as best you can, how the other person's thinking differs from yours.

2. Seek out a more compatible view of the problem / purchase / investment / decision.

3. Be sure of the other person's SWIIFM (in this case the Colonel's enjoyment of TV exposure).

4. Propose the new view, don't force it. The other person has to decide to accept.

The reframe must have worked as we (just) managed to get everything done; I kept my job and Colonel George bored people for years afterwards with his expertise in Stress Corrosion Cracking!

PREFRAMES

A "Preframe" is the set of filters that a buyer often constructs *before* they've even engaged with you – whether that's face-to-face, or simply by phone or email. They may build a model that's inaccurate and hard to shift, but it's likely to be based on things that are important to them. These might include your age or gender, the company you work for, experiences with your offering– even the fact that they see you as 'selling'.

The actions that you can take *before* you engage with your buyer to make this model favourable to you are limited only by your imagination and experience. In every case, whatever you do, you should take actions that will *make them want to talk with you openly* at the moment you walk through the door or they pick up the phone. The Buyer Discovery in chapter 6 can be a good basis for this.

Tactical and strategic Preframes can include:

- Email a short agenda with clear outcomes and timings.
- A quick confirmatory phone call to confirm these.
- Finishing that call with an open question about what *they* want.
- Emailing a link to a 30 second video of you talking on the subject.
- Organising a 'supporter' to mention you in a good light.
- Visible reputation of expertise via blogs, interviews and articles.
- Send a short, digestible article that you or a colleague has written.

Many of the actions that we take unconsciously are actually Preframing – being Consciously Competent and knowing what you're trying to achieve can really make them effective.

IN SUMMARY:
YOU CAN 'REACH INTO YOUR BUYER'S MIND'

There's a lot of power from simple ideas in this chapter. Chunking and reframing are amazingly productive techniques that make life easier and more predictable – and not just in influencing someone to buy. They are also fundamental human communication skills.

Chunking and reframing are at the heart of finding out whether there is business to be done. Without seeming to be 'selling', you can move the conversation to a discussion about each possible TakeAway that you know you can deliver. Once you confirm a TakeAway is needed, you can then further explore its size, timescales, and relevance – again using Chunking, challenges, and reframes.

If your buyer has no need for a particular TakeAway, then OK – just move to the next one and develop that. Once you've visited each TakeAway and know what can be delivered, you can say:

"Well that's great, that's exactly what we do"

When you can truthfully state that, then you're well on your way to *Turning Selling into Buying*.

Go out and have some fun with these two skills. Practice, experiment, be respectful so that you get lots of feedback, and you'll wonder how you ever survived without them.

The *"I wish I'd learned this at school"* remark has come up many times at the end of this section in my seminars. You may feel the same.

CHAPTER 5:
REVIEW QUESTIONS & SELF-DEVELOPMENT ASSIGNMENTS

Navigate Your Buyer's Mind – see Annex B for Answers

To print a copy of this section, download it directly from goo.gl/GqcnT or select it from the TSB Download Page at goo.gl/p0Ajn.

Self-Test Questions

1. What are the two skills covered in this chapter? What makes each of them so very productive commercially and how?
2. What is the Hierarchy of Ideas and how many levels does it have?

Chunking

3. Give an example of two generic Chunking Up questions.
4. Create two Chunking Up questions that will be of use in your situation.
5. Give an example of two generic Chunking Down questions.
6. Create two Chunking Down questions that will be of use in your situation.
7. Give an example of two generic Chunking Sideways questions.
8. What can you do if your Buyer's answers are going down the wrong vector?
9. Describe how Lateral Chunking works and what it can be used for.
10. What three attribute of a Buyer's Model of the World can Chunking reveal?
11. What is the most important verbal key to successful Chunking?
12. How can you use these new-found skills to help another person?

Reframes

13. What is a Frame? What is a Reframe? Are they statements or questions?
14. There are the three places in any path of thought or communication where we all apply our own Frames (of reference). What are they?
15. List and describe three of the six most common reframes.

Self-Development Assignments

Ch 5 Assignment 1 – Fun with Chunking

Pick two or three of the 13 generic Chunking Up or Down questions and try to use them in normal conversation – and be very consciously aware as you listen to the answer. What is their Chunk size? Are they happy going in that direction? Do they have a 'preferred level'?

NOTE: It's important to use a *varying group* of questions, since asking *"Can you give me an example of that?"* over and over can lose you friends quickly!

Ch 5 Assignment 2 – Serious Chunking

Now try it in a real influence meeting. Start by *consciously* using the questions to elicit information. Then begin to be aware of the direction you're moving the discussion and take more control.

Once you're confident of your own TakeAways (see chapter 7), you can then use the same techniques to navigate your Buyer to the TakeAways that you can *potentially* provide. If they have a need, you can develop them, if they don't, then move on.

Ch 5 Assignment 3 – Reframing – Little by Little

Now you're ready for reframing. Firstly, listen to other people. Look for the few natural reframers that are around us. Maybe someone in your team doing the same job has some useful ones you can use. Another excellent source is watching the best political interviewers – these are a goldmine!

TV Soaps are often a great source of 'negative reframing' where an accidental phrase causes misunderstanding and either hilarity or tragedy – driven by the conflict between the models run by the two people involved.

Once you've got a 'shortlist' of reframing questions and statements that you're happy with – go out and use them. You'll have to bide your time a little more than with Chunking, but when the opportunity comes, give it a try.

When I started, I focussed on one specific type (e.g. 'Change Frame Size') and I'd spend a week looking for opportunities to solve problems and change opinions by using it. Then I'd move onto another, the next week.

When the time is right, sit with some colleagues and brainstorm some commercial reframes for statements and objections that may come from your buyer – then you're ready for 'prime time' – and it will go well

PART TWO

"Readiness"

*The right Analysis...
so the right Buyer
buys the right Offering
for the right Reasons*

In Part Two, you're going to use all the techniques and insights you just learned. You'll apply them to your Offering – the idea, product or service – that you need someone to buy.

You'll generate everything you need to Build a Willing Buyer as you:

- Analyse what would motivate anyone to buy what you offer.
- Understand what makes any Buyer stick with a buying decision.
- Learn how to get them to take action – with an order or a decision.
- Use a simple, powerful tool to generate a robust financial case.

Most of all, you'll gain the *confidence and belief* that makes TSB such a game changer.

Part Two is very practically based, and each chapter starts with a downloadable self-test and development worksheet for you to write on.

You're strongly advised to read Part Two through first without doing any exercises. Then go through it again, with the worksheets beside you, to understand the whole approach and build extra information on your buyer, your offering, and the situation.

Enjoy...

CHAPTER 6
Buyer Discovery

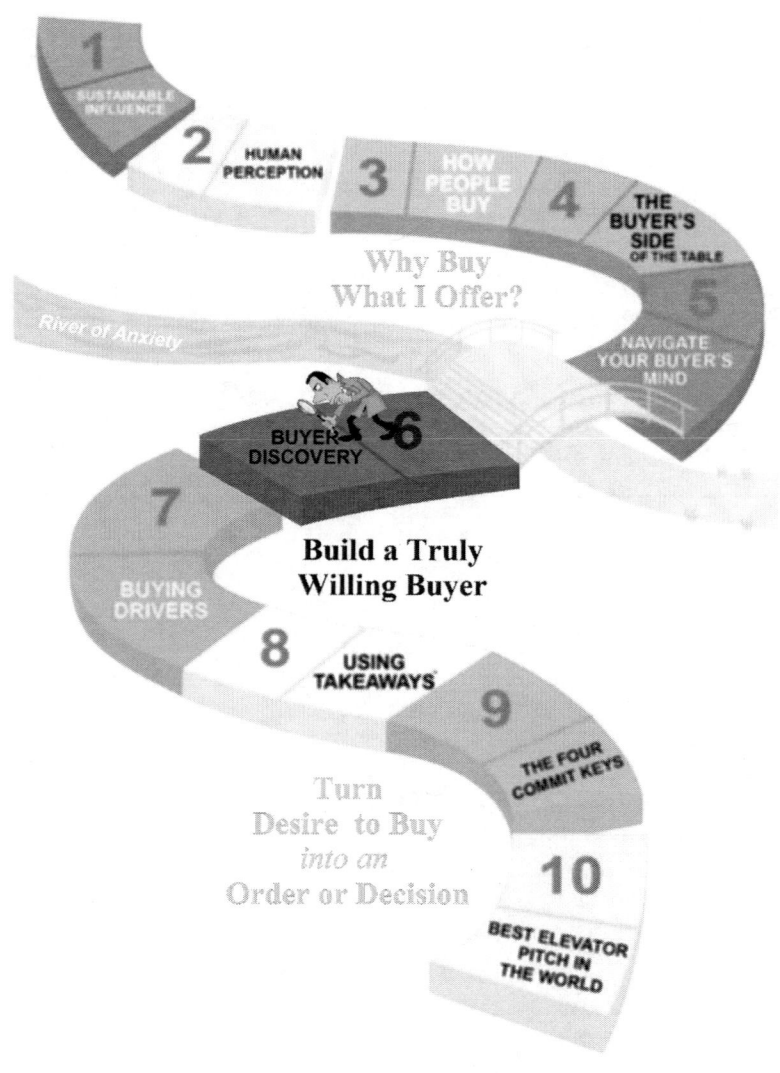

BY THE END OF THIS CHAPTER, YOU'LL UNDERSTAND …

- Why 'Discovering Your Buyer' before you meet is so useful
- A wide range of new research methods and tips
- Ways to uncover information – ethically, legally and productively
- How to minimise anxiety and boost confidence when you meet

HOW WILL THIS HELP ME BUILD A WILLING BUYER?

Turning Selling into Buying is about seeing a decision from your buyer's side of the table and doing what's necessary to generate a Desire to Buy within them. It's about leaving behind much of your own need to 'make a sale' or 'get a decision'. It also teaches how to gain your buyer's confidence that you can deliver their TakeAways.

It's hard to think of a better way to understand your buyers' real needs than through research. Some of that research will be factual – age, school, job history, etc. Some might be subjective – personality, how they make decisions, communications styles, etc. Some can be objective – corporate procedures, buying limits, technology rules, etc.

The right research will also change how you relate to your buyer. Are you confident when you're with them? I still remember how nervous I was when, as a junior salesman, I met a senior banker in Zürich. When you've performed a Buyer Discovery, it's much easier to feel confident going into a meeting.

This chapter's techniques uncover objective answers to questions such as:

> "Is the company decision making process available on their website?"
> "Has my buyer published an expert paper on what I'm offering?"

But much of the benefit of Buyer Discovery is firing up your mind – familiarizing it with the buyers' situation – well before you actually engage with them. Practice this chapter's techniques every day, so that they become second nature, and your confidence will grow in direct proportion.

The speed of change on the web means some of the resources used in this chapter may change. Look for updates and newly emerging resources at goo.gl/p0Ajn.

Time Spent in Reconnaissance is *Never* Wasted....

I was taught this 50 years ago by my Dad, who learned it serving in WWII; my own time in the Army reinforced it. I've passed it on to many people since then, including my own kids. But what I didn't realize for some time was that not all of the benefits of reconnaissance come from the facts themselves.

Much of the benefit is psychological and comes from confidence and familiarity – with the location of a meeting, the type of company, the logistics of getting there, the people who work there, how they get to work, etc. If you have a good insight into this, then you avoid making assumptions that can be shattered when you encounter reality – to the detriment of your confidence and your ability to influence. In chapter 3 we saw that the three biggest things that create 'sales fear' are:

- Anxiety at being asked about something you don't know.
- Personal embarrassment at being too aggressive.
- Fear of rejection.

Each of these issues is tackled head-on by Buyer Discovery. Just knowing what you know (and even understanding what you don't know) will go a long way to removing fear, uncertainty and doubt – releasing room for confidence, clarity, and creativity.

SO FOR WHAT PURPOSE PRECISELY DO YOU NEED TO RESEARCH YOUR BUYER?

A key success factor is for you to become, to the best of your ability, *genuinely interested in your buyer* – as a person, or as a company – what they do, their pressures and their daily problems. There's no perfect, mechanical way to do this, but you can at least feed yourself plenty of information to help you along the way.

> I was selling a high capacity messaging system (EDIFACT if you know what that is) to a multi-national paint company – so I made it my business to become genuinely interested in what they did. I'd been selling similar technology to airlines for some years and was pretty sure of my ground there, but knew I needed some 'Buyer Discovery' before I approached a very different business.

When I eventually met with the IT Director at the paint company, I'd learned enough (from some of the sources below) to be able to ask her much better questions than just *"So tell me about the paint manufacturing industry"*. I was able to ask her about some recent changes in data security regulations that I'd discovered – and how it would affect their international business. I'd also found out that she was on the committee that managed the standards and would know her stuff – so I used this as a lead-in to the conversation.

The unexpected result of our good discussion was my identifying – at our first meeting – one part of the EDIFACT messaging standard that our software *didn't* support. This would have been harder to manage if it had happened later in the project when the extra work would have increased our price. Identifying it so early allowed me to get her used to the fact, right from the start, that there would be extra development cost, not an off the shelf solution.

As a direct result of conducting Buyer Discovery, I protected our pricing and was seen as a partner. We even added new functions to our software which we were able to sell on to other customers.

Ethics

You're about to learn a powerful group of research techniques to find information about companies, individuals, institutions and industries. You'll then use that knowledge to influence them to buy your offering. In every case, the process is legal, ethical and in my opinion, completely proper.

Your test must always be whether you're happy
to truthfully answer a buyer's question

"Where did you learn that?"

As we saw in chapters 2 and 5, it's often really useful to ask your buyer directly. You may sometimes think you know the answer, but even if you do, you're likely to learn more about their mental filters and Frames– as they answer you in their preferred representation system or favoured words.

If you phrase the question correctly, you'll probably even get credit for your research or knowledge *and* still get their version.

Support for Your Mind

There are also some 'mental triggers' you can fire that are more personal.

I, for instance, know that I perceive the world very visually, while some people are more auditory – and some rely on their feelings. For me, being able to see a picture of the person I'm phoning or emailing can be a big help in relating to them while I'm talking or writing. It's rare to not find someone's picture somewhere on the Internet – add it to your information about them and you may find you immediately become closer.

Combine your research and imagination to create a Willing Buyer

- Your knowledge of the buyer's situation within their organisation – position, timeline, activity, publicity, influence and history – will allows you to ask questions that are more likely to be answered. This will help you to explore and create bigger projects and include other stakeholders in the decision-making process.

- Your knowledge of the wider commercial situation – industry trends, world markets, the legal Framework, and so much else – is useful in building a bigger buy from the customer you are trying to influence and may lead to other customers and partners.

- Learn about the buyer's personal situation – local community activity, age, gender, number of children, sports interests, etc. This not always available and you need to be careful to not come across as 'creepy', but it can be a way to start a good conversation and build a relationship.

If you find a good customer, research others who are 'like them'. That doesn't just mean the obvious targeting of their direct competitors or peers. It means answering the question:

> *"Which other companies or individual have a similar structure to my buyer – and so might need similar TakeAways?"*

Let's suppose for example, that your offering is a profitable premium consignment delivery service that's used by large pharmaceutical companies. These medical customers use your fast trucks and secure national distribution network because it saves time for their high-cost staff and also reduces the risk of them being sued for late delivery.

If you Chunk Up, you might well find that those exact same TakeAways fit a legal operation with the same needs for speed, security, and reliability – but in their case, for critical legal documents. On the face of it, law firms and pharmaceutical companies do completely different business, but they may well need to buy similar services to keep their customers happy and costs down.

Same service – different offering ... think laterally

Write down what the TakeAways for the pharmaceutical buyer might be:

```
```

Write down what the TakeAways for the lawyers might be:

```
```

Keep your mind open at all times to the possibility of spotting a match like this.

GOOGLE ADVANCED SEARCHES

This is a wonderful area for creativity, with many uses. One great resource is _googleguide.com/_. There's more detail at _goo.gl/nCyO_.)

TSB Tip One

You want to find out a person's job title within their company. It's time to use the **site:** Google Search function. Type (including the space):

>   gary site:holisinc.com

into your Google search engine or Chrome browser. You'll see several documents and pictures in the result. Not all are available via links from the normal Holis Inc. website.

One of them is a PDF document. Open it, then use **CTRL-F** to search for **gary**.

You'll find his name and his job title is shown in one of our press releases. Not only that, but there's also his email and phone number – what a bonus!

If you also click **Images** on the Google Sidebar, you'll see there are also several pictures of him (see my point above about visuals). Add these to your buyer information.

TSB Tip Two

You want to find out the phone number of your buyer's assistant in a subsidiary office, but you don't know their address. Here's another variation on **site.** Type:

>   +44-20* site:holisinc.com.

The *star is what is known as a 'wild card' and the query will return you every single variant of phone number that starts with **+44-20** (which is the international code for London). As a source for unpublicised phone numbers, this is just great.

There are also variations you can use when the buyer is in a large company with direct dial codes for each extension. In that case, you can enter the whole corporate number with only the last 4 as a wild card (e.g. **+54-11-4300***). This would return all the extensions that are recorded in any document on the website, often with the name and title of the owner.

TSB Tip Three

For much more specific searches the query can be made more complex. Try the search:

> "buy OR sell" site:holisinc.com filetype:pdf

You'll get back a list of all the Adobe Acrobat documents that contain either the word **buy** or the word **sell**. Use your imagination and check out what else you can find on your favourite website.

TSB Tip Four – Your Faithful Servant

All the previous tips can become time-consuming if you use them a lot. So (surprise, surprise) there are software tools out there to help you. Here are a couple that work well together. If you join my Twitter feed, @sellingtobuying, you'll be sent more as we find them.

The first tool is _rapportive.com_. This is an add-in for Gmail which, completely automatically, finds any information it can on the person you've selected in the 'To' box of your Google Mail. It looks in your Gmail account, in Facebook, Twitter, LinkedIn, Google+ and YouTube (and you can add others) – without you needing to do anything.

It then replaces the ads on the right hand side (which is also a good thing) with a simple display of everything it's found about that EMail address. This is pretty useful, and I leave mine switched on all the time. It currently works with the following browsers: Chrome, Firefox, Safari and Mailplane (GMail on a Mac).

TSB Tip Five – The Permulator

When you're trying to find a specific person in a company (perhaps to connect with them on LinkedIn) it's time to add to the power of Rapportive by using the EMail Permulator at _goo.gl/HqbzJ_. Full credit must go to Rob Ousbey of _Distilled.net_ for his hard work in building and debugging this great tool.

This very simple spreadsheet is the basis for this sequence:

- Enter the first, middle (optional) and last name of the person you're seeking to contact.
- Add the extension of their corporate/personal EMail provider (e.g.@holisinc.com, @gmail.com, etc.).
- Automatically generate the 46 EMails they're most likely to use (in descending order of likelihood).
- Select them all from the spreadsheet and press ctrl-C to copy them.
- Go to Gmail, *COMPOSE* an EMail and then press ctrl-V to paste all 46 permutations into the 'To' field.
- Click on the top entry. Rapportive will immediately dash off to find what it know about that EMail and display what it's found.
- The first combination may reveal nothing, but keep pressing the down arrow to move through the combinations, pausing each time to let Rapportive do its work.
- When you hit a good EMail, you'll get a clear indication with pictures and details appearing. In almost every case, the first successful search is the one you want.

Try it with Trevor, Graeme, Wilkins and @holisinc.com. My correct email appears within the first few lines.

NOTE: Do *not* just populate your GMail with all the permutations that the Permulator creates for you – this is anti-social and unethical. Use the power of Rapportive to find the one that shows you the person you want.

Once you've installed Rapportive, you can extend its reach even further with add-ons, called *Raplets* which you can get from the rapportive.com site

TSB Tip Six

If all this technology is just too scary for you.... go to www.google.com/advanced_search and simply fill in the search form!

LINKEDIN

What a joy LinkedIn is. It has quickly become the 'de facto' standard for business connections and for presenting yourself to the commercial world. It's also a valuable tool for non-business situations. One of its greatest strengths (unlike Facebook) is its self-regulation by peers.  If I claim to have been the CEO of Apple, it would only take a few hours before this untruth was spotted by an employee at Apple who would have reported my abuse to LinkedIn.

There are many sites that are similar (Viadeo, Xing, Ryze, ECademy, etc.) and detailed functions and use are constantly changing. But most of what follows is fairly universal. So if your area of life or business uses a different networking hub, just pick what's best for you. LinkedIn is presently still the 'big brother' but the smaller, more specialised networks will always have their place.

TSB Tip Seven – Basic LinkedIn Searches

At a basic level, LinkedIn allows you to see the job history and geographical movements of your buyer. This is useful if, for instance, you've both worked in the same location, or if you've been a supplier or partners to one of their employers. If your buyer has a lot of recommenders, drill down into that list and see what you can find there. You may well know someone there who can help you with useful insights. Your buyer may also have, in turn, recommended someone you know. There may even be a recognisable industry or geography pattern to the people they recommend or where they work.

Check out your buyer's education – can you see any pattern there? Have a look to see whether they have their own websites or twitter feeds. These can reveal a lot more about the sort of person you're influencing. You may even find they have several jobs at the same time! Have they written any papers or articles? The great thing is that they have posted everything there themselves and want you to see it. No mistaken Facebook 'tagging' from photos at crazy parties on LinkedIn!

TSB Tip Eight – Advanced LinkedIn Searches

LinkedIn allows you to go much further than this if you really use it properly. Sometimes you can learn much more than is apparent on the surface. How often do they move jobs? Are they a 'flitter' or have they worked in the same location or job for 20 years? Look at the pattern of their promotions – have they unfailingly put their entire career progression into LinkedIn? Or does it just show 12 years in the 'Admin Department'? Do they have a single geographical bias or are they citizens of the globe?

What LinkedIn Groups do they belong to? If it's just professional groups related to their work, go and see if they've actually been posting there. What is your buyer an expert in? What questions are they asking and answering? Look at the people who've joined those posts and the subjects. Are *they* in turn Linked to your buyer? Do you know them? If your buyer is a member of non-work groups (e.g. 'Darts', 'Cycling' or 'Charity') as well as professional ones, you know LinkedIn is important to them. Go and check out the list of Connections and Groups that you share with them – this may also reveal useful insights.

I have sometimes joined a Group for a few months during a sales campaign to get the inside line on what's happening in (for instance) the paint manufacturing industry. Sometimes actually joining, posting and asking a few questions can add even more insight into the industry pressures and opportunities of your buyer.

TSB Tip Nine – Wider Horizons

Another area worth looking at is the Companies section of LinkedIn. Enter the name of your buyer's company and see whether you're connected to anyone who works there.

Not only does this give you a great source to tap for information, but it can also give you an insight into the company where your buyer works .

Take a look at what groups and discussions are being posted to – by other people in your buyer's company. This is often a fertile source for 'discussion prompters' about industry gossip. It's particularly useful when you need to know what the latest issues are in the paint industry!

Another fertile place to seek someone who may know your buyer is to check whether you have 1st or 2nd level links to anyone in their Groups or the Companies where they've worked in the past. It's a small world out there and the *degrees of separation* can often be very small. Use your imagination and don't be afraid to drill down using the *advance search* offered by LinkedIn.

If you discover or create great new techniques, please share them with the TSB Online Community at *goo.gl/dth17*

TSB Tip Ten – The 'De–Anonymiser'

I must thank Mike O'Hara of *highfrequencytradingreview*, for this excellent variation which combines LinkedIn with the **site:** command.

When you search via LinkedIn, you often get results that contain 'anonymised' names (with only an initial in place of their surname). This happens when the people within those results are more than two connections away from you. But the anonymised results *do* contain a job title and company details. This means that you can take those details and use them in a standard Google search, using the site:*linkedin.com* qualifier.

For example, if my LinkedIn search brings back the result Damian K – Lead Trainer at ElementK (i.e. I don't know his family name – just that it begins with K)

I now have two choices. I can type in

> site:*linkedin.com* Damian "Lead Trainer at ElementK"

(note you must use quotes to search for the exact string of letters)

The answer I get is that that his full name is Damian Martin.

Alternatively (particularly if the job title is something more distinctive than 'Marketing Manager') I can enter the whole job string (in this case "Lead Trainer at ElementK") into a normal Google search. This can produce some interesting results and information about the person. Once again, a variation is to put a website name after **site:** rather than LinkedIn.

Good luck and happy hunting! I won't give you Mike O'Hara's email, phone number, or picture – I'll leave you to use the techniques you've just learned to hunt him out and contact him for yourself. He is the guru of telephone sales training that *Turns Selling into Buying*.

TSB Tip Eleven – Competitors

If you're in a competitive situation, take a look at information about your competitors on LinkedIn. See who's working for them – do you know any of them? Who *used* to work for them? Who's following them? Do you know any of them?

See who else is LinkedIn to senior people at your competitor. If the person you're influencing is LinkedIn to your competitor, it may not mean anything – or it might mean everything. But at least you now know that there is a good chance your buyer knows what your competitor is offering.

Companies are now putting their own description on LinkedIn. Sometimes the descriptions/videos/slide shows of your competitors can be really helpful in strongly framing your offering with your buyer.

Industry Alternatives

Specific industries sometimes create their own 'LinkedIn Lite' but these are often blunted by the sheer power of LinkedIn. One example is the CAPS website where I am a member. It has some good stuff on it for members, but most of the really useful conversations now take place in the CAPS Groups on LinkedIn.

But where (say) a 'paint industry' group covers your buyer (and thrives), visit and use it in exactly the same way as LinkedIn. You may not be able to join, and your view of the data may be restricted, but they're often useful to help you become genuinely interested in your buyer's industry, needs and challenges.

Prospecting

This book's purpose is to teach you how to turn influence people to buy from you, not how to find buyers for your products, services, or ideas. But it would be crazy to ignore the power of LinkedIn for finding buyers.

The center of this prospecting power is the _Advanced People Search_ page. Here you can use the three golden parameters – Industry, Job Title, and Keywords to find the right target to buy what you offer.

But LinkedIn should not be overlooked as a source for other powerful allies such:

- Distributors.
- Value Added Resellers.
- Investors, Angel Groups or Professional Funds.
- Development Partners.
- Management – for your start-up or just day-to-day recruitment.

BUILDING YOUR NETWORK

The more connections you have, the better your results will be when using LinkedIn. Building your network is not something I want to cover in detail here, but here are a few thoughts.

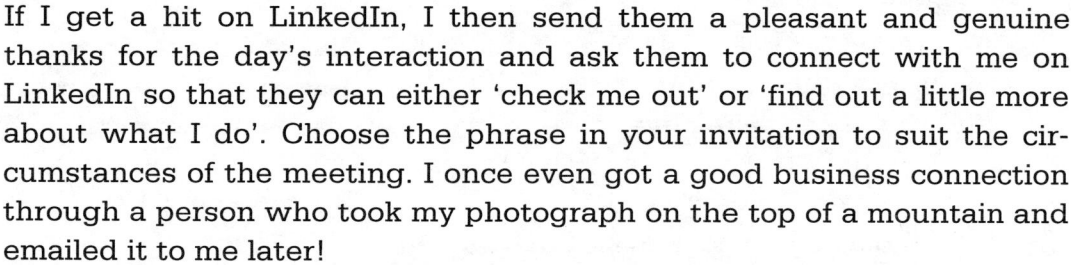

Make it a strict rule at the end of each day to search on LinkedIn for any and every person on the business cards you've collected – whoever they are. If you've jotted down other names on the card (perhaps referrals) do the same search with them. Also search the names of any new people you've connected with by phone, email, blog, or messaging into LinkedIn. Another reason I love Rapportive!

If I get a hit on LinkedIn, I then send them a pleasant and genuine thanks for the day's interaction and ask them to connect with me on LinkedIn so that they can either 'check me out' or 'find out a little more about what I do'. Choose the phrase in your invitation to suit the circumstances of the meeting. I once even got a good business connection through a person who took my photograph on the top of a mountain and emailed it to me later!

Integrate this approach to network building into all of your business life. I now have over 1000 _good quality_ LinkedIn connections – all of whom

I've had real contact with. This genuine connection hugely improves the quality of my outreach and my ability to learn about my buyers.

I very seldom accept invitations from people I don't know. But I usually check who they are and sometimes, instead of rejecting them, I may send them a message asking who recommended me. Depending on their response, I may then accept their request.

As you might have guessed, I'm not a fan of 'Super Connectors'. These are people whose business is to collect a massive number of Links and then, in turn, give access to a wider number of people. But that's a personal choice. For me, quality is more useful than quantity when it comes to the subject of 'know your buyer'. Quantity can be useful in setting a telephone calling campaign, but not here, where you're learning what might influence others to buy your offering.

> I'm really proud of my success in building my own strong 'Regional Networks', so here's one example that you might find useful.
>
> When I decided to emigrate from Europe to Canada, I realised that my connections there were limited to the one sale I'd made there, and to the reseller and buyer involved. So I started to use the Advanced Search function on LinkedIn vigorously. I paid a little extra for a few months of Premium Service and searched for people with the right job title (Sales Director, Business Development Director, etc.), who worked for medium to large companies, and were within 100 kilometres of my new home.
>
> I did a TakeAway Analysis (SWIIFM) and realised that I had one thing of potential interest to most of them – a diverse set of senior connections – and *all outside of Canada*. So I wrote some friendly, well-targeted InMails (also included in the Premium Service) to the people that I'd found from my searches. I suggested that they connect with me and take advantage of my wider network – and bingo – it worked! With the exception of two non-replies, every single person I mailed connected to me. Several people later became customers and a couple have even became personal friends.

Do the same research and outreach whenever you move into a new commercial territory – and do it primarily to get local information, rather than looking for buyers. Look at your own situation the way I did. Maybe your asset is (for instance) that you have a good set of connections amongst Chinese graduates. Decide whether those links would be a useful enough TakeAway for people in the area that you're interested in, and then ask them to connect to you and take advantage of what you offer them.

CRMs (Customer Relationship Management) systems

I don't even try (consciously) to remember anything that can be put into my CRM. I'm totally dependent upon it – even though my business is so very personal. For that same reason, it's absolutely imperative that, whatever size you are (individual, start-up team, independent business unit, etc.) you have the right CRM. Whatever amazing analytics, real time graphics, and forecasting it may have, it must:

- Be accessible from *anywhere* (notes added directly after a meeting are so much more accurate).

- Combine free format text with a user history (when exactly did I add that link to her research paper?).

- Be well synched to different devices (when I check it just before a meeting, I need to know their CEO just phoned).

- Give me 'single click' access to other sources about them or the opportunity (e.g. direct click to LinkedIn, a related news services and our project file).

One last point – make sure that you nurture your 1st Level LinkedIn connections. If it's at all possible, 'pay it forward' by sending them something they'd value – for free. Maybe give them a free invite link or useful (non-sales) videos or articles. Then, when the time comes to ask for help with your buyer research, you'll feel much more relaxed about asking and they'll be more inclined to help you.

SEARCHING WITH POWER – AN ETHICAL WARNING

I hope I've made it clear in all my writings that I strive to maintain high ethical standards. As I mentioned in chapter 1, the sales influence profession often has a strong negative aura about it. If we each act correctly on all occasions, it will help to dispel this reputation.

Don't abuse the power of this research. The test of ethics is very simple – your gut will tell you. If you think you might be doing something unethical – use this test:

> *"If it looks like a duck, walks like a duck and quacks like a duck…*
> *… it's probably a duck!"*

The same applies to what looks or feels wrong to you – if it looks or feels wrong in any way – it probably is. I urge you to take an ethical approach in your use of any of the tips and advice I give here.

BUYER'S STAFF & COLLEAGUES

It's important to always stay on good terms with as many people you meet as is possible. For me, that's a strong personal value, so it's pretty automatic. You never know when it will be useful to just pick up the phone and ask for advice and guidance on how to influence a person or organisation. So make sure you stay in a position to be able to do that.

LinkedIn is only one of several sources. Here are a few more:

- Many websites have a staff list (if it's not immediately available, use the **site**: function above).

- If you and the buyer are members of the same industry or leisure organization, see if there's someone there you know

- (My favourite) Send an email around your team or company explaining (for instance) that you're 'about to have an important meeting at …xxx… to influence them to become a reseller'- has anyone had any experience of or (better still) worked for them? Then swap coffee for great inside information.

Another route is actually very simple and risk-free once you've done it a few times. Why not phone up your buyer's gatekeeper (secretary, executive assistant, or colleague) with whom you've worked so hard to book the meeting? After a normal social opening, say to them directly:

> *"I want this to go well and make best use of your boss's time. So can you tell me the way she prefers to take things in? Does she prefer pictures or numbers? Is she chatty or reserved?"*

As long as you introduce the request properly (the 'Positive Preframe' of 'saving her boss's time'), the very worst you're likely to get is *"I'm sorry, I can't help you"*. But if you happen to get someone helpful who loves to chat, then there are fewer better ways of Buyer Discovery!

A DAY IN THE LIFE OF....

One technique I've used successfully on several occasions is to brainstorm '*A Day in the Life*' of my buyer. I usually do this with colleagues – I once even had it facilitated by someone outside the group. We usually make it a '*Business Day in the Life of*', but there's no reason not to make it wider than this. It need take no more than half an hour or less.

Our usual approach is to start by identifying key people who might be involved in influencing the buying process and assign each role to a person in the group. Examples of these roles might be the CEO, a buying department rep, the finance manager, the IT director – whoever you believe to be useful to your cause. Your team members then go off and do their own research (hopefully having read this chapter).

When you reconvene, you can then carry out an (often entertaining) role play with your buyer's day unfolding. I always assign one especially imaginative person as the 'THIRD & FOURTH POSITION' (see chapter 4) to challenge us with questions as we go along – about process, motivation and objective facts. This exercise throws up a lot of new information and, just as importantly, important questions that we can't answer. These can then be researched further.

At the end of a 'Day in the Life of' session, your team will have a much better understanding of the buyer's true situation on the other side of the table. This will benefit greatly the way your team goes on to generate TakeAways, the ROI Framework, Convincers and the Delivery Narratives (see chapters 7, 8, and 9). They're also likely to have become very familiar with the company or individual. This alone can bring great benefits of confidence and knowledge for when they actually need to engage with the buyer.

PERIODICALS/NEWS SITES

These are generally a great source of up-to-date background information – and not just as useful conversational openers. It's clearly useful to be able to ask about 'the hostile takeover' which you read about in the local business paper, but sometimes even more useful gems are hidden in the pages. There are, for instance, sometimes quite detailed industry case studies or stories in these sites. The figures from these might even feed directly into the ROI or cost justification for your offering.

Canadian Paint and Coatings Association

Public news is also an excellent source of company and individual names that you can feed into LinkedIn to see whether you have a connection. These periodicals usually choose senior, influential people for their articles – the very best people you can have as contacts, allies or sources of information. Another great source is to open an account at Newsle – *newsle.com/about* – to email you news stories about your contacts.

It can also help with your professional credibility when you're open and honest about your research in this area. By preframing a question with:

> "I thought I ought to find out what's happening in the paint manufacturing industry and spent a bit of time on the abc journal website. I found an article there about the xyz legislation and wondered if you could explain ... "

Not only does this give your buyer an opportunity to discuss what they're experts at (which most people love) but it also demonstrates that you're a professional who takes meeting preparation seriously. It's even better if your buyer actually wrote the article!

TSB Tip Twelve – A Press Release 'Back Search'

A great source for News is to click on the **News** button that is always shown on the sidebar of any Google Search you've made for a company or organisation. Other sources are to use the **site**: Search and look for Press Releases.

Then take some unique or distinctive phrase (six words or so) from the Press Release or News item and feed it back into a Google Search. The result will very often be an accurate list of all the periodicals and sites that have been sent the press release and have then decided to publish it – almost always verbatim.

Search those new sites, and they, in turn, will have other news and names about related companies, individuals, and issues that may be of interest to your buyer.

CONTACTS

Do not forget the business and personal contacts that you've built up – however and wherever you keep them. If you don't keep them electronically, take some time in lateral thinking to identify someone who might know your buyer's industry, company, or job type.

Do you store your contacts electronically (as so many of us do now)? If so, get into the habit of spending an extra 20 seconds whenever you create or modify their record. Add those all-important notes about the person – who introduced you, the date you met, what you spoke about, personal interests, sports, etc.

It takes so little time, but in three months or three years it can become a source of valuable information. I can't remember how often that 'who introduced us' has helped me. I should mention that free text search is so good nowadays that you don't need expensive re-configuration and new fields in your records. I just put INTRO in capitals in the note.

As a sidebar, you should also automatically classify your contacts as you enter them – for the same reason. As your connection with them increases, their classification may change. I also generally keep an audit trail of changes as well, rather than just changing the status. I even have one person in my contacts database that has gone from Acquaintance to Client to Friend and then to Family!

As I've mentioned before, I believe that you should maintain a healthy degree of conscious 'paying it forward'. If the only time your contacts hear from you is when you're asking for something, they may soon move backwards from Client to Acquaintance – not the direction in which you want them to move!

> While I was deeply involved in completing this book, I had an important appointment booked with a potential partner. This had been set up many weeks earlier and couldn't be cancelled. But my schedule on the day became very tight. I arrived directly from another meeting and had been flat out all morning, so I'd had no time to prepare for what might be a key influence opportunity.
>
> However I was saved by the system I've just described. When the CEO of this organisation had told me (several weeks earlier) that I should connect, I'd noted down the contact's name. That evening, I found his entry on LinkedIn, uncovered some press releases about his activity, grabbed a picture and found several mentions of directorships he had. I went and had a quick look at the websites for these companies as well. He'd also published two documents that I quickly scanned and summarised.
>
> It took me less than three minutes to do and I stored the results into his record on my system. Since my trusty Android phone is synched automatically, this tiny amount of effort paid dividends over a month later. Despite the great time pressure I was under, I popped his record up whilst walking to the meeting. Reading through it allowed me to construct my opening questions and (in my head) run my potential TakeAways past what I now knew about him. I also recognised him as soon as I arrived, too!
>
> We struck a chord and dived into discussing what his organisation could TakeAway from working with me. The meeting went well, he was influenced to make the decision I wanted, and we each went away happy.
>
> Without the preparation, I'm sure that I'd have been more anxious, I might well have made incorrect assumptions and there would have been a stronger chance of the meeting going badly.

OTHER SOURCES

Blogs, RSS and other Subscriptions

When you do a Google Web or Site Search, you'll always also get a sidebar showing different results – **Images**, **Maps**, **Videos**, **News**, etc. They're not always so obviously displayed, but don't forget to click on **Blogs**, **Discussions** (or maybe even **Patents**). If your buyer is there, then you can discover a lot about a lot about them – their pressures, their beliefs and their accomplishments. Rapportive makes this even easier.

If your buyer has a blog, that's a great place to find out what they believe in. You can even subscribe to it – but be aware that they may be alerted that you are a subscriber. So again, be open and honest about your research on them.

> It may also be worth your while signing up for a newsletter, RSS, or similar feed in the industry area where your buyer works. When we were looking for funding for our start-up, I signed up for several Venture Capital newsletters and immersed myself in industry talk about start-ups. This was not an area with which I was hugely familiar, but doing this definitely helped my verbal fluency in front of those tough financiers. I didn't claim to be an expert, but I was comfortable – and we got a finance term sheet!

Social Media

Facebook, Twitter, Google+ ... the list is long. It's also possible to be sucked into these in a way that will stop you being properly productive at what you're trying to achieve. It's worth remembering that in most cases, if your buyer has an entry in these social media systems (and many others) the result of your Google enquiry will almost always include their entry on these systems – so there's usually no need to go to each site separately. Again, Rapportive can be a great help here.

At this point you need to make another decision about intrusiveness – particularly with personal pages on Facebook and any personal or family websites that you may have found. I generally take a cursory look, then leave. If, however, you feel it's appropriate to 'Friend' or 'Like' someone, that's your decision – but it should be consciously made, not automatic.

However, if your buyer is actively tweeting, that must be with the intention of being followed – so go ahead – follow and retweet as you wish. Just be careful if your meeting doesn't go well and they tweet to the world what happened!

Wikipedia and other Wikis

Wikipedia is another great source for industry and situation information. The huge number of links there also means that it's possible to wallow around in background detail for a long time – so give yourself a time limit or a specific set of deliverables (e.g. every peer company of your buyer).

Once again, the names in Wikipedia are real and almost all peer reviewed, so they can be plugged back into LinkedIn or Google for valuable results.

Video

YouTube and other video sites like Vimeo are increasingly worth visiting. But the sheer volume of material can make it hard to find useful information. If you know your buyer is active in a particular area, it can be useful to use some keywords, find them on video, and watch them in action. At the very least, you'll learn a little about how they communicate, with the rapport benefits that brings. If what they say is provocative, it can be a great basis for a conversational opener or shortcut to their TakeAways.

If they have their own YouTube Channel, it's worth spending a little extra time checking out who's subscribed to it. Do you know them? Is there an identifiable demographic? For what purpose precisely does your buyer maintain their own channel? Is there something there that you can ask them about?

Conventional Sources

'Old school' libraries can still be a source of valuable information on companies and industries, but scanning and online projects are making these less and less useful. If your buyer is a government or institution, there may be a historic or legal reason for you to walk away from your PC and visit a real town hall or chamber of commerce!

Events & Publications

If your buyer appears in a search as speaking at or attending an event, take a look around that event. Look at the event's associated industry and attendees, and maybe plug a few into Google or Rapportive. Likes attract, so the chances of other attendees similar to your buyer are quite high.

Once again, cross-reference and drill down to the people you may know. If your buyer is a writer, find out everything you can about their published work. Does the book have its own website? Is there discussion there? Who's doing the discussing? Check out the book's genre, their publisher's site, and even 'Look Inside' if it's on Amazon.

IN SUMMARY:
ARM YOURSELF WELL TO MAXIMISE SUCCESS

To sum it up, *Buyer Discovery* is about weighting the odds of an influence meeting as strongly as possible in your favour. It's about minimising the chance of poor luck affecting what happens. It's about taking control through your own efforts.

Of course, you could trust to luck. You could accept that sometimes 'you'll drop one'. But in today's tough markets, with more and more people competing for the same opportunity – can you afford it? Even away from work – do you really want to leave your family's future to luck? Do you really want that job, or is it just a casual interest?

- Be(come) genuinely interested in everything and everybody around you.
- Let it become second nature to collect and store information.
- Use your imagination and roam widely for information.

I can't leave without a story – you know that by now!

> When I started at the London Stock Exchange, my buyers were the original 'open outcry' floor traders (who have almost disappeared today). Prices were requested verbally; the answers came back the same way; orders were written on a note pad – by a Blue Button (a trainee stock broker). It was a completely new world to an ex-army officer.
>
> Before I got very far into my new job, I decided to do some Buyer Discovery. I arranged to spend a day on the Stock Exchange Floor as a Blue Button. I truly sat on their side of the table (well, their side of the security doors anyway). It was a great experience and I gained a lot of objective knowledge about the Exchange's procedures and rules.
>
> But the difference for me went much deeper than that, once I got down to the business of influencing brokers to buy electronic trading systems. I'd now experienced (a little) what drove these people. I understood how their day ran. I knew which bits they enjoyed and which they didn't.

All of that made *such* a difference to the questions I was able to ask and the conversations I developed when I finally engaged with their senior partners. It also, incidentally, made a difference to the way they related to me – I'd actually gone to the trouble of sitting on their side of the table – which they respected.

Since then, I've repeated the exercise often. At the exotic end of the list, I've made sure that I crewed a race on board a world class racing yacht when I was writing navigational software for them. I've spent a night shift in the British Airways Flight Operation in a secret bunker in Heathrow when they were buying my reservation software. I've sat with the customer service team at Cosworth F1 Engineering when I was selling them an internet phone service.

Yes, it was a lot of fun, and that's one of the reasons it worked – I became genuinely interested in what they did. You can do the same – and enjoy the same great results.

CHAPTER 6:
REVIEW QUESTIONS & SELF-DEVELOPMENT ASSIGNMENTS

Buyer Discovery – see Annex C for Answers

To print a copy of this section, download it directly from *goo.gl/ANvUY* or select it from the TSB Download Page at *goo.gl/p0Ajn.*

Self-Test Questions

1   What are the three most common causes of sales fear?
2   What is the key success factor in researching your Buyer?
3   Give one example of a Google Advanced Search and describe how you would use it to help you Build a Willing Buyer
4   Describe three useful LinkedIn searches and what you can achieve from them.
5   Describe three other productive sources of Buyer research data.
6   Why is acquiring a picture of their Buyer so useful for some people?
7   Describe two ways to tap into the expertise or knowledge of friends and colleagues.
8   What should you do with your new contacts at the end of every day – no matter how late you get back? Do you? What will you change so you do it tomorrow?
9   Devise and describe one new off the wall way you might research *your* Buyers.

Self-Development Assignments

Ch 6 Assignment 1 – Dummy Run

Use these techniques to find out about people you already know well (including yourself!). You'll be surprised how much data many of us put out there for the world to see. Compare what you learn with what you know. How accurate is the impression you draw about them? Are there any people who are harder to research than others? What can the world see about you?

Ch 6 Assignment 2 – Live Use

Pick one person that you're going to meet and use every technique above to find out about them before you meet. Don't do anything special to change what you say or do, just notice the difference in your confidence and awareness. Once you're happy that you're not doing anything weird, try the next step on. Phone contacts, ex-colleagues and co-workers who used to work at the same company.

Ch 6 Assignment 3 – Team Use

If you have a team working on a project, share these techniques with them. Then assign two or three names from team at a customer or prospect and give them a specified time to find out the maximum possible about them.

Then sit down and merge information for the project, pool techniques (correcting errors, new extensions, etc.) and in particular, share any *new* sources of information that will allow everyone's data to be expanded with some extra research.

CHAPTER 7
Build your 'Buying Drivers'

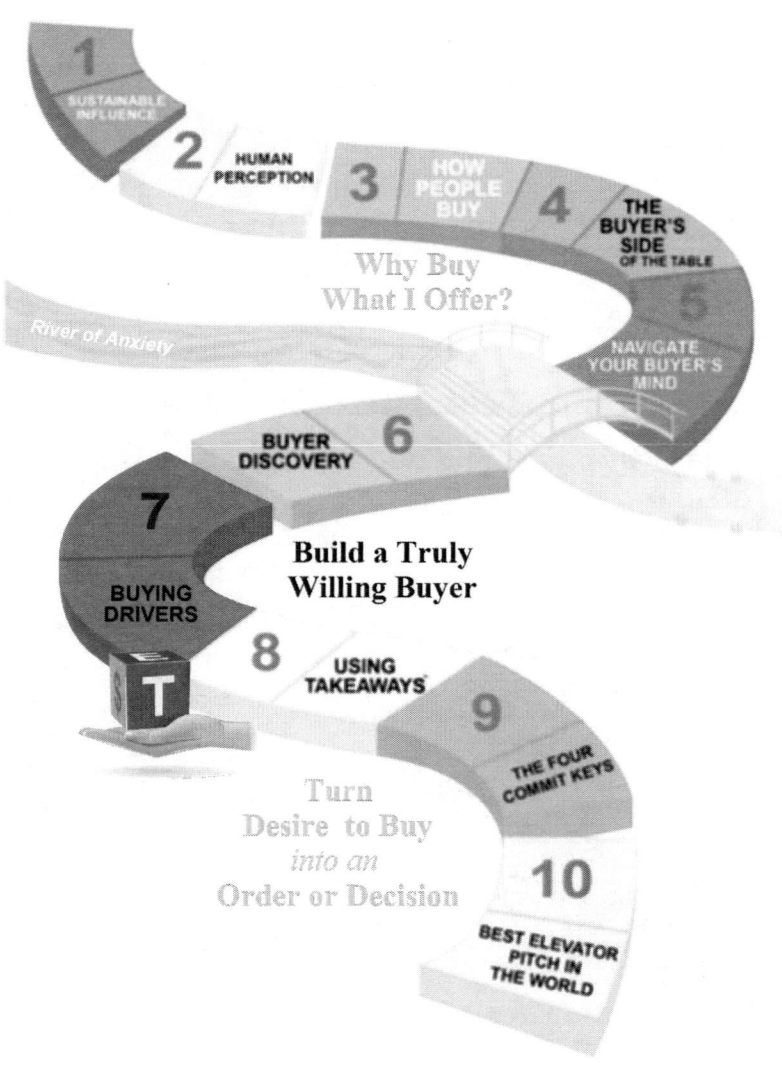

BY THE END OF THIS CHAPTER, YOU'LL UNDERSTAND …

- The importance of a *Core TakeAway Analysis* of what you offer
- The power of "So What?" and "So What Else?"
- How to strengthen, broaden, and deepen TakeAways
- How TakeAways vary from Buyer to Buyer – even with the same offering

HOW WILL THIS HELP ME BUILD A WILLING BUYER?

Whenever you influence someone to buy from you, you want to maximise your chance of a favourable decision. Buyers who can be helped to recognise, early on in the process, *"What's in it for me?"* are much more likely to accept your proposal than those left to work it out for themselves.

The most powerful and consistent way to do this is to analyse in advance, *all the possible motives* that might drive a specific buyer (e.g. an individual or company) or a Buyer Group (e.g. everyone over 25 years of age in Buenos Aires) to make that positive decision. These are the *Buying Drivers* you were introduced to in chapter 3 – How People Buy.

To be effective, the Buying Drivers must be driven by Time, Income, Risk, Expense, or State (the TIRES) Get this right and you'll get the result you want – get it wrong and your sales anxiety, unpredictability, and stress will remain.

The Hidden Qualifying Power of TakeAways

What does it mean if you ascertain that your potential buyer *definitely doesn't* need any of the TakeAways that you've so carefully analysed? Well, as long as it doesn't happen too often, it's good news. It means you're not going to waste your time on a wild goose chase. In sales this is one of the key components in *qualifying an opportunity*, but it can be used in many other situations.

If I'm trying to influence my local bank to resurface their potholed car park – but I discover there's nothing in it for them to do so (since no one else has complained), I should give up and use my time better – or maybe start a petition so that more people complain and the bank does have a need (to stop the complaints)!

The same applies when you're applying for a job and they *really* have no need for the great skills you can deliver – just move on and find someone who does need your skills.

In business, I may find in talking to a potential distributor for my new widget that they couldn't care a bit about the unique and effective training my company gives its partners. They just want to shift as many as possible as quickly as they can. At this point, it's time to talk to another distributor – or perhaps change what we offer.

Each of these is an example of qualifying out an opportunity – and the earlier you can do it the better! Accurate, early qualifying saves you time and reduces your stress (classic TIRES).

You regain time you'd have lost chasing something that was never going to happen. Because you're not beating your head against a wall (and believe me, I've done it too often in my sales career) life is sweeter and you can use your time more profitably.

Health Warning 1

It's very easy to get carried away with enthusiasm for a really strong set of TakeAways that you've built for your offering. Because *you* can clearly see the TIRES, the TIRE Compounds and so much else, *you're* impressed enough to buy it – but you're not selling to yourself! You must stay in SECOND POSITION (see chapter 4). It can be very productive and enlightening to complete a Four-See exercise before doing a TakeAway Analysis.

NOTE: Remember you're generating *potential* TakeAways – not every buyer will need them. Even if you've done a great Buyer Discovery, you'll only be guessing or assuming – and both are dangerous. You need to engage and elicit their *actual* TakeAways.

The greatest mistake you can make in TSB is to create a great list of TIRES-checked TakeAways and then simply pitch them at your potential buyer. This is a little better than spraying features at them, but only just. It still:

- Doesn't differentiate you from all the other 'pitchers' and their feature lists.
- Doesn't engage buyers to tell you the details of their situation.
- Leaves them to do the work of selecting from your pitch what's right for their situation.
- Doesn't allow you to draw out (elicit) their true Buying Drivers and their value.

- Sounds glib and unproven: "Our software improves customer retention by 30%."
- Limits the opportunity to your list – what if they need something else you can supply?

So, in summary, the only time you can move a TakeAway from *Potential* to *Confirmed* is when you've heard it from the actual buyer. Anything else is a dangerous, expensive, or embarrassing assumption.

Talk to them. Gain their confidence. Drill down into their situation. Draw them out.

To do this well needs preparation – and that's what this chapter is about.

The work is best done in a group, with plenty of whiteboards. A digital camera is also helpful to capture the results of your creativity. You'll use two important documents that you'll be introduced to in the second half of this chapter.

Throughout this chapter, there will be exercises that give you hands-on experience with these important tools. If you use an e-reader or don't want to write in the book, download them from *goo.gl/k0WzU*.

WHAT'S A TAKEAWAY ANALYSIS ALL ABOUT?

In this chapter, you'll use all the techniques you've learned so far to generate an accurate list of *potential* Buying Drivers for your Buyer/Offering combination. You'll then enrich them even further – making them more and more 'buyable'.

In chapter 8, you'll then save them in an efficient document you can always refer to as a support for Building a Willing Buyer.

In chapter 9, you'll add the final three powerful commercial drivers that will convince your buyer to take the last step and *spend time or money* – and remain convinced enough to follow through with actions.

The skills you'll learn in this chapter are simple, easy to understand, and can be used over and over again, formally and in-the-moment.

Once used in life and work, they'll quickly become second nature whenever you need to:

- Decide what might motivate anyone to buy a new product, idea or service from you – great for marketing, product development, consultants and entrepreneurs.

- Engage and explore what they need and then match that to what you can supply – great for sales, account management, consultants and entrepreneurs.

- Build a new, more powerful offering from your products, services and features – great for product development and marketing.

- Take an existing offering into a new market, geography or to a specific buyer – great for business unit and sales managers.

- Create focussed marketing material that will drive the *right* buyers to your door – great for marketing leaders and consultants.

- Differentiate yourself from competitors or alternatives early in a buying process – great for sales, entrepreneurs and consultants.

- Create attractive and convincing bite sized value statements – great for everyone.

- Spread a single, productive statement of *"This is what we do"* across your organisation – great for senior management and entrepreneurs.

DOING YOUR OWN 'SO WHAT TO TIRES' ANALYSIS

This powerful exercise is very simple. Until it becomes second nature (which it soon will), it's best practiced with your colleagues, your friends, and your family - whoever is most appropriate and knowledgeable. Start with the following exercises, then do it again with another offering. Follow *all* the steps each time. The real power comes when you dig out every possible TakeAway.

Go to Figure 17 for a diagram of the full process or download it from goo.gl/DKB1a, print it out, and keep it beside you for the rest of the chapter.

Once you've done a *So What to TIRES* exercise a few times, and got a positive result, it will quickly become integrated into your thinking and actions – you'll soon be Unconsciously Competent!

There are eight small steps in the process. To work on them, we'll use an easy example. Pick something simple that you know about and need to sell.

For my example, I've chosen a service – Window Cleaning. This sounds trivial but it's as suitable for TakeAway Analysis as the most complex technology (and quicker, too).

> Write out the simple title of what you're selling here:

Step 1 – Define your Buyer/Segment/market/geography

Every TakeAway Analysis has two variables – what might be bought, and who might buy it. You need to define these well. Clear thought at this stage reaps huge benefits later.

Always start with a *specific Buyer* or *Buyer Group* in mind. The more tightly you can focus in on them and their situation, the more effectively you'll generate strong, attractive TakeAways that you can supply.

If you define your buyer group very widely (e.g. *everyone aged 35 to 55 in East Asia)*, you're likely to generate a *lot* of TakeAways. This will happen because such a broad buyer group covers a large number of personal situations, incomes, stages of life, etc. As a result, the Buying Drivers will be variable and there will be a lot of them to draw out from any potential buyer.

If you have a focussed, tight definition (e.g. *everyone with a government pension living in Berlin*), you'll to get a much shorter, more useable list of potential TakeAways that you can confirm with a buyer much more easily.

The ideal is, of course to have a single, specific person or company as your buyer. You should always do this with a key account (in fact, with every account early in a start-up). I actually recommend running through your existing TakeAway Analysis before *every* customer meeting if possible. Even if it's quickly in the car park before the meeting, it's worth doing. I still try to do this (even briefly) on every sales call I do.

If you're not yet sure what your best Buyer/Offering combination is, this is a great opportunity to loop through different permutation until you find the most productive. This is an important early step for start-ups.

Even a tightly defined buyer group (e.g. Southern US paint manufacturers) will vary in its business by location, age, or size of company, direct/indirect distribution, etc. As you move your offering into different markets, your analysis should constantly be reviewed and refined as it's the basis for all your sales and marketing activity. The same applies if you're seeking funding or partners in different places – do a quick review every time.

At a more personal level, the same variables apply. If, for instance, you're influencing someone to vote for you in an election, the Buying Drivers of voters (for 'buying' what you offer) will vary widely from person to person.

If you want to be chosen as a member of the management board of your local canoe club, the TakeAways from voting for you will be different for the coaching staff than they will be for the accounting staff – or for the athletes themselves.

> My Buyer Group is 'anyone in the Westboro district of Ottawa, Canada'.
>
> Write your Buyer or Buyers here:

Step 2 – Define Your Offering

The other side of the TakeAway Analysis equation is your "Offering". So what do we mean by an offering? It's certainly not meant to be religious, although in some situations a little praying can help you feel better!

Essentially, your Offering is *everything* that your buyer can draw on for the value in their TakeAways.

Offering Example

I'm the owner of a Canadian company that manufactures top-class ski bindings for downhill racing in our Québec factory. On the face of it, my offering appears to be an expensive version of the biparallel bindings used by top skiers.

But my sales team has been on a Fearless Selling Workshop, and their offering doesn't stop at the tech specs for the binding and the cool name – Super-Bind!

What they offer includes the following:

- An R&D department that owns its own patent for the binding design.
- Preferred financing from a global bank to finance the purchase for buyers worldwide.
- Attendance by the company's engineers at every World Cup ski event.
- An overnight priority repair scheme run with UPS.
- A strong sporting connection with North American skiers.
- A strong cultural connection with French-speaking buyers.
- A free X–ray foot mapping service on first purchase.
- An Internet community for owners to share experiences, hints, and tips.
- Three Olympic medallists on the board of directors.

Now that's a heck of an offering! Yet not one of them passes a TIRES check, and it's the TIRES that drive a Desire to Buy – not the strong sporting connection. It would be completely legitimate to look at the list and say *"So What?"* That's precisely what we're going to do in the rest of this chapter, but with something a little simpler than ski bindings.

At the end, come back and do the analysis you've learned on the ski binding above.

So let's give our Offering a title:

> My Exercise offering is named '**VIP Windows**'.
>
> Write the name of your Offering here:

Step 3 – Declare Features from your Named Offering

Look at the Offering you've just named and make as long a list of *positive* traditional sales features as you can. If this list is massive (which it often can be), group them together so that you start this analysis with 15–20 features. I always do this on a whiteboard to be as quick and creative as possible.

Remember the ski–binding company above, and all the extras they included? Yours might include your update policy if you sell software; your partnerships if you're a solution provider; your customer support, etc.

Working with a colleague, you become person No 1 (the Influencer/Seller) in Figure 17 below. You declare (*proudly*) a factual, truthful, *positive* feature from your list, such as:

> "*The cases of our hydraulic motors are made of ceramic-metal composite*"

or

> "*Everyone in our company is a fully certified facilitator*"

or

> "*Our investment bond is linked to the Central Bank Rate*"

or

> "*The processor in our GPS unit runs at 8 Gigahertz*"

or

"*We have a money–back guarantee on all our seminars*"

or

"*I can start working here on Monday*"

> My positive statement for '**VIP Windows**' is:
>
> "*You pay for our service with a small, monthly direct debit*"
>
> Write yours here:

Step 4 – Challenge

Your colleague (No 2, Challenger in Figure 17) responds to your statement with:

SO WHAT? (It's extremely important to use these *exact* words.)

Say it out loud NOW: "*So What?*"

Step 5 – Response

You (the Influencer at No 1 in Figure 17) then answer with as strong a *reason to buy* about the feature as you can devise. But here's the trick that makes this so effective – you're not just giving random answers …

… your reply to SO WHAT always steers the conversation towards delivering TIRES!

It may take several SO WHATS and several responses to get there, but the number of loops doesn't matter. In fact, we'll see later that small steps are usually better than big leaps. (Remember the 'big leapers' in chapter 5?)

Step 5 Example

Look at the three statements below.

Statement No.1: *"This oil contains synthetic polymers"* is a feature, not a TakeAway – so I've put **N** in the box and challenged with *So What?*

I then get Response No 2: *"The oil takes longer to fail"*

This is still not quite a TakeAway, so I put an **N** in the second box.

I then challenge a second time with another *So What?*

Response No 3: *"You pay for..." is* a real, solid TakeAway. It delivers a cost saving (**E**xpense) and a reduced frequency of doing the job (**T**ime) – so I wrote **Y** and **T,E**

#1: *"This oil contains synthetic polymers"*	**N**	
So What?		
#2: *"The oil takes longer to fail"*	**N**	
So What?		
#3: *"You pay for an oil change half as often as you do presently"*	**Y**	**T,E**

Step 5 Exercises

Here's a small test of your ability to spot whether you've reached a TakeAway – exactly as I did in the example above.

Each exercise in the grid below consists of a first statement which is definitely not a TakeAway – then a challenge – finally a response to that challenge. Your job is to decide whether the second response (e.g. *"They won't split under pressure"*) is a TakeAway. If it is, what are the TIRES that drive it? Put the answers in the boxes on the right.

The first (square) box is **Y/N** to whether the statement describes a TakeAway. If the answer is *"Yes it is a TakeAway"*, then write the TIRES that the TakeAway delivers into the second (larger) box (as I did when I wrote **T,E** in the example above).

CHAPTER 7: BUILD YOUR 'BUYING DRIVERS'   181

> *"Our pistons are ceramic-metal composite"*
> SO WHAT? → *"So they won't split under pressure"*

> *"Our team are all fully certified facilitators"*
> SO WHAT? → *"Decisions are quicker and more profitable"*

> *"Our interest rate is linked to Central Bank rate"*
> SO WHAT? → *"So you always know your loan rate"*

> *"The processor in our GPS runs at 8 Gigahertz"*
> SO WHAT? → *"So calculations are done rapidly"*

> *"Our seminars have a money–back guarantee"*
> SO WHAT? → *"So the risk of wasting your money is zero"*

> *"I can start work on Monday"*
> SO WHAT? → *"I'll start earning revenue for you earlier"*

If the response is *not* a TakeAway, try to find a response to *SO WHAT* that is closer to being a TakeAway. Repeat until you have a TakeAway.

Step 5 – With our TakeAways

> My response to SO WHAT is *"Our team clean your windows even when you're not home."*
>
> Write yours here (but don't jump straight to a TakeAway)

Step 6 – The TIRES Check

Check whether the statement is a TakeAway or feature by checking if it will:

- **(T)** make something happen earlier, more or less frequently, more controllably, etc.
- **(I)** increase income, 'shape' it better, make it more predictable, etc.
- **(R)** reduce or control risk, make it more visible, make it more controllable, etc.

- **(E)** reduce expense, cap it, assign it elsewhere, etc.
- **(S)** reduce stress, make you smile, put you in a better light, more satisfied, etc.

Step 7 (Loop Back if statement fails TIRES check)

> My response of *"Cleaning when you're not home"* did not quite pass the TIRES check. It did not demonstrate any clear improvement in Time, Income, Risk Expense or State. Does yours?

If the second statement *still doesn't* describe a true TakeAway (i.e. it still doesn't pass the TIRES check) then the Challenger simply asks *So What?* – Once again, use these exact words and say nothing else – this must be a mechanical process. The discussion comes later!

Repeat this loop until you reach a statement that (at last) contains a TakeAway. As the influencer, you must use your creativity and knowledge to steer your answers, slowly and surely, towards a statement that passes the TIRES check - with answers that are *truthful and accurate*.

> My loop back response is "**So that means** you don't have to take time off work to be at home to pay the cleaners and you never have dirty windows that offend your neighbours"
>
> Write your loop back response here: "**So that means** ...

Keep looping through the 7 steps until your positive statement *does* pass the TIRES check. See Figure 17 (or *goo.gl/DKB1a*) for a complete *So What to TIRES* flow:

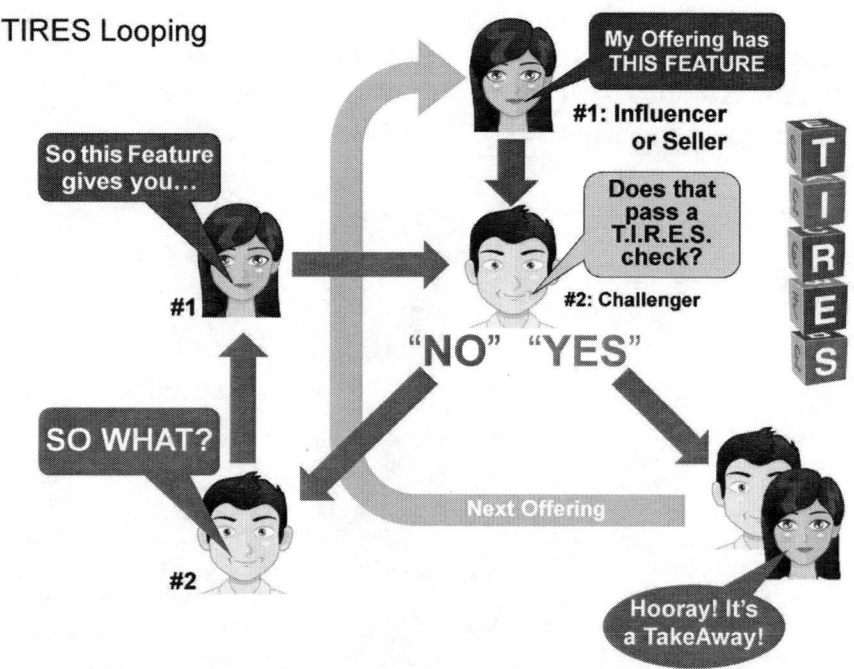

Figure 17

Go to *goo.gl/tdWX0* to watch the result of a successful TakeAway Analysis.

How far to go?

If you *genuinely* can't get to a TakeAway, then either:

- It's a worthless feature you might consider dropping from your offering.

or

- The feature is worth keeping but need not be mentioned in discussion or material.

or

- The feature needs to be improved so that it does deliver some TIRES-checked value.

So here's the interesting thing – the nearer you get to a TakeAway with your answer, the easier you'll find it is to make a TIRES-passing statement.

In fact, once most people have done this exercise a few times, they really enjoy the positive vibe they get as they approach a live TakeAway – it's a good moment.

At goo.gl/j7Wxh there is video sketch of a woman using a SO WHAT challenge in a different way with her husband. He has clearly not done any TSB training and is attempting to influence her by spraying facts. She leads him gently to the TIRES that drive the decision.

Figure 18

In our seminars we use TIRES cubes as teaching aids (see Figure 18). As the students feel their answers approaching a TakeAway, they enjoy reaching for the cube and turning it to the right TIRES face. Watch the video at goo.gl/kvUqy to see an enthusiastic student with some of the blocks we use beside him. (You can also make these from the template at goo.gl/8RniN or order them from our website shop.)

Step 8 (If your statement *does* pass the TIRES check)

Firstly, give a sigh of relief or a whoop of joy – you've completed your first SO WHAT sequence and caught yourself a live TakeAway!

> My loop back response does pass the TIRES check – **Time** is saved, and the **Risk** of a bad **State** (embarrassment) is improved. How did your loop back response fare?
>
> Respond here to SO WHAT until you pass the TIRES check:

Health Warning Two

I can't over-emphasise how important it is to stick with the rules. In our seminars, the coaches can jump on rebels who say more than SO WHAT – but you'll need to police yourself. This exercise isn't a marketing strategy discussion or an old school sales pitch - we're generating simple, solid, TIRES - tested Buying Drivers!

But there's one last danger – being yourself. If you're selling to a Japanese shipping company, it's *that* buyer who must be in the mind of the Influencer/Seller who is responding to the SO WHATS - not the buyer's *own* model. In fact, the influencer must, to the best of their ability, *become your buyer*. Now you can see why the Four-See exercise and Buyer Discovery can be so useful!

The more tightly you define your buyer group the easier it is. Temporarily thinking as a retired Berliner is much easier than being every 35 to 55 year old in Asia.

Spray & Pray or Engagement?

> I was brought in to help a software company fix their broken sales process and improve their forecasting. Their cutting-edge air traffic control software was worth its high investment cost, but sales took too long and were hard to predict.
>
> I started by asking them to *sell to me* – as if I were a prospect – and it was really boring! I watched an impressive and expensive multimedia show with films, demos, and simulations. Sure it was cool, and it left me impressed – but confused.

It took an hour before I could ask my first question, and they never once asked me anything about *my* operation. I sat there, glassy-eyed as features and functions flew past me at such a rate that I couldn't spot what might be useful to me and what wasn't.

They had left all the effort to me – on the buyer's side of the table.

Watching this presentation as a potential buyer, I was able to spot a few of my Buying Drivers, but they didn't stand out from the detail of the presentation. So to reduce my exposure, the first part of my buying decision would inevitably have been to say *"Let's agree a process to evaluate this properly. "*

This would have required a lot of people and resources (on both sides) and consumed a lot of time. Both sides would get excited, but neither would know SO WHAT'S IN IT FOR ME – SWIIFM – until much later. The sales teams confirmed that they often faced exactly this time-consuming scenario.

They badly needed an ABC Analysis to distil out a few, powerful Potential Buying Drivers – ones that would pass a TIRES test.

The sales team arrived with a list of over 2000 features and functions! A list that long is OK for ticking boxes in a Request for Proposal (RFP) – but it doesn't work for *Turning Selling into Buying*.

We began by grouping the features and functions together to determine how many were duplicates. This got us down to about 300 strong statements – and we started the SO WHAT analysis. As we progressed, it became clear that a very large number of features or functions drove exactly the same business TakeAway. The pattern emerged so quickly that we didn't need to go through all 300 – we just checked for exceptions.

The final answer was six! There were actually only six basic (i.e. TIRES-checked) motivations to buy their software – and any single one might be a strong enough cost justification on its own.

A bit surprised, we went back to past sales and confirmed that *in every case* the final, real life, TakeAways for their live clients could be fitted to this short list.

So what changed for the team as a result of this analysis?

1. They no longer *'ask to give a presentation'* – they go *'to talk about your business'*.
2. We worked up a set of questions that would quickly and simply allow them to determine which of the six Potential TakeAways applied to that buyer's situation.
3. The 90 minute presentation was split into six sections which were made more interactive and only deployed *after determining which TakeAway(s) were needed*.
4. They built six well-crafted financial cases – one for each TakeAway, rather than taking a lot of time and effort to reinvent the wheel for each client's ROI.

And that's pretty much all they did. Since doing this work, the company has shortened their sales cycle and become a market leader in its sector.

The main lessons are already in the story. But I can't over-emphasise that, whether you're selling ideas, products, or services, your life will be much easier if you teach your buyers how to buy and make it easy for them to do so.

I've even sometimes shared my raw TakeAways list with a customer – to help them understand the decision and justify a purchase or investment.

THE TAKEAWAY GENERATOR

To record your *So What* sequences easily, use the *TakeAway Generator Sheet*. Copy Figure 19 or download it from goo.gl/CvdPy (8x10 Letter) or goo.gl/8RXoo (A4). It allows you to record the answers to *So What* in the center column and then review the route the sequence takes to a TakeAway on the right hand side.

You can then very simply backtrack to create the TakeAway pairs that you'll learn about in chapter 9. We call these powerful groups of words Value Statements.

188 PART TWO: "READINESS"

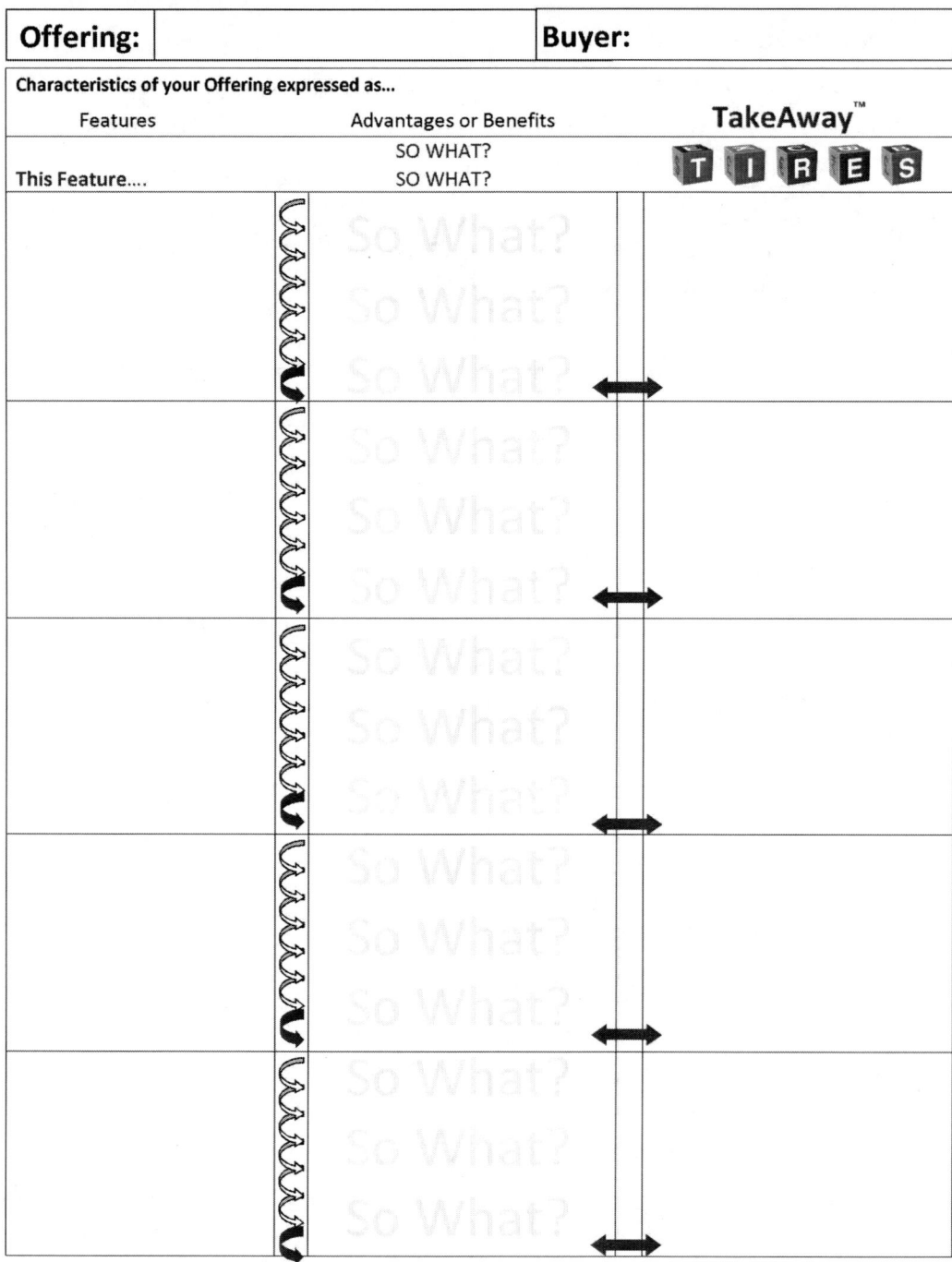

Figure 19

For our corporate workshops, we use a large pre-taped whiteboard with this layout. It allows us to be very quick and creative. We also take photographs which we can share, print out, or use later. This works well and allows a real creative energy to stay in the room. If you're in product management and will use this process regularly, you can create a permanent version with some tape and a whiteboard.

If possible, it's effective to appoint a 'whiteboard jockey' whose only job is to record the *So What* sequence. This job is harder than it appears as they *must* understand the process and write down *exactly* what's said. If they don't, their own filters can delete, distort, or generalize some powerful insights.

Some people are really good at this and enjoy it. If you find someone like this, nurture them well! Figure 20 is another example of a real TakeAway analysis. The top TakeAway sequence has been completed – try filling in the ones beneath it.

TakeAway™ Generation Example

Offering:	Sat-Is-Fire GPS System		Buyer: Engineers
Characteristics of Your Offering expressed as...			
Feature	Advantages/Benefits		**TakeAway™**
This Characteristic....	SO WHAT? SO WHAT? SO WHAT?		Passes TIRES Check? **T I R E S**
e.g. **Hardened Steel Shaft** =	Resists high temperatures Requires less lubricant flow Resists wear in all conditions Lasts longer Breaks down less often... ...Very Seldom Requires Repair	TakeAway Pair = Value Statement	Less down **TIME** for repair No **EXPENSIVE** late penalties Fewer **COSTLY** breakdowns
24 Hours Support Desk			
Used by all major Emergency Services			
User Replaceable Parts			

Figure 20

PEAK POWER FOR YOUR TAKEAWAYS

Lessons from 1000s of So Whats

Here are a few tips to make this process generate more powerful Take-Aways to use with a potential buyer.

Little, Dumb Steps

When you're responding to SO WHAT don't make big jumps to reach a TakeAway more quickly. This is not a race! Jumping from a feature like *"This camera has a much faster shutter speed"* directly to an **I**ncome TakeAway – *"I can earn more money shooting Formula One races"* – is too big a leap. You may miss important TakeAways along the way.

In this case, the faster shutter speed might reduce the number of lenses you need to purchase, which would reduce your investment cost – a significant **E**xpense TakeAway.

State

When you do this analysis, it may only be once per Buyer/Offering combination, so *do your best to ensure you're in the same* State *your buyer will be in*. At the very least, do a Four-See to get on their side of the table and help you to answer SO WHATS as the buyer. If you have a specific buyer, not a group, then make sure you do the Buyer Discovery in chapter 6 just before the analysis. This will make your answers even more relevant.

Don't Overthink

Once you start, the responder should say the first thing that comes into their head – even if it's crazy or obvious. There's no right answer here – you're trying to generate a strong list of potential TakeAways. They may not apply to this specific buyer, but they are ready in your quiver for another potential buyer.

If a wacky answer ends up in a TakeAway dead end, then you've only lost a little time. But a wacky answer may well generate a unique new TakeAway that your buyer (or your competition) has not even considered. At the least, it will strengthen your TakeAway list. At best, it might add to the ROI and thus support your pricing.

Bring in the Buyer

Well, someone similar to your buyer anyway ... to act as the Responder to your *So What* questions. What about a colleague in your team/group/company who used to do a similar job? How about someone of the right age? I've even brought a Generation Y person into a group of older Baby Boomers a few times, when Gen Y was the buyer group. I once even paid a consultant with knowledge of the buyer's company, industry, and pressures to join us for a TakeAway exercise.

Enter the Buyer's room

Sometimes it's good to do the TakeAway analysis in a place similar to your buyer's environment – where they work, live, or play. Bring in props, pictures, industry journals, the tools of their trade, etc. I even once brought in a big picture of my buyer and hung it on the wall.

With imagination and determination, you can drive out some great TakeAways - and enjoy doing it! This process is also a great warm-up for an influence meeting you have planned with a buyer. Your mind will loosen up and steer smoothly to the possible TakeAways.

Enrichment - Go Wider & Deeper than Competition & Alternatives

Once you've reached a TakeAway, there are four more enrichment steps that are described below. These will make your Buying Drivers even wider and deeper (creating more reasons to buy and spend). Why is this important?

The key reason is that your competition won't have done it! Even if the alternative is do nothing or do it in-house, your TakeAways will be so much more attractive.

Enrichment 1 – *So What Else*?

Let's suppose you're doing a TakeAway analysis of a garage's offering (something I've actually done). You have challenged one of their features and your *So What to Tires* leads to a nice TakeAway pair – *"Our garage's Premium Service reduces the risk of serious accidents"* (clearly an **R**). You can now expand that TakeAway even further by asking:

"*So What Else* does your Premium Service Package deliver?"

You could also ask the same question but relate it to other TIRES. This allows you to specifically check whether there are any other TakeAways clustered around the first.

In this same example, asking the (slightly less open) question:

"SO WHAT ELSE that *is not* related to Risk?"

might result in 'Peace of Mind' (definitely an **S**). Another blunter way might be:

"SO WHAT **T**, **I**, **E** and **S** might also be delivered?"

A third way to enrich a TakeAway is to ask a 'closed' question':

"SO WHAT ELSE is there that's related to **Expense**?"

The reply might be *"Lower insurance costs"* (certainly an **E**) since insurance companies give a discount if this brake is fitted. Then repeat the closed question with **T** and **I**.

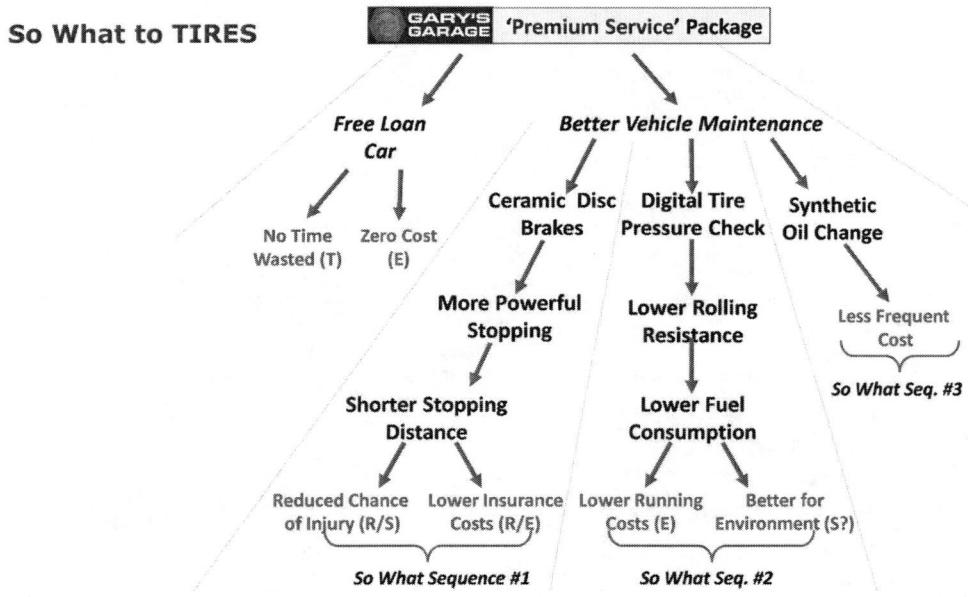

Figure 21

This is illustrated in Figure 21 where each arrow indicates a SO WHAT.

Enrichment 2 - Reverse Back

...then SO WHAT ELSE?

The second enricher is to reverse back one or two steps in the TakeAway sequence that you've just followed, and once again look for TakeAways by saying SO WHAT ELSE?

In the garage example above, the statement that preceded it in the SO WHAT sequence might have been "*We fit Ceramic Disc Brakes.*" Go back to this point and ask SO WHAT ELSE? The answer might now be "*We also do a digital tire pressure check*". This would start another SO WHAT sequence ending in a TakeAway.

These further SO WHAT questions might get you to "*Lower fuel consumption due to lower rolling resistance in the sidewalls*". Just one more SO WHAT will get to saving money, which is definitely an **E**.

Go back up to "*Better Vehicle Maintenance*" again – this might produce yet another SO WHAT sequence and a third TakeAway.

Follow the SO WHAT sequences #2 and #3 in Figure 17.

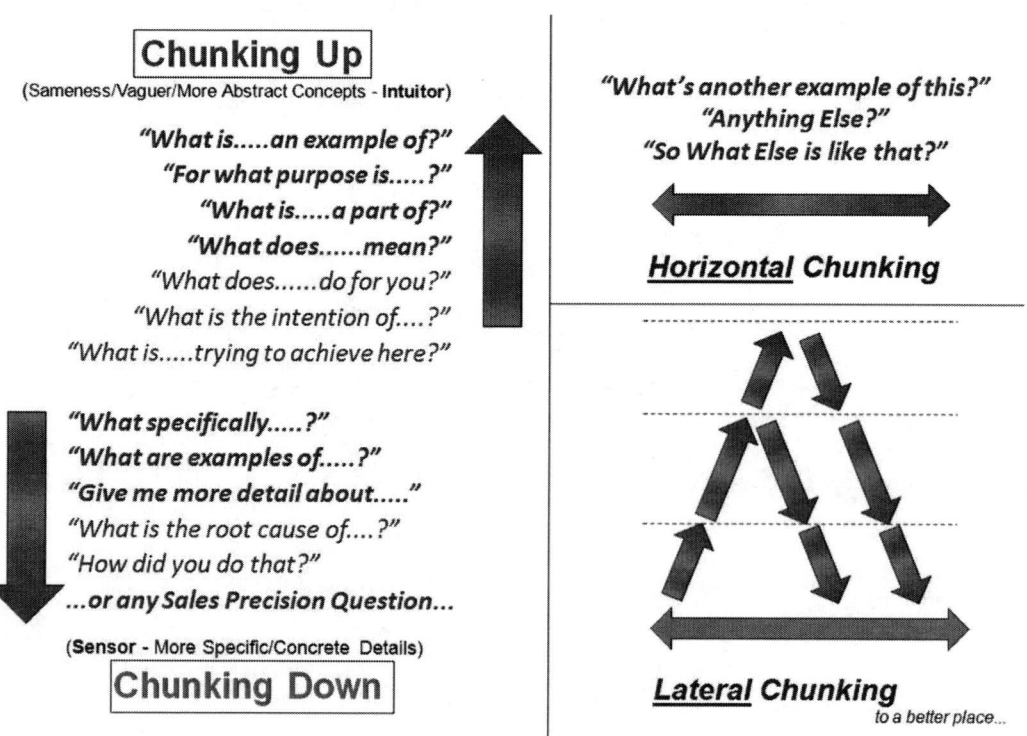

Figure 22

Enrichment 3 - Challenging the TakeAways

In chapter 5, you mastered Navigating the Hierarchy of Ideas (usually known as *Chunking*). Once you've cracked this technique, it's a really great addition for powerfully expanding the TakeAways at the end of the TakeAway Sequence. When you get to the TakeAway, you can squeeze the last value out of it by *challenging* what's been said.

The Chunking challenges (see Figure 22) are just more focussed forms of SO WHAT questioning. In fact, SO WHAT ELSE always was in the list. If you're confident with Chunking, then use it. If you're not, you're going to get the full TakeAways 80% of the time anyway, so don't worry – in time, it'll become natural and easy.

The best way to illustrate the power of a Chunking challenge is to follow through the examples in Figure 23.

Statement in "So What?" Sequence	Buyer's Chunking Challenge ... then Response	Answer
"We save you money by removing transport costs from your business model"	"Can you give me a specific example of how that saves me money?"	"Well, our service removes the need to deliver to your local post office..."
	"Ah! So I wouldn't need to pay them the quarterly retainer that I do now" **(E)**	
"Our software always stores data in 'The Cloud'"	"For what purpose do you do that?"	"To allow our worldwide processing systems to access it from anywhere"
	"Ah! So that means that my staff won't need to wait until the next day - they can access it from anywhere as well..."	
	"...so that will allow them earlier access to profitable deals!" **(T/I)**	
"We save money through economies of scale"	"What does 'economies of scale' mean?"	"Well, mostly we can buy equipment at lower prices because we buy so much of it"
	"Ah, so that means I could get a discount if I ordered more!" **(E/R)**	

Figure 23

Enrichment 4 – Combining TakeAways

Once you've processed all of your features by looping through multiple *So Whats*, a useful pattern always emerges:

- A few TakeAways will be connected to *many* features. This may make those features valuable to a buyer when it comes to pricing. At the air traffic control software company in the story, it turned out that two TakeAways connected to 30 features – so they drove most of the buying decisions.

- A single feature is connected to many TakeAways (the reverse of above). Did the product manager know just how powerful that feature was in TIRES terms or did they think it was just 'cool'? Does your marketing expose its value well enough? Does everyone know about it? Can you change the pricing to reflect its value?

- A few TakeAways will stand alone. If they stem from unique features of your offering that your competitors don't have, they might benefit from extra marketing emphasis. Maybe they need special pricing.

- Certain features will end in dead ends – we've dealt with the product management issues of these already. Either remove them or let them wither on the vine.

- Many features will quite naturally collapse down into one high level TakeAway.

SAME PRODUCT – DIFFERENT OFFERING TO DIFFERENT BUYERS

All of the questions in the previous examples have a *specific* Buyer/Offering context. This is critical to create buyable TakeAways. Different buyers, in different situations, are very likely to be motivated by different TakeAways.

A brightly coloured, breathable rain jacket, with a fluorescent finish might be considered for purchase as a safety feature **(R)** to one potential buyer – perhaps they sail.

To another buyer – perhaps my daughter – it may be buyable because it's bright and fashionable **(S)**.

A third buyer may not be interested in fashion, but wants to prevent an expensive jacket being ruined by the rain **(E)** – that's me!

Same Product – Different Offering

So, let's look at a fictitious example. I'm product manager for a hydraulic piston manufacturer, and my team build a single product – a high-powered hydraulic ram. The product is the same, but our offerings into three distinct markets are very different, even though they're based on the same core hardware.

Example 1 – The 'Away From' Buyer

This offering is branded as 'The Bucket Nursemaid' for the construction industry. It's aimed at fixing the frequent failures that occur on construction sites through abuse and which cause costly production problems. The offering includes a rapid-response service delivered by a local partner who works overnight to replace and recalibrate the broken ram – all in time for work the next day. The TakeAway pairs we supply include:

- *Saved time and late penalties* (**T/E**)
  – through reliable overnight delivery of replacement parts.

- *Fewer expensive errors* and *faster response* (**T/E/I**)
  – through a centralised customer equipment registry.

- *Stress free reliability for customer* (**S/I**)
  – thanks to our ISO 9000 manufacturing and delivery.

- *Low cost option* (**E/T**)
  – through a recurring monthly fee structure.

My sales teams focus on looking for buyer companies that have:

- Aggressive contracts with heavy late penalties.
- A small administration that needs to reduce extra work.
- A pressured, independent workforce.

Example 2 – The 'Towards' Buyer

The second way of offering my hydraulic rams is branded the 'Bucket Booster'. It greatly improves the performance of any earth-moving excavator it's fitted to. It's marketed very differently from the Bucket Nursemaid and has different buyers. The same crew delivers it, but not as an overnight rush job. Furthermore, it's paid for on easy terms. The TakeAway pairs of this offering are:

- *Larger, more profitable jobs, and sooner* (**T/I**)
  – via a skills upgrade evening class for operators.
- *More frequent higher-margin jobs*
  – not available with lower ram power (**T/I**)
- *Squeezing extra work (= profit) out of each operator-day.*
  – through the increased ram power (**I**).
- *Minimised lost revenue*
  – since a 'hit team' upgrades the bucket power overnight (**R/E**).
- *Early profit*
  – since revenue appears immediately, but cost is spread out (**T/I/E**).

NOTE: the very different TIRES patterns between 'towards' and 'away from' buyers.

The buyers that my sales team look for include companies that:

- Are busy, aggressive, and looking to expand their opportunities – but tight on cash.
- Have a workforce that's prepared and motivated to learn new skills.
- Work in an environment that needs these extra capabilities.

Example 3 – The 'Cautious' Buyer

The final way of selling my hydraulic rams is without a specific title for the offering. My buyer is a civil engineer whose job is to design lock gates operated by hydraulic rams.

She's very conservative and balances 'towards' and 'away from' characteristics. Expense is much lower in her priorities as she's primarily employed to 'get it right' – it's a quantity surveyor's job to monitor the costs.

The civil engineer's TakeAways include:

- *Low risk of failure* (**R/S**)
  – for the gates, the downstream damage – and her reputation.
- *Reduced risk of cost* (**R/E**)
  – the massive cost of lock repair, and of her being sued!
- *Time saved* (**T/E**)
  – accurate, performance data for specification and order.
- *Reduced Cost to her client* (**E**)
  – quicker and cheaper than a custom build.
- *Confidence* (**S**)
  – key for a consulting engineer who has to justify her decisions to a client.
- *Reduced Cost to her* (**T/E**)
  – doesn't have to chase around for the solution.

The buyers my sales team look for include companies with:

- A busy design office under a lot of pressure.
- Knowledgeable engineers who will 'get' this aspect of their product.
- Contracts in a high value environment that invest in safety.

In each example case, the actual hardware delivery is much the same, but the TakeAways they deliver are very different. Because my account team had been trained to Turn Selling into Buying, they discuss each client's business, not the machinery.

Rather than tell clients about the ceramic coatings and high powered hydraulics within the products, they discussed their problems and then discussed:

- The correct offering for the client.
- The TakeAways it would deliver.
- The TIRES that drove those TakeAways.

> Write here what you think are the components of each offering? (see chapter3 – 'So What is an offering' for details) How can you extend or multiply **your** offering?

IN SUMMARY: DETERMINE THE FEW, SIMPLE REASONS PEOPLE TRULY BUY FROM YOU

TakeAways are all about SWIIFM – *So What's In It For Me*. It's not necessarily immediate – it may be hours, days, or years away. The buyer may not even be conscious of their real Buying Drivers – until you tell them!

Features, advantages, benefits – all of these are what we used to pitch in old school sales. Focus now on exposing the TakeAways that drive the decision – whether they're buying stuff, or services, or buying into your great vision.

The list of *potential* TakeAways you've made is a great roadmap for any buyer discussion. They'll be what drive your buyer – and they'll love talking about TakeAways.

> As the conversation moves along and visits each TakeAway, confirm whether they're needed; develop them and determine their value; then discover who else might benefit from them, and when they're needed.

People buy for simple reasons, even if they wrap them up in complexity.

That's why TakeAways are simple. Even the most complex software process, chemical catalyst, business outsourcing, investment strategy, or consulting project is only able to deliver change in five things:

- **(T)** make something happen earlier, more or less frequently, more controllably, etc.
- **(I)** increase income, 'shape' it better, make it more predictable, etc.
- **(R)** reduce or control risk, make it more visible, make it more controllable, etc.
- **(E)** reduce expense, cap it, assign it elsewhere, etc.
- **(S)** reduce stress, make you smile, put you in a better light, more satisfied, etc.

...or for those with a visual preference see Figure 24:

Figure 24

Picking the right TIRES story

After years of working in the commercial outsourcing business, Charlie decided he needed a change. He joined LogicaCMG, a company with a great reputation in the finance and telecommunications industry – an area he'd never worked in. On his first day, he was told that his sales territory was the clients that were being poached from LogicaCMG by incredibly cheap offshore outsourcing companies. His friends said that Charlie had been given a poisoned chalice, but he was determined to prove them wrong.

He realized what he'd bitten off when he went on his first call to a bank – the competition was savagely undercutting him on price, charging 40% less than Charlie's best price!

He lost that deal; but Charlie was determined and knew there was more to winning business than just the price – he'd always believed in getting inside the heads of his customers. The ideal situation for him involved becoming a trusted advisor, one who understood the client's business – transport, claims processing, or local government – whatever it was. When that happened, he could bring flexibility, creativity, and shared resources to the problem – and deliver Take-Aways quicker with less effort than doing it in-house. So why should finance be any different?

He set himself the task (with the help of LogicaCMG's existing customers and colleagues) of finding out about the detailed workings of his prospects' businesses. He soon realised that their operations had many *more challenges than just the monetary cost of their call center*. He could offer fast, onsite project support and staff training. He could offer extra integration that actually removed the need for much of the manual processing. Because of LogicaCMG's project management skills, he could reduce risk by offering delivery guarantees with strong penalties – which he was sure they'd never need to pay.

He visited his prospects again and engaged with them. He challenged their desire to simply *"cut call center costs"*. He discussed the big picture of their operation and worked with them to create an all-inclusive route to their business goals. He helped them to see what they were trying to achieve from another perspective. And he began to win business – not just beating the 'poachers' in existing accounts, but also winning new business against the cheaper offshore companies.

Of course, he didn't win every time – some situations were too much about cost for that. But the ones he did win usually ended being bigger than they originally looked – and that was why he won them.

So what can we learn from Charlie's experience? Well, it goes right to the heart of *Turning Selling into Buying*. He won the business because he:

- Got on his buyer's side of the table and truly understood their business. If he didn't know, he found out – most people love talking about what they do.

- Analysed a TakeAway set that addressed more issues than just **E**xpense reduction.

- Challenged his clients to look at a wider horizon than just cost cutting, and to look at the problem from a different place and over a longer time.

- Qualified out prospects that only had (or could only see) an **E** need that he couldn't satisfy as cheaply as the offshore companies.

- Used the same techniques to drive more revenue at existing accounts while building bigger, later sales at new accounts.

CHAPTER 7:
REVIEW QUESTIONS & SELF-DEVELOPMENT ASSIGNMENTS

Build Your Buying Drivers – see Annex C for Answers

To print a copy of this section, download it directly from goo.gl/k0WzU or select it from the TSB Download Page at goo.gl/p0Ajn.

Self-Test Questions

1. What are the Five Buying Drivers? Why aren't features and benefits enough?
2. What is qualifying an opportunity? It might be an opportunity for a partnership, for a sale, for an investment, or even a job.
3. Why don't you just pitch your TakeAways? After all, they're so much stronger than features and benefits.
4. Describe Steps One and Two in a TakeAway analysis. Why are they so important?
5. What do you do if your feature list is very long (perhaps several hundred)?
6. When do you stop saying SO WHAT in response to the answer?
7. Name and describe as many of the Success Hints as you can. Go back and re-read the ones you can't remember.
8. What form can you download and use to make this job much easier?
9. Describe each of the four Enrichment steps once you've uncovered your initial set of TakeAways.
10. What are the three types of Buyer you can encounter?

Self-Development Assignments

Ch 7 Assignment 1 – Visual Acuity

Next time you're in the office watch out for someone (with whom you have a good relationship!) making a statement to justify something. Then say (with a smile) SO WHAT? and see what reaction you get. Once the person realises that you're being serious, you'll see them 'go inside their head' to give you an answer.

You'll find two very distinct types of reaction as you repeat the *So What* and build up a TakeAway Sequence with them:

- The first is the person who completely intuitively moves towards **T**ime, **I**ncome, **R**isk, **E**xpense or **S**tate improvements as a reason for 'buying' the statement they've just made. If that person works in your company, they either are or should be working successfully in sales, marketing, or customer service – their Model of the World lets it come naturally!

- The second type will tend to struggle to reach a reply that will convince you. They may stick at one level. They may move towards features and functions (a common trait with techies). They may freak out at the whole idea of being made to sell.

The good news is that if this second type learns this chapter and practices, they can become just as good at generating TakeAways.

Ch 7 Assignment 2 – Simple Practice Runs

Make sure you re-read the Success Hints first. Practice initially on products or offerings that you know well. If you're a start-up, this may be hard, but perhaps make some up or chose some things that have been sold by others in the group before. Take as many goes as you need to get used to saying (out loud) *So What* until you get to the TIRES moment. *Most importantly,* experience the mental satisfaction of getting nearer and nearer to TIRES. Be wacky!

Ch 7 Assignment 2 – Real Live Runs

Again, re-read the Success Hints first and if there are some that seem particularly appropriate, take action. Then simply follow the rules and use the TakeAway Generator sheets. The difference between an 'OK' TakeAway analysis and a spectacular one comes in the Enrichment. Really push it when you get there – see what extra TakeAways and Value Statements you can drive out.

Most important in a live run is to have one person assigned to write everything down. Sometimes really powerful gems can be missed. I now video and photograph all my important TakeAway analysis sessions, in addition to taking notes. I can then review the session once I've completed writing up the results.

CHAPTER 8
Using TakeAways to Influence

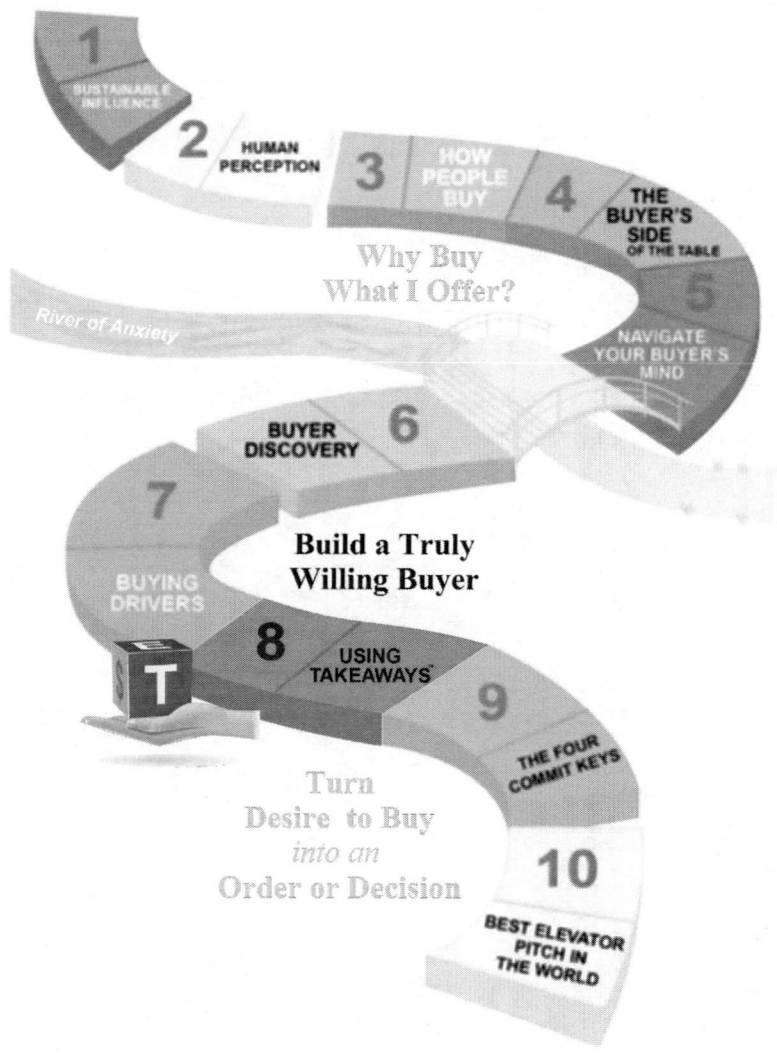

BY THE END OF THIS CHAPTER, YOU'LL UNDERSTAND ...

- How to carry out an ABC Analysis
- What comprises an Offering
- How to generate and use Value Statements

HOW WILL THIS HELP ME BUILD A WILLING BUYER?

It's now time to engage with your buyer; to drill down into their problems, their targets and the desires they have – explore them, challenge them and then, in a relaxed way, convert them into TakeAways. If you can match the TakeAways they need with TakeAways you can offer, then great, tell them so – clearly and confidently.

ABC Analysis

Over the years we've used front-line feedback to create two essential add-ons to the basic chapter 7 analysis. These make TakeAways even more usable in real, commercial situations. The add-ons make your job much easier when you're face-to-face with your buyer. They'll stop you from ever being lost for words, facts, or ideas and keep you fear-less.

The first add-on is the TakeAway Quadrant; the second is the Value Statement. Chapters 7 and 8 together comprise an ABC Analysis.

TAKEAWAY QUADRANTS

So how do you record and then use the TakeAways you created in the *So What* exercise? You use a very simple sheet called a TakeAway Quadrant (examples are shown on the next few pages). In any influence situation, you need only one sheet that relates to your specific Buyer/Offering combination. If you personally generated the TakeAways, you don't even need to learn them - the sheet is just a good prompt!

Before we look at some examples, there are two powerful new factors added by using a TakeAway Quadrant. They both relate to the way people are convinced to change – and to stick with that decision. As you learned in chapter 3, everyone has their own detailed buying strategy, but they are ultimately driven by the TIRES that will be delivered.

There are two additional questions that need to be answered which will affect how easily your buyer is influenced by what you offer.

The first question is:

> *"Is this a personal TakeAway, or driven by company aims?"*

The second is:

> *"Will this TakeAway achieve something new, or prevent something happening?"*

Corporate v. Personal

This defines the *actual* beneficiary of the TakeAway that's driving the decision. Is it something that affects your buyer, their family, friends or society? Or is it just their employer or organisation that will profit from the TakeAways? If it's a combination of the two, what's the ratio?

When you generate your TakeAways using the *So What to TIRES* exercise, you'll quickly spot whether it's the buyer who benefits or their company/organisation/team. There is, of course, no reason why it can't be both – as it should be in a well-motivated company.

Examples

'*Reduced staff turnover*' is likely to be a Corporate TakeAway. In fact, it delivers the (**R/E**) part of the TIRES check – since it would reduce the expense involved in replacing those staff. If your discussions indicated that your buyer (who in this case is the business manager) is suffering from overwork as a direct result of high staff turnover, then it would also be a Personal TakeAway (**S**).

If the TakeAway was '*less painful eye strain from staring at the screen*' (**S**) then this looks like a good *Personal TakeAway*. But of course it may also be a *Corporate* one – since the company may be responsible for paying for staff's eyewear (**R/E**) and your buyer might generate profit faster with better eyesight (**T/I**).

An opposite example comes from the '*enhanced speed of our new report writer software*'. This may, on the face of it, appear to be a *Corporate TakeAway*, since more time would be released for other, more profitable activities (**T/I**). Sometimes, there may be a *personal* aspect to this as well: suppose your buyer's extra workload from the current report system means that they constantly get home late? If that's the case, they'll become a strong advocate of buying, even if they're not the decision maker – as long as you really can get them home earlier!

'Increased income' can also be interesting. Sometimes there's no direct linkage between a buyer's personal income and the organisation's revenue or profit. In that case, the personal Buying Driver would be small. However, if the person is on commission, on a bonus, or is a stock or option holder, then they'll benefit directly as well. This is just the sort of thing that Buyer Discovery or a good personal connection can reveal.

When you're discussing TakeAways with your buyer, it's usually fairly clear whether a Buying Driver is *Corporate* or *Personal*. But if in doubt, just ask!

There's nothing offensive in asking

> *"So besides the business unit benefitting from this, will it affect you personally?"*

The answer might be a gem of a need that you can satisfy – and no one else may even know about! It might even be a need that your buyer hadn't realised existed until you asked! It's a great moment when this happens – your buyer will have created a uniquely strong link with you, and only you.

Away From v. Towards

In chapters 3 and 7, I mentioned briefly that one of the decision making strategies people use is a *'Towards' or 'Away From'* preference. Let's now look at this in more detail. *Towards* is a motivation to achieve a specific goal, or produce an outcome, and can be deeply embedded in a person's character. Away From is pretty much what it says. It's a drive to prevent unpleasant or undesirable things happening. It's a need to reduce the 'what if?' risk. It's a desire to *prevent* an outcome, rather than *making* something happen. It can be a very central part of the person's character, whether it's a personal Towards or a personal Away From.

In fact, the best balanced teams contain a mix of Towards people (the drivers forward) and Away Froms (the checks and balances) who are needed to prevent rash decisions.

This trait can often also be recognised in a company's identity – usually driven by the specific business they're in. A trading operation is likely to be driven to *achieve* profit targets and happy to accept *risks* along the way. A cooperative pension fund may be much more likely to be motivated to *protect* their members' investments from reducing in value through a *wrong* decision.

Why is this *Towards/Away From* trait so important? Well, there are several reasons:

- The TIRES that drive the two types will be different. It's not a hard and fast rule, but Away From TakeAways tend to involve **R** or **E**, with negative **S** or **T** in their statement. 'Towards' TakeAways will tend to create specific **I** and positive **T**, and be generating a positive **S**.

- When you're discussing Towards TakeAways with a Towards person, they're more like to lean forward, connect with you and pay attention. When you discuss Away From TakeAways with them, they'll be a lot less engaged – and vice versa for a Buyer who's Away From.

- It's almost the same when you present your Delivery Narrative (see chapter 9). If you present your beautifully crafted statement and it emphasises the opposite driver to those of your buyer, they won't be convinced. Get it the right way round, give them a view they like, and they'll want to buy.

Using TakeAway Quadrants in real life

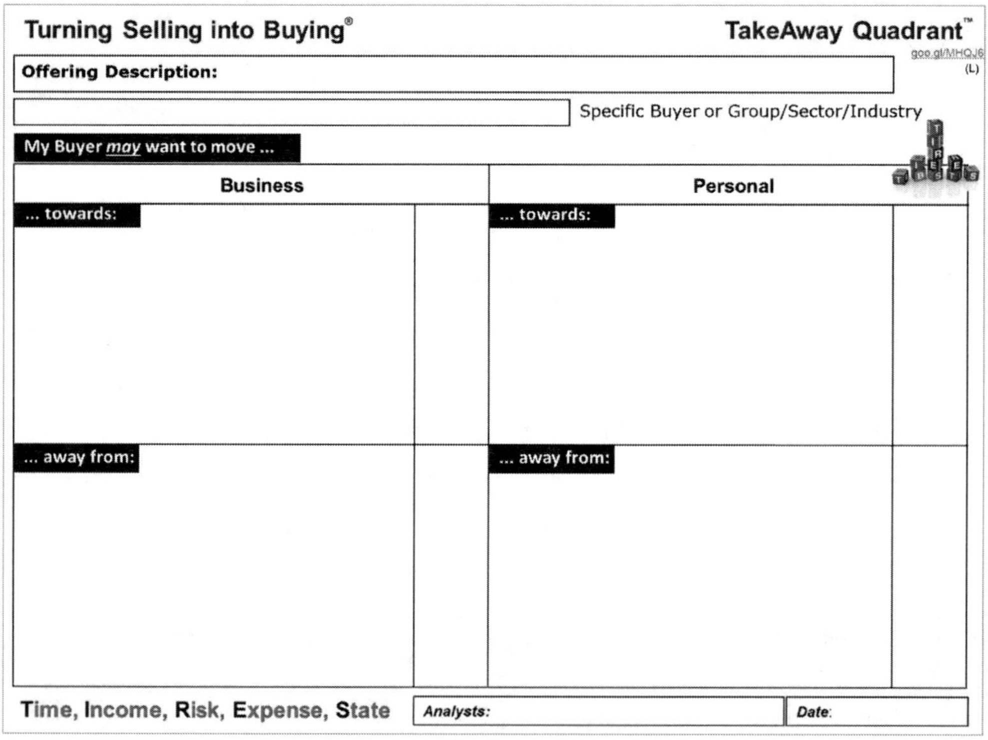

Figure 25

The TakeAway Quadrant (see Figure 25) is a simple document that holds ALL the Buying Drivers you need for a specific Buyer/Offering combination. It has two columns (one for *Business*, one for *Personal TakeAway*) and two rows (one for *Towards* and the other for *Away From TakeAways*). This creates four quadrants:

NOTE: The same TakeAway (e.g. predictable revenue) can be in several different quadrants at the same time.

I keep a copy of my TakeAway Quadrant as a 'cue card' on my cellphone and in my day book – one for each of my offerings, and the four types of buyer I encounter. Sometime, I even share it with my buyer – but that requires a high degree of rapport.

Beside each quadrant is a vital component – the (narrow) **TIRES** column. This will contain a letter denoting whether the TakeAway beside it is one that:

- Improves control over **Time**.
- Increases **I**ncome.
- Controls or make **R**isk more visible.
- Reduces **E**xpense or transfers it elsewhere.
- Improves **S**tate of the buyer, observers and stakeholders.

A TakeAway can have multiple TIRES (although it's rare to find all five). The column may also contain TIRE Compounds. A simple example of a TIRE Compound would be **T/I**. This indicates 'Time to Income' – in other words, *earlier revenue*. **R/E** would indicate changed *risk of incurring an expense*. **R/S** might indicate the *reduced risk of fear and anxiety* (as occurs when using TakeAways!).

At the top of the quadrant are the all-important offering and Buyer details. If you're analysing a market, geography or industry group, this is where you put it. Put *as specific a title as you can* for your offering. This means that simply entering a product or service name is usually insufficient. 'Statutory Reporting Solution for Small Airlines' is much better than just 'Accounts Software'.

In chapter 7, my window cleaning offering was a very specific package of services which I called '*VIP Windows*'. That had a very clear definition of the offering behind it.

If you're doing a TakeAway Analysis in preparation for influencing a specific person, group, or company, then put their details in the Buyer box. It may also be useful to add their Buyer Group as well, for context.

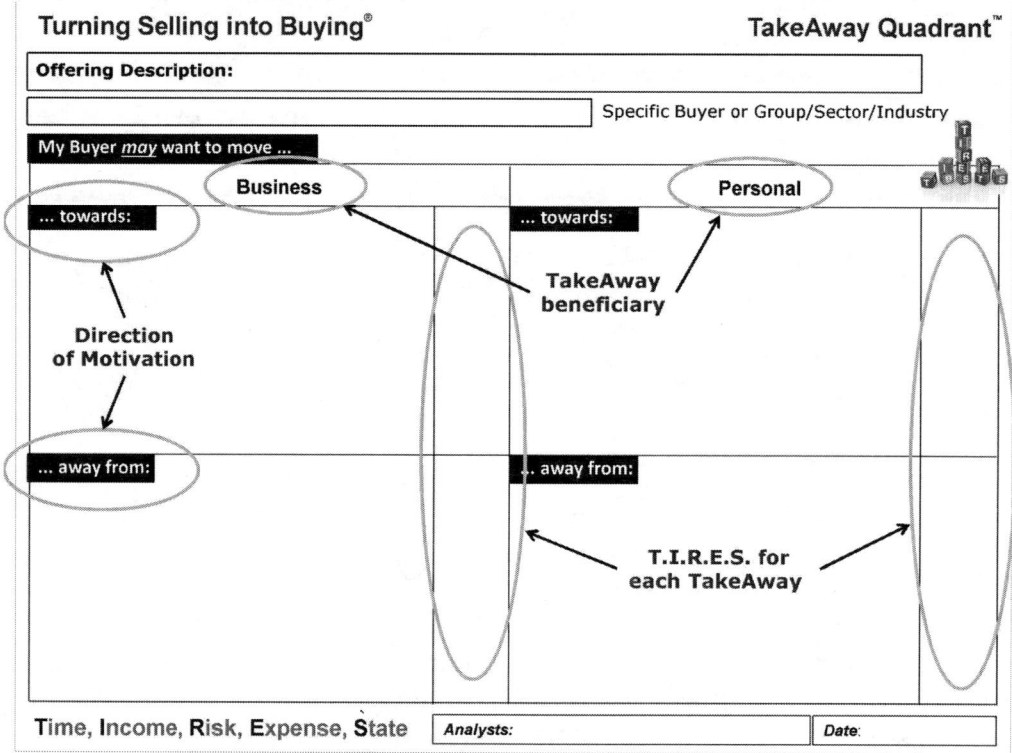

Figure 26

Last but not least, at the bottom are the analysts and the date. This is important to track as TakeAways for the same offering can change over time.

A change in TakeAways can happen for many reasons including:

- Changing legislation.
- The economy.
- Technology changes.
- Competitor pressures – their new offerings.

- Changing personal or market needs.
- A change in your offering that improves its 'buyability'.
- Exchange rates.
- Fashion trends, etc.

Figure 26 shows an annotated version of the Quadrant I've just described.

Quadrant Examples

Technology Example

First is a technology example – a very specialised business GPS that is offered to professional transport companies – not the more normal consumer GPS. For a full description download the Sat-Is-Fire product description from *goo.gl/XZ2zj*.

In the TakeAway Quadrant in Figure 27, I've entered the TakeAways generated from the *So What* challenges we made to the features and functions of the Sat-Is-Fire offering. Believe me, I had a few to pick from – this is one of our classroom exercises and imagination boils over from the students when they do this!

All *you* need to do is look at each TakeAway, think about where it's positioned in the quadrant (Towards/Away From, Personal/Corporate) and decide what goes in the TIRES column. Then go back and see what TIRE Compounds you can add to the basic TIRES entries.

If you want an example of this completed Quadrant, download it from *goo.gl/HSTrL.*

Non-Technology Example

The second example is at the other end of the scale. It's an outsourcing offering for small and medium sized companies who do a lot of travel and also need irregular but high value shipping.

At present, all these tasks are done as an added extra by whoever is free within the admin team. The time taken up in arranging travel and supervising the parcel carriers has to be made up for outside of normal hours. There is not sufficient work to take on full time staff, but there is a definite need to do something about it.

Turning Selling into Buying®		TakeAway Quadrant™	
'Sat-Is-Fire' GPS System		**Offering Description**	
Medium Sized Transport Companies		**Specific Buyer or Group/Sector/Industry**	

My Buyer *may* want to move ...

Business		Personal	
... towards:		**... towards:**	
Reduced fuel cost through better routeing	E	Less pressure on transport management	
Lower maintenance through lower mileage	I	Less stress for drivers who know arrival time	T/S
Customer loyalty through faster delivery	R/I	Employee pride at improved service	S/I
Revenue from high value 'express pickups'	I		
... away from:		**... away from:**	
Fuel waste through inefficient routeing	R/E	Tired, lost drivers having accidents	R/S/E
Fuel waste from traffic jams	T/E	High driver turnover on complex urban routes	R/E
Overtime payment for over-run work		Late delivery complaints upsetting drivers	S
Costly penalties for late delivery			

Time, Income, Risk, Expense, State

Analysts: Dave Perfect   Date: 14 August 2012

Figure 27

Imagine that you have an outsourcing service that solves exactly this problem. Write down what the features of your Offering are – how it's accessed, how it operates, what it covers, etc. and then decide on the characteristics of your buyer (keep it simple).

Then using *So What* and some imagination, see just how many TakeAways you can generate and enrich – put your answers into a copy of the blank quadrant at Figure 25.

Then look at Figure 28 and the notes below it.

CHAPTER 8: USING TAKEAWAYS TO INFLUENCE 217

Turning Selling into Buying®   **TakeAway Quadrant™**

'Take–It–Away' Outsourced Logistics		Offering Description	
Small to Medium Sized Transport Companies		Specific Buyer or Group/Sector/Industry	

My Buyer *may* want to move ...

Business		Personal	
... towards:		**... towards:**	
Reduced cost through cheaper fares	E	Less frustration doing non–mainstream jobs	S
More profitable face–to–face sales meeting	I	Reduced staff turnover	R/E/I
More chance of 'overnight' sales business	R/I	Greater job satisfaction & productivity	S/I
Happier, more productive staff	S/I		
... away from:		**... away from:**	
Buying high priced tickets at last moment	E	Frustration of late working without warning	T/S
Time wasted chasing transport companies	T	Having to chase late deliveries	S
Overtime payments	E	Needing to take flights at inconvenient times	S
Management time spent on unhappy staff	T/E		

Time, Income, Risk, Expense, State   *Analysts:* Ida Allsop   *Date:* 14 Sept 2011

Figure 28

Take a look at each quadrant boxes in Figure 30 and compare them with *your* TakeAways. Do you agree with what's there? What else did you add? Are your TakeAways in different quadrants? Why? – Is it the Buyer or the offering that's different? What other Buyer Group might have been interested in these TakeAways? Write your answers here:

To play around, download and print some double-sided examples from goo.gl/MHQJ6 (A4 format) or goo.gl/XeIwO (Letter format) – or get them from the TSB Download page.

Miscellaneous Examples

Figures 29 and 30 show two more completed TakeAway Quadrants. Read these carefully and think about how you could navigate a conversation to each TakeAway there. What opening remarks would you use? What questions would you ask? What stories would you tell? What information could you ask for?

Web Software TakeAway Quadrant

My Buyer may want to move ...		Analysts: Dave Perfect		Date: 14 August 2012
Business		**Personal**		
... towards:		*... towards:*		
Faster database query writing	T	More time working, less time waiting		T/S
More profitable queries	I	More friendly interface		S/T
Access to risk data in overseas offices	R	Access to risk management datafeeds		R
... away from:		*... away from:*		
Accurate answers needing multiple queries	T/R	Working late due to slow reports		T/S
Missing data causing expensive errors	R/E	Failure to hit personal monthly targets		I
Need for expensive hardware to run queries	E			
Last minute calls to overworked support staff	S			

Global Insurance Asset Management
Flin Flon Assurance

Buyer group/sector/industry
(Optional Specific Target Buyer)

Time, Income, Risk
Expense, State

'HyperQuery' Report Writing Web Service

My Offering to Buyer

Figure 29

Disaster Team App TakeAway Quadrant

My Buyer may want to move ...		Analysts: Jevin Maltese		Date: 14 Sept 2012
Business		**Personal**		
... towards:		... towards:		
Faster access to incident details	T	Citizen energy & creativity able to be used		T/S
Ability to target resources effectively	R/S	More people rescued, more quickly		S/T
Less cost for permanent infrastructure	E	More equipment saved, more quickly		E/T
More efficient routeing for crews	T/S			
... away from:		... away from:		
Expensive video cameras and flood sensors	T/R	Inaccurate deployment of tired crews		S/T
Inaccurate, garbled phone updates	R/E	Crews given inadequate details		R/S
Overworked, jammed call centres	T/E	Citizens with key info unable to send it quickly		T/S

Government Flood Relief Agency	**Buyer group/sector/industry**	
Mantario Plains Province	*(Optional Specific Target Buyer)*	Time, Income, Risk Expense, State
Mobile App for Emergency Services	**My Offering to Buyer**	

Figure 30

TAKEAWAY GENERATION EXERCISE

An exercise we do in seminars is to analyse a simple, un-technical product – a winter tire (tyre). You may not need winter tires where you live, but there's no need to have experienced minus 30°C to understand the tire characteristics in Figure 31 below (or from goo.gl/An2jB). You should use the generator sheet at Figure 19 or download it from goo.gl/6qGZZ.

Do this exercise with a colleague who has read chapter 7 and understands TIRES. If you can't arrange that, then at least get someone else to say *So What* to you at the appropriate times. Doing this is very much more productive than talking to yourself!

Here's a summary of what you've learned to do:

- Write a Feature in the left hand column of the Generator Sheet, then read it out.
- Next, hear the words *So What* (preferably from someone else).
- Then generate another feature that edges closer to a TakeAway.
- Once you've looped enough for it to pass the TIRES check, write down the TakeAway.
- Enrich it as in Section 5 of chapter 7 and add the new TakeAways you've created.

Turning Selling into Buying® - Winter Tires Exercise Brief

Features of your Offering

Winter Tire that conforms with 2010 Highway Safety Code

'Super Blocks' tackle every possible tough winter condition safely

'Hyper-Hysteresis' construction reduces road noise over normal winter tires

Carbon-Filled Polymer (CFP) allows less wear than soft winter tires

Stiffer Sidewalls allow, higher cornering speeds and better handling

'Lo-Flex' design keeps blocks firmly planted even under heavy braking

Unique 'A-Syn' sidewall design has a lower profile than conventional winter tires

Backed by the country's largest distribution network

Includes free storage of summer tires when used

24 month warranty

In the top 10% in recent 'Wear-King' longevity tests

Made in a plant owned by us in China so that the savings can be passed on to you

Installed and supported by local contractors with ISO9001 certification

Commercial versions backed by National Puncture service

Weighs only 18 pounds

Has unique white sidewalls

Available in all popular sizes

Figure 31

Then move to the next feature in the list.

Now look for patterns or grouping opportunities within the TakeAways you've created. Then place them in the correct places in the quadrant, remembering that a TakeAway can go in multiple quadrants (e.g. Personal/Towards and Corporate/Away From).

Less Is More – A Profitable Variation

Franco Caccia had a problem. His company had built the 'Rolls Royce' of internet collaboration solutions. But it wasn't selling … well it was, but each sale took so much effort that it was barely profitable. He had great sales teams who were working their hearts out, but his software offering was five years too early. The market couldn't get its head around the idea of what he sold. In TSB terms – they couldn't recognise their own potential TakeAways.

So the management team sat down, went back to basics, and focussed on the business TakeAways that they could offer a customer, rather than highlighting how technically smart their software was. They knew their backs were against the wall. They needed to make it a *business investment* for their customer – not just a technology sale. They worked through different scenarios and found many combinations of use, users, and situation – all of which generated strong and buyable business TakeAways. But then the moment of truth came – there were now *so many* TakeAways that to explain each one would overwhelm all but the smartest buyers.

So they made the decision that many successful start-ups have been forced into. They decided to sell less than they could actually deliver. They switched off or hid many of the 'cooler' functions. They picked a simple, business problem that their offering would solve – one with hard facts behind its return on investment. They pared down their marketing material, changed the scripts of their cold calls and engaged in discussion with their customers in *only one area*.

Their offering was simple and based on the **E** of TIRES – it would reduce customers' phone bills! No more talk about spotting more profitable deals (**I**) by using smart collaboration, or saving time (**T**) by connecting people as soon as necessary, or reducing the risk of costly errors (**R/E**) by sharing vital documents.

They were also smart enough to realize that changing their offering meant that it was time to change which potential customers to target. So they focussed only on buyers who were in industries with high phone costs and with many regional offices.

It worked. The customers liked the simple new offering and could commit easily. Franco changed the whole pricing structure and users quickly gained confidence in the system. They could then switch on (and be charged for) 'premium features'. Franco's concept is still going strong today – and cost reduction (not the cool screen sharing) continues to be a mainstay through times of economic uncertainty.

So what did Franco teach us?

- Don't get caught up in how cool or clever your product or offering is.
- Be prepared to radically change direction if it helps people to 'get' your TakeAways.
- Sometimes, letting the clients ask you for TakeAways can be very powerful.

GENERATING VALUE STATEMENTS

TakeAways are invaluable for navigation when you're drilling down into a buyer's situation. You'll eventually get to a point where you've revealed either:

- What your buyer's need or problem is and know you can deliver something (which is great).

Or

- You know for sure that there's no business to be done (the opportunity is qualified out – which is also useful).

So what do you say next? Well that's where "Value Statements" come into their own. They're not just conjured out of the air as so many marketing and sales teams do. Nor are they made up in the moment during a meeting. TSB Value Statements are simple, objective, and generated directly from the TakeAways.

A Value Statement is sometimes called a TakeAway Pair, but this is not a very buyer-friendly title. The TIRES delivery (save **T**ime, improve **I**ncome, reduce **R**isk, improved **S**tate) is just a baseless claim on its own. To give it credibility, it needs to be *paired with the feature or function that created* it in the *SO WHAT* chain. That feature or function may, in turn need to be supported by the one that created it, until there is no need for proof or justification. Most Value Statements need only the last one or two links in the chain to be added to the TIRES. A few need three or even four.

Here are a few examples:

Value Statements/TakeAway Pairs:

- *"Our overnight delivery service reduces repair **T**ime."*
- *"Satellite imaging made the fire fighting **R**isk much more visible."*
- *"Objective Analysis puts a consultant in a productive **S**tate."*

So how do you generate these Value Statements? Well, since you've carried out your TakeAway Analysis so well in the last chapter, it's really easy!

Select your TakeAway and reverse back up the *SO WHAT* sequence (exactly as you did in the Enrichment tasks), but this time the purpose is different. This time you're gathering evidence to add to your TIRES assertion that makes it *provable, convincing* and *persuasive*. This is best illustrated in these two examples.

Example 1 – 'Hi-Pro Driveshafts'

Stated TakeAway from your Product: *'Reduced Cost'* (i.e. Delivers **E**).

How can we justify that statement?

Here (in reverse) is the TakeAway Sequence that generated it:

- Reduced cost – *comes from* – Fewer expensive repair callouts.
- Fewer repair callouts – *comes from* – Less frequent driveshaft failure.

- Fewer failures – *comes from* – Patented surface treatment of metal shaft.

- Patented surface treatment – *comes from* – Our R&D Laboratories.

- R&D Laboratories – *comes from* – 25 years well-funded, reinvestment in the company.

There is no fixed format to a Value Statement. They can be varied according to context or buyer. Here are a two more examples generated from the five statements above.

> *"Our world class research team has created a new treatment for driveshafts which dramatically reduces failures and the associated costly repair."*

> *"Our customers' loyalty has funded our unique product development which has given them back ultra-reliable equipment which costs less to run."*

Value Statements that are generated from this reverse SO WHAT exercise are powerful, accurate, and compact. They contribute strongly to building a Willing Buyer.

Create different Value Statements based on the five bulleted steps in the Hi–Pro Driveshafts TakeAway chain above:

Now write some for **your** offering (from its TakeAway Analysis):

Example 2 – Trading Support Software

Stated TakeAway from your software: *"Faster, more profitable results"* (delivers **T/I**).

Sounds good – but how do I achieve it?

Here is the TakeAway Sequence that generated it:

- Faster Profit – *comes from* – Profitable trading decisions based on a complete picture.
- Trading Decisions – *from* – Real time view of trading positions from all offices.
- Real-Time View – *from* – Secure, web-based connection to every trader's system.
- Secure Connection – *from* – An unobtrusive 'plugin' app on any and every computer.
- Simple plugin app – *from* – Patented financial middleware built by a PhD genius.
- Financial Middleware – *from* – Start-up team of ex–traders frustrated by IT support.

This example is one I've come across many times. All too often, a clever piece of technology is 'sold' to non-technical business people – traders, grocers, lawyers, whatever. Even though many of them could benefit from the technology, they can't make the link to their day-to-day business problems.

Here's my attempt at a Value Statement from the previous *So What* chain:

> "Funded by expert ex-traders, we deliver unobtrusive software that connects decision makers in a global business to the trading information they need for profitable minute-to-minute choices."

Create different Value Statements based on the six bulleted steps in the Trading Support Software TakeAway chain above:

Now write some for **your** offering (from its TakeAway Analysis):

IN SUMMARY:
PREPARE ONCE, USE MANY TIMES

The ABC Analysis described in this chapter is where your work and learning in the previous chapters comes together. The TakeAway Quadrants you create will let you productively re-use the results of your preparation.

If you have several different offerings, they can get you into the right frame of mind. You can use them to brief specialists who are supporting you. You can use them to differentiate yourself. You can use them to start conversations about monetary value. Properly introduced, you can show them to your buyer.

Value Statements (or TakeAway Pairs) put real meat on TakeAways. Anyone can say "*What I offer will make you more money*", but your ability to quickly, objectively, and repeatably trace the route to that money is highly convincing.

Deriving your Value Statements directly from the TakeAways means the statements you make are always relevant, accurate, and effective.

CHAPTER 8:
REVIEW QUESTIONS & SELF-DEVELOPMENT ASSIGNMENTS

Using TakeAways for Influence – see Annex C for Answers

To print a copy of this section, download it directly from goo.gl/Om929 or select it from the TSB Download Page at goo.gl/p0Ajn.

Self-Test Questions

1. What is a TakeAway Quadrant used for?
2. What are the four classifications of TakeAway in a Quadrant?
3. How many Quadrant Sheets for each Buyer/Offering combination?
4. How does a Value Statement differ from a TakeAway?
5. When would you use a Value Statement?

Self-Development Assignments

Ch 8 Assignment 1 – Have Fun

Print out the blanks quadrant sheets and TakeAway generator sheets in chapter 7. Then try what you've learned in this chapter on as many things as you can:

- At work – what would your boss TakeAway from reorganising the department?
- At home – what would your son TakeAway if he actually passed his driving test?
- At play – what would your gardening club TakeAway from having its own website?

Ch 8 Assignment 2 – Just Do It

After your first dry run analysis, take the final results and place them in a TakeAway Quadrant. Remember the same TakeAway can go in more than one quadrant. If there are a lot of TakeAways on the sheet (more than 12 perhaps) check that you've not got duplications. If there are a lot, you may need to consider simplifying your offer to make it more buyable (remember Franco?) or tightening up your Buyer Group.

Ch 8 Assignment 2 – Just Use It

Next time you go to an influence meeting, take a look at the Quadrant Sheet for the appropriate Buyer/Offering combination just before you go in. There's no need to learn it by rote. You've generated it yourself, so trust your unconscious to guide you. You'll find getting the conversation around to the TakeAways so much easier.

CHAPTER 9
Your Commit Analysis

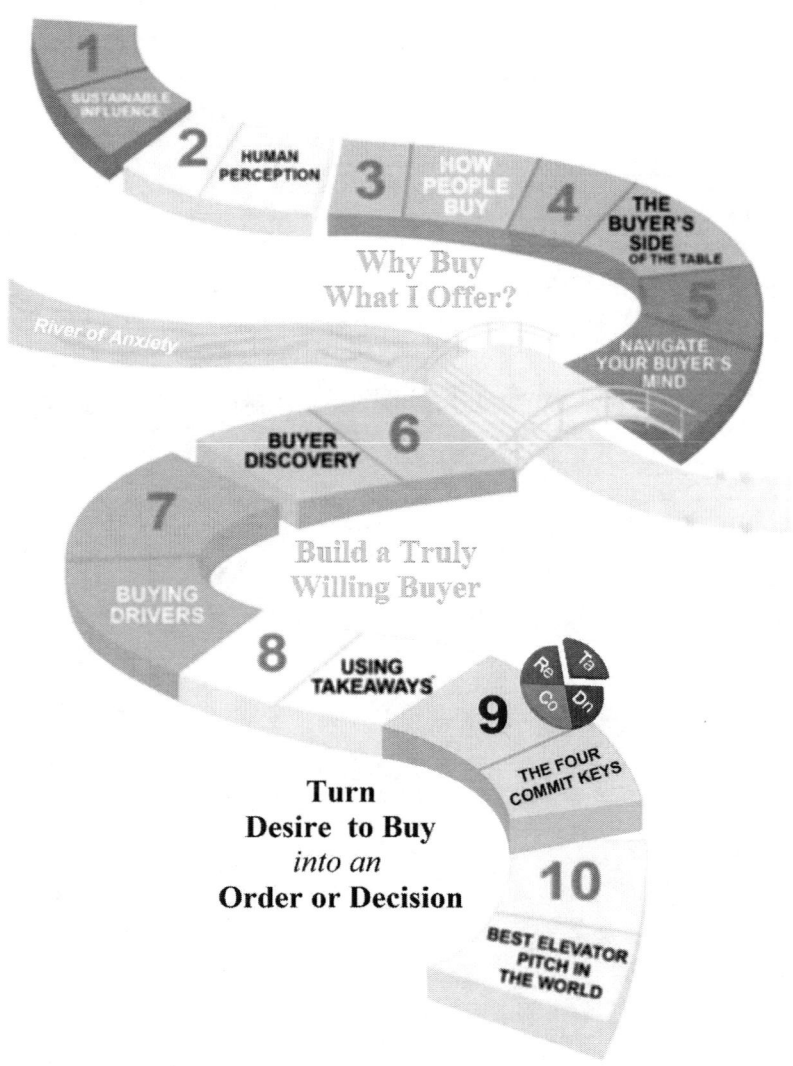

BY THE END OF THIS CHAPTER, YOU'LL UNDERSTAND ...

- The Four 'Commit Keys' needed to produce a Decision or Order
- Ways in which a person or organisation becomes 'Convinced'
- The most powerful financial justification possible for your Offering
- Simple ways to help your Buyer 'step into' a purchase decision

HOW WILL A COMMIT ANALYSIS HELP BUILD A WILLING BUYER?

In the last chapter you learned how to create a Willing Buyer. That's a great thing to be able to do, but it can leave you one step short of the finishing line.

You need to take action to turn a Desire to Buy into Action – action that actually generates an order or a decision. That desire for **action** must also be strong enough to maintain its own momentum – even when you're not with your buyer.

Your Buyer needs four **Commit Keys** to do this:

- Identify the TakeAways they need or want – analysed in chapter 7, developed in 8.
- Become sure TakeAways can be delivered – their "Convincers."
- Identify themselves with the process – their "Delivery Narrative."
- Build and agree a cost justification – their "ROI Framework."

Figure 32 illustrates these Four Commit Keys.

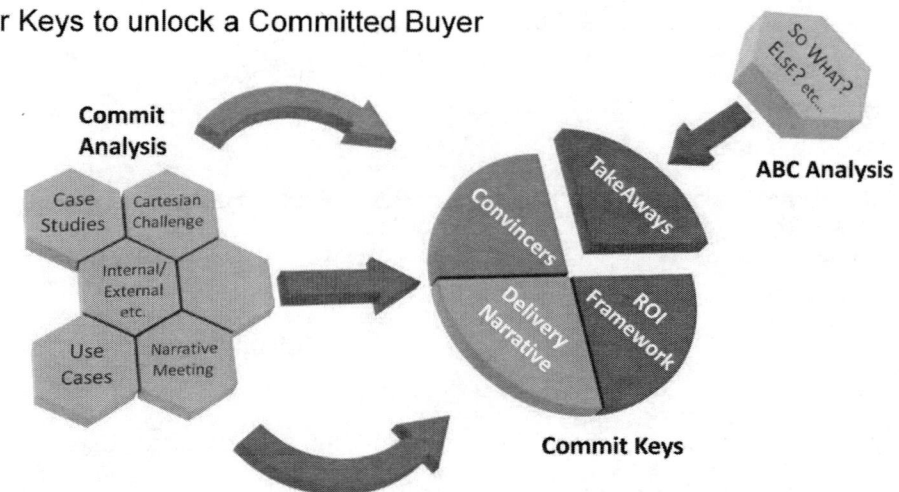

Figure 32

A "Commit Analysis" is the industrial strength extension to the ABC Analysis that you learned in chapters 7 and 8. The outputs cut through the assumptions, guesses, and untruths that can be so expensive for both established and start-up operations.

This chapter delivers the tools that move your buyer from 'buying into' the idea to actually spending money – and doing so willingly. It also gives you the confidence to fearlessly and successfully tackle what are sometimes the toughest nuts to crack:

- Nailing a financial justification to support your pricing.
- Face-to-face sales and influence discussions.
- Negotiation of terms, prices, and deliverables.
- Keeping the momentum in your favour – even when you're not there.

Just some of the questions you'll be able to answer at the end of this chapter are:

- Would anyone in my new market be willing to buy what we're offering – at this price?
- Would anyone pay for what our R&D department wants to create?
- Will our price deliver the desired return to the buyer?
- What do we need to do – to actually prove our assertions?
- Should we continue to sell this offering, at this price, in this market?
- Can this failing product be turned into a fuller, more buyable or profitable offering?

What a Commit Analysis adds to an ABC Analysis

Your chapter 7 & 8 ABC analysis created the first "Commit Key"– the TakeAways.

You can build upon this work to generate the final three Commit Keys. To achieve this you'll learn:

- How people become *convinced* – of anything – and stay that way.
- The power of well-prepared *story telling*.
- A simple tool for generating powerful *cost benefits*.

HOW PEOPLE BECOME CONVINCED

It's a great feeling when you have a Willing Buyer in front of you, and you know they're motivated *at that moment* to move ahead with the positive decision you've influenced them to make.

But it's not such a great feeling to realise that very same buyer – who was so keen to buy from you three days ago – has just changed their mind. They may now appear to believe in very different things after only a short time. That's the effect that overwork, a bad cold, or a disagreement with a partner can have!

To avoid this, you've got to actively *lock in their Desire to Buy* so that it still exists long after you've left. *Making a buying decision stick* is what Convincers are all about.

Convincer Strategies

Humans are remarkably consistent in the way they decide whether something is true. We're each different, but there's seldom much variation in the sequence of steps we individually take to *build a belief* (or change it). Each time, we tend to follow the same, familiar path.

Which is the right car to buy? Which consultant is right for us? Which new suit makes me look great? Which air conditioning unit should I get installed? Each of us uses our own "Convincer Strategy" to create these new beliefs. Understanding this is essential to taking the uncertainty out of influencing someone's decision to buy your products, services or ideas. It's not a fine science, but it *is* a practical model that works well to greatly increase your chance of success – and your ability to predict it.

Once your buyer has successfully completed their Convincer Strategy, they will have made a decision, and their Model of the World will have changed in your favour – perhaps for ever. Before the strategy is run, their model will not include (for instance) the true statement *"This supplier is reliable and financially stable enough to buy from."*

Once their strategy is successfully filled, their model *will* include that statement – and it will do so until something convinces them otherwise.

But here's the catch – the evidence that *you* find so convincing may not work for someone else. As we saw in chapter 2, we all perceive the world differently. If you demonstrate practically to a person that something is true – but their Convincer Strategy means that they're only truly persuaded if they *read about it* – your chances of changing their belief are much reduced. So how do you deal with this?

The 3 'Convincer Components'

There are three parts to any person's Convincer Strategy. Knowing how your buyer likes to complete their strategy can help enormously to influence them. The first is the way they prefer to receive the information they respond to. We call this their Convincer Channel. It describes the way they prefer to find things out. Do they like to read about it? Do they always ask someone else? Do they need to see it demonstrated?

The second component is their Convincer Mode. This describes the internal schedule they use to become convinced – once they've received what they need through their Convincer Channel.

Third is their Convincer Frame. This is the mechanism used to change their Model of the World from *"Doesn't include this idea as true"* to *"Does include buying…"*

You learned that TakeAways can satisfy both personal and corporate Buying Drivers. The same is true of Convincers Strategies. Behind the buyer or buyer team in front of you may be an organisation with its own preferred Convincer Channel, Mode and Frame – these also need to be exposed. They won't call them that, but they'll be there!

Let's look at each in turn, to understand how to use them.

Your Buyer's 'Convincer Channel'

When my wife and I are buying a car together, we use different *Convincer Channels*. I like to know what people are saying about that car – and I prefer reading it to hearing somebody say it. My wife much prefers to search out lots of numbers and study them carefully before making a decision. Those aren't the only channels we each use, but they're our first choice. For both of us, 'how it feels' (i.e. drives) is very important but comes narrowly in second place.

As a result, a car sales person who wants to convince us both to buy also needs to present us each with different evidence. If they read me as a car nut and focus on giving me a great test drive, they won't *complete my Convincer Strategy*. If they only give my wife well-written road tests, that won't be enough, either.

There are five Convincer Channels which cover most people and groups. There will usually be one which strongly satisfies the need for evidence, and another which will has almost no effect. Some people specifically need two channels at the same time. *"I need to watch it and hear it to make a decision."*

Looks Right

Visual buyers need to see the evidence before they change their belief in something. That proof might be a picture, a model, or seeing the actual thing itself. If it's a conceptual idea, then a diagram or a pictorial metaphor works well for them. The language that these people are most likely to understand clearly will include the words: *"…picture this…, …see it working…, …watch a demo…, …get some perspective…"*. Looks Right is sometimes combined with Reads Right.

Feels Right

Kinaesthetic buyers need to get their hands on and actually experience something before they'll believe in it. Ideally, they'd like to experience exactly what they will feel after the decision or purchase is made – the TakeAways. They need to try it out for themselves. The language these people are most likely to understand clearly will include *"…see how it feels…, …hands on…, …have a go…, …real-life experience…"*

Sounds Right

Auditory buyers need to hear something before believing it. They can also be sensitive to the tone or authority of a voice. The language these people are most likely to respond to will be *"…does that sound OK?…, …hear at first hand…, …listen carefully…, … pay attention to …"*. Sounds Right is sometimes combined with Makes Sense.

Reads Right

These buyers are most influenced by *reading* the evidence before they'll believe it. They usually need some space to take in all the information – they need to 'Research it properly'. The language that these people are most likely to understand clearly will be *"…read into it…, …study what other people have said…, …see it in black and white…"*. Reads Right may be combined with Looks Right or Makes Sense.

Makes Sense

The *Internal Dialogue* buyer is the one who need to understand and make sense of it inside their head before they'll believe it. They may Chunk Up and focus on the more abstract, or they may Chunk Down and look at the detail. Either way, to them it's analysing that's important.

They'll always want to acquire logical information. Then they'll have a chat with themselves and come to a conclusion, usually very firmly. The language that these people are most likely to understand clearly will be "...make sense of..., ...evaluate logically..., ...run the numbers..., ...run that by me...". Often combined with Reads Right.

Your Buyer's Convincer Mode

Your buyer's Convincer Mode is driven by their personal traits or character. There are five main Convincer Modes, and most people are consistent in their use of a preferred mode – unless a significant event occurs and they're convinced to change it.

Automatic

These buyers take the information that they're given (and it may only be a small amount), and fill in the gaps – from the Model of the World that their experience has built for them. They make up their minds (literally) very quickly and are not easily influenced to change their minds back. They survive what can be a rather dangerous strategy by usually giving people 'the benefit of the doubt'. If your offering delivers strong TakeAways, these are great buyers, but it is the least common mode.

One challenge with this buyer is that if a competitor gets to them, they can quickly swing away from what you're offering. They need to receive strong Convincers – and early – to make a decision stick.

Time Period

This buyer needs either a flow of new Convincers or to be consistently reminded of the original ones. For them, the gathering and the evaluation of the evidence will always take place over a period of time. They can be frustrating to influence, as there may be no external feedback to you that your buyer's 'Convincer clock' is ticking – or that you might get a positive result at the end!

Number of Repeats

This is probably the most common mode. The buyer needs to reach a critical mass before flipping from unconvinced to convinced. The majority of repeaters need three repeats before they decide to change their minds. For some, this may be the same information repeated, for others it may need to be different each time.

Never

These buyers are *never* fully convinced. Every opportunity to re-valuate their decision is a joy to them. They can be very frustrating to turn into Willing Buyers, but once they're there, they can be a committed and loyal source of new information and opportunities.

Consistent

These buyers need to be re-convinced each and every time you interact with them. Their natural outlook is to demand proof on every occasion. They're sometimes even more frustrating than the Nevers – at least with a Never, you know where you stand – Consistents can be a real grind.

Your Buyer's Convincer Frame

Your buyer's Convincer Frame is probably the piece that has the strongest influence in most commercial situations; the personal traits are important, but only as parts of a bigger jigsaw puzzle. Convincer Frames are usually a strong corporate characteristic – where there is an clear 'personality' to the procedures and rules the company follows.

Here are some examples of Convincer Frames. Some buyers can be placed at one extreme or another, most are to one side or other of the middle:

Internal/External Frame of Reference

Do your buyers look inside themselves for confirmation that they've done well? Or do they ask someone else outside for a pat on the back? The same can apply to how they are convinced of a new truth.

These people will almost always ask for a reference or a testimonial. The detailed content of the call (as long as it's positive) is usually much less relevant than the fact that they're talking to a third party. Their Convincer could be written, or a video – it's not always necessary to connect the parties.

Towards/Away From

Which motivates your buyer most? Are they energised by achieving a goal? Are they more driven to prevent something happening? We saw this in chapter 7 (the indicators in a TakeAway Quadrant). These people are usually easy to spot when they talk because of the way they describe situations. "*What we really need is to quickly achieve ...*" would be a clear sign of a Towards buyer. "*What I want to stop is ...*" would indicate an Away From buyer. If you convince your buyer that you can deliver a set of outcomes that are compatible with the way they think – then you're on the way to Building a Willing Buyer.

They are sometimes described as possibility v. necessity people. Are they motivated by what's possible or do they react to what's necessary? As with all the strategies here, it's not a fine art. The key skill to build is calibrating how your buyer or their organisation make decisions – and then adjust what you say to give them what they need (as long as your offering actually meets their needs).

SWIIFM – Internal or External

How much of your buyer's strategy is *personally* driven by SWIIFM? How much is driven by the needs of the company or organisation? How much is an altruistic desire to make things better for others? The answers to these questions will strongly determine the best way to convince them.

If you can detect and satisfy a personal, internal driver, (and they're not always obvious) that's likely to be useful. An external SWIIFM will need to see, hear, or experience the benefits to their organisation – and, although that may take more effort, at least you know it's necessary.

Detecting Convincers

As I've mentioned previously, this is not a precise art. It will depend how close your connection is with the buyer, how much they are prepared to reveal, and often simply the luck of what happens while you talk. Sometimes your buyer will drop classic phrases such as '*it has to look right*' or '*only if it makes sense*' into the conversation. These can be good indicators of their Convincer Channel.

You can sometimes check the strength of this indication by offering a couple more different Convincer options. If they repeatedly pick the one they've already flagged, you've probably got their primary channel.

Another possibility is simply to ask. But, in a commercial situation, this is not always easy. Classically, you ask questions such as *"the last time you hired a consultant, how did you make the choice?"* If the opportunity arises to do this, then go for it. When they answer, then you have a great opportunity to develop and extend the information they're offering.

More often than not, however, detecting Convincers needs to be done subtly and indirectly, without questions. Sometimes the only way will be to offer them several different Convincers or make sure that the Convincer that's offered contains different channels of information. Their reaction to being offered a multi-mode Convincer may also help you to detect and develop their preferred mode.

In the next section, you'll be introduced to Delivery Narratives – the compelling story you can tell to your buyer of how they will attain their desired TakeAways. Stories are compelling events for most of us, and can be amazingly powerful ways of learning about your buyer and detecting what's important to them:

- Which areas of your story are they most interested in?
- Where do they lean forward and listen?
- Where do they ask questions?
- Are they Chunked Up, big picture questions?
- Are they looking for detail?
- What is their reaction to your Convincer Detection question? (see next Section)

Convincer Detection Example

I'm a keen motorcyclist, and if I see evidence in a buyer's office that they ride a motorbike, I'll quite naturally bring it into the conversation. This starts as a genuine and enjoyable rapport builder – that puts them at ease before I drill down into their TakeAways.

But this example shows it's possible to turn it into a neat Convincer Detector:

> "So I see from these pictures you do Track Days…when did you start going?"
>
> "OH I'VE BEEN DOING IT FOR ABOUT FIVE YEARS!"
>
> "How often do you go?"
>
> "AT LEAST THREE TIMES A YEAR. I'M A MUCH SAFER RIDER FOR DOING IT"
>
> "And how long did it take you to decide to start doing it so regularly?"….

How your Buyer answers that question	Convincer Detected
"Well, I went along with a buddy to see what it was all about and it looked great. It gave me a whole new perspective right away. It was clearly something that made riding much safer"	'Looks Right' Channel – probably a One Time Convincer
"Well, I was really energised by doing a couple of different training levels with California Superbike School. They made me feel really good about my own abilities and it felt so right"	'Feels Right' Channel – probably a two times Convincer
"Well, I'd listened to the boys in the club talking about track days, then my riding buddy said it was great, but I wasn't convinced. Then I heard on Top Gear that it was a great thing for rider safety. So I decided to go for it"	'Sounds Right' Channel – probably a Three Times Convincer
"Well, I'd read about if for a long time in various magazines, but I wasn't convinced. Then I read a few articles online and thought I'd give it a try. But although I keep going, I'm still not entirely convinced it improves my safety"	'Reads Right' Channel – probably a Never Convincer
"Well, I thought about it for a long time – a couple of years actually. But it made more and more sense considering the safety aspects, and now my insurance premium is down too…"	'Makes Sense' Channel – probably a Long Time Convincer

This example is not a hard and fast rule. You need to utilise what's happening around you. But if you get the opportunity ask an open question like this, it can be most productive.

COMMIT KEY ONE – POTENTIAL TAKEAWAYS

You created these in chapters 7 and 8. But remember – the work you've done is *not* a list that can be 'pitched'. The *potential* TakeAways in your quadrant are navigation marks for a buyer conversation. They can be ticked off or crossed out as you engage and discuss with them, but don't spray them at your prospect.

TakeAways that have been agreed with your buyer are a strong foundation, to which you can return to time and again. That is why they are Commit Key One. You can extend them in time, you can bring in other stakeholders, you can look in detail at how they'd operate. All of these are great precursors to being able to say to your buyer:

> **"Well that's great – that's exactly what we do."**

Once you get to that point, and the response is positive, the other three Commit Keys come into effect. Anyone can make a statement like the one above and, for a moment, your buyer will believe you. But the other commit keys are also needed to make an order or decision happen.

COMMIT KEY TWO – MAKING THE DECISION STICK

How do you ensure your buyer's *Desire to Buy* remains as strong when you're gone?

How do you deal with

> *"Well, you would say that wouldn't you? You're just a salesman…"*

This is the point at which their Convincer Strategy need to be satisfied. You can do this in four ways:

- *Immediate Convincers* – that you can give your buyer, there and then.
- *Deferred Convincers* – events you can agree to arrange for later.
- *Assembled Convincers* – not at hand but can be organized.
- *Management Commitment* – you know what might be demanded, but don't have it yet.

NOTE: Unlike old school sales, we only deploy Convincers that are necessary to prove the TakeAways the buyer has confirmed they need – no spray and pray of demos and visits here!

Let's look at them each of them in turn.

Immediate Convincers

You're going to have to satisfy buyers who may each have different Convincer Channels, Modes, and Frames. So you need to build up a good portfolio of goodies. If you're confident your buyer is running a particular Convincer Strategy, then go with it. But don't forget to mention that you have other Convincers available as well. Once you get to the Buying Plan, there may well be others involved – and each will have their own Convincer Strategy.

NOTE: Remember that *Convincers are always about TakeAways* – the TIRES your buyer will achieve. Convincers are *not* about proving features and functions – proving factual statements can come later in the Buying Plan. So don't get sucked into discussions about processors speed or output rates at this stage. Your aim is to convince your buyer that they'll get the TIRES they need – not the strength of the fibres they're buying!

Here are some Convincers to deploy in different situations:

Case Study

This is a real life customer (a company or an individual) *ideally with similar characteristics to your buyer*. A case study should start and end with TakeAways and contain both a Delivery Narrative and a financial justification. It should follow this sequence:

- Background and the buyer's situation.
- The problem to be solved (the desired TakeAways).
- What was delivered (see Delivery Narratives in section 5 of this chapter).
- The final result – in TakeAways.
- The final result in money terms (see ROI Frameworks in section 6).

If you don't have a case study yet, it should come under the heading of Management Commitment below. You must build a portfolio of these for each Buyer/Offering combination. In the early stages of a start-up, you should be crafting a case study in your mind – even before you receive the order from your first buyers. The creation of a good case study may even affect what you deliver to buyers. For instance – how you provide training or what support deal early buyers get.

Use Case

This has an identical form to the Case Study above. But it is actually a well-crafted illustration of an *imaginary* company or individual, with similar characteristics to your buyer. It contains the same Delivery Narrative, TakeAways, and ROI.

Because it's fictional, a Use Case is generally most effective where the biggest Buying Driver is a financial TakeAway. It's a valuable tool for start-ups with few or no customers.

If you're asked *"Is this a real client?"* please don't be tempted to say *"Yes"* – an untruth will always come back to bite you later!

Independent Report or Audit

This is probably the most powerful external Convincer you can provide. Ideally it will have been crafted by you to highlight the TakeAways and Financials at the end.

Sometimes a report over which you have no control will stop short of the TakeAways by only focussing on the features and functions. In this case, simply 'wrap' the report in a header and add a couple of paragraphs and a table to complete *your* picture.

Whitepaper

Whitepapers generally focus on the detail *behind* an offering – how it works, the R&D that created it or the theory behind it. A whitepaper should be treated with care. An awful lot of time and effort can be put into them with little effect on the outcome. If its sole purpose is to convince a *Makes Sense* person or as part of the proof stage in the Buying Plan, then great. But do not be sucked into the trap of thinking that everyone will be impressed or convinced.

Financial Whitepapers are a variation that I have often used to great effect. Unlike the more solution-focussed one described above, a financial whitepaper dives deep into the financial justification and (by implication) its connection to each TakeAway.

Video Testimonial

With the easy, instant access we all have to video nowadays, this is a powerful and compelling Convincer. But you do need to do some careful preparation. A general testimonial such as the one at goo.gl/gkW6n is unlikely to be useful as a Convincer because it's simply not specific enough. A good example of a highly focussed testimonial is shown at goo.gl/QaECL. It deals with three issues – a technical person's view of their sales training; whether a Francophone is comfortable with the English used in the course; and the specific problem addressed – monetising social media technology.

A video Convincer is a highly effective tool. It is great for both the *Looks Right* and *Sounds Right* people. Even better, if you can script a customer to mention the numbers or point at a diagram or talk over a slide, you'll bring in the *Makes Sense* buyer as well.

Written Testimonial

This has the same *"Is it focussed enough?"* health warning as above – it must address specific issues. Ideally, the person who wrote the testimonial is also available for a phone call to satisfy the *Sounds Right* buyer as well as the *Looks Right* one.

ROI Framework

We'll look at this in much greater detail in the next section, but it's essentially the financial return from buying your offering. It combines figures that are industry norms (e.g. error rates, daily salary, accident statistics) with space for the buyer's figures. Your buyer can then quickly and easily *build for themselves* a strong justification for the purchase, even if their own figures are confidential.

One of the greatest strengths of a well-built ROI Framework is that you continue to have some degree of control over the decisions and discussions, *even when you're not in the room*. This is because the Framework for the conversation and associated calculations has been supplied by you.

Pictures

These are great for *Looks Right* people. There is a fashion to combine numbers, text and pictures in one piece of sales collateral. Sometimes this is compressed even further into an infographic.

This is OK for marketing as it offers several channels at once and the reader can self-select. But if you want to strongly influence one-on-one, you might consider offering three powerfully focussed documents – one perhaps entitled 'The Numbers', another 'The Words', and a third called 'The Pictures'. Your buyer can then select the one that attracts them most –you then have an insight into their Convincer Strategy.

Deferred Convincers

These are the classic proof activities that every corporate sale generates – visits, phone calls, running the customer's data through your own test rig, etc. You should have these ready to organise. (**NOTE**: always paired with a *specific* TakeAway – not with features and functions)

When you're asked for them, it's key that you also know the answer to the question

> *"Are we providing this as a Convincer or as a step in a buying process?"*

If it's the latter, you should ideally defer it until your buyer has agreed that

> *"If you can prove delivery of this TakeAway is possible, I have a cost justification to make a favourable decision."*

If what's asked for is a Convincer, then you don't yet have a Willing Buyer. That means that it needs more of your focus than a simple process step. If it *is* a Convincer, and you don't spot it – *and it fails*, you may waste a lot of resources without knowing that you're not going to win. If it *is* confirmed as only being a step in a buying process, that usually means they're a Willing Buyer, which is good news.

Synthetic Convincers

If you're asked for Convincers that have not been requested before, this should set off some gentle alarm bells. What's changed? Is this buyer unique and unusual? If so, in what way precisely? Should you put some extra effort into servicing this need with another client? What is the competition saying? Again, you should also know whether this is a Convincer or simply a step in their buying process.

> When I sold trading software to banks, I was often asked for reference visits. We would go to a lot of trouble (and expense) to create these and they'd often involve an overseas visit, usually with one of our sales people in attendance. We'd always do the best we could to give the customer what they asked for, but I began to wonder whether it was really necessary.
>
> We were asked by one customer if they could go on a reference visit to an identical operation to theirs – trading the same instruments as them, with the same sort of traders, and the same size of team – but overseas. Unfortunately, that didn't exist – they would be our first customer using our software in that specific way.
>
> So I used my (recently learned) precision questioning skills to ask them what specifically they wanted to TakeAway from the visit. After some initial reluctance (and, I suspect, some desire to go on a free trip), I drilled down to three specific things that they needed to determine:
>
> 1. Could we cope with the multi-currency accounting required?
> 2. How good was our online support for non-English speakers?
> 3. Would our central bank reporting work in other jurisdictions?
>
> Well that was wonderful news – I could supply him with proof of *each of these*, quickly and simply, with (in order) a local visit, a phone call and a demonstration. Once we'd discussed it, my buyer was OK with joining them together to become convinced (which he was, and we got the deal).

This taught me a lesson that I now always insist my sales team do whenever they're asked for a reference, a test, or a demonstration. They must always Chunk Up to the TakeAways the buyer is looking to check for. This is also yet another opportunity to learn more about their Convincer Mode, Frames, and Channel.

If your buyer asks for an opportunity to discuss something with a reference that's clearly strategic (e.g. *'I'd like to discuss how they feel about having a long term commitment to you as a supplier'*), do the opposite – Chunk Down to the specifics of what is motivating them to ask that.

If you make it a rule to *always* identify the drivers for the demo, visit, or call, you will be able to better prepare and you'll learn far more about what drives your buyer's Convincer Strategy. It's also demonstrates your genuine interest in giving them what they really need.

Management Commitments

Sometimes you just don't have the ability to supply the Convincers that the buyer asks for. If you find that you can't supply Convincers for specific statements (e.g. *objective proof of your claimed data rates on a buyer's hardware*), you must put two actions in place.

Creation

The first is to get a management commitment to creating that Convincer (or at least its constituents). This may take time, money, and resources, but it is likely to be far more useful than yet another whitepaper!

The reason for making it a management commitment is that it won't be driven by a sale and is likely to be a low priority. By the time the need arrives again (but driven by a sale this time), it may well be too late and another opportunity may be lost. I've seen this cycle happen too often.

One very common management commitment is obtaining or generating figures to strengthen the Return on Investment (ROI) Framework. If you're using old industry averages that are open to challenge, why not sponsor an up-to-date survey before you're challenged? If you don't have baseline technical data for (say) 'Mean Time Between Failure' for your hydraulic rams, get your management to invest time and money in getting that data – with the TakeAway of speeding up the next sale!

Underwriting

The second (closely linked) action is to cover the exposure until the Convincer is available. A classic example of this might be the data rate problem above. If you know that the required performance can't be demonstrated in the time available to win the business, then a senior person within the company must be ready to *underwrite* the statement.

This might be in the form of a money-back guarantee, free development of a capability if there's a shortfall, and many others. In each case, the exposure to the company or organisation needs to be evaluated by management. If you happen to be the CEO of a start-up (which often means you're also its lead salesperson) the job is simpler!

COMMIT KEY THREE – THE DELIVERY NARRATIVE

A "Delivery Narrative" does one thing – it 'tells the story' of how you'll provide the TakeAways your buyer wants.

If your offering is a staff training workshop, your Delivery Narrative *is not* a detailed list of the day's agenda. The Delivery Narrative must describe in convincing detail the resulting staff behaviour changes and the TakeAways and financial benefits those staff changes will deliver *a significant time after the workshop*.

The Delivery Narrative isn't merely a dry project plan which finishes with a delivery sign off – it compellingly leads the buyer through the experience of getting to the TIRES they seek.

Most important of all – it's not just an enthusiastic story of how great everything will be once the job's done or the decision implemented – that's very old school. It's the story of *the experiences your buyer will have on the way to their TakeAways*. It should also explicitly address any issues or objections raised by your buyer during discussions.

Everyone loves a story, especially one that's well told. Your Delivery Narrative must be the compelling story of how your buyer will move from where they are today to where they want to be. With all the information you've created so far, it's easy to do. Most importantly, you can tailor it to fully address any concerns and issues your buyer brought up during your meetings – and using their preferred Convincer Mode.

With this very engaging approach:

- You'll minimise the risk of errors and assumptions (on both sides).
- Both of you will enjoy and engage with the process more.
- You'll get direct access to more of their Convincer Strategy.
- Your statements are more believable and memorable.
- The degree of rapport between you will increase.
- The degree of accuracy and preparation will make you look even more professional.

By the end, you'll have brought your buyer to the point of being convinced and can start discussing the detailed route to a purchase order or decision – their Buying Plan.

Delivery Narrative Examples

In the four examples below, the narrative is tuned to resonate with a specific buyer's Model of the World and the problems or objections they've raised during discussion.

In a personal situation, a narrative is just as powerful. The third example deals with an aged relative rather than a commercial sale, but it follows exactly the same pattern.

Joinery Contractor

> "Our team only starts when you're completely happy and have agreed to and signed off on the plans and price. We achieve this by sending out a team of two people – a layout designer and an engineer. Between the three of you, and using our design software on their tablets, you'll agree on a design for the new deck for your garden that will supply your TakeAways. We'll confirm a fixed price there and then. One third is payable up front.
>
> We always deliver all the equipment and material the day before, to ensure nothing is missed. While the deck is being built, our quality manager visits once a day to check in with you. As the job nears completion, the manager will bring in the original plan to ensure it's as you agreed and check whether you want any variations.

Once your new deck is complete, you pay the next third of your investment. That's when you can start enjoying the time you're saving by not cutting the grass, relish the fact that you won't need to treat the wood for another five years, and relax knowing that your children are safe [all TakeAways that you'd discovered while talking with your buyer].

The third instalment is due one month after completion. We'll visit again (with your agreement) to take another look at our work after six months."

> Write down the Buyer's Issues and Objections that the story addressed:

New Reseller/Distributor

"We'll start the partnership with a combined planning and training session with sales, marketing, delivery and customer support staff from both companies.

During this session, we'll look in detail at what you as a company want to take away from the partnership and how we can supply it. We'll then work through what we as a supplier need from you as a distribution channel. After that, we'll break into working groups to craft an operating agreement which will become part of our contract – particularly in the area of technical presales.

Once the legal agreement is agreed on and signed, we'll train all of your sales, presales, delivery, and support staff and set up a three month mentoring programme to ensure that the first sales they make are both profitable and a useful learning experience.

Once we have an operation that's generating revenue, we'll have biweekly sales calls for the first three months, built around our Channel CRM system. We'll then transition to your normal monthly sales meetings. At all times, we'll both have an escalation procedure to bring management into any situation, but only when it's necessary, and only with all the correct information."

> Issues and objections that the story dealt with:

Elderly Relative moving into a Nursing Home

> "You'll start by meeting with the director of the home and their director of health. Together, we'll create a tailored care plan for you – particularly to deal with all the medical issues you mentioned. At the end of the meeting, you can agree to the next stage or walk away.
>
> If you're happy with that, you, I, and your brother will sit down and take a good look at what we should do with your house, your car, and your investments to make sure that you're absolutely confident that you can afford it – and you'll get the lifestyle you want. If you're not happy with the result, we'll look for somewhere more affordable.
>
> If you do decide to move in, we'll take on the whole worry and effort of selling your place and will put it on the market after you're happily settled into the home.
>
> Once you get there, you'll not have to worry about your garden – you'll be able to enjoy theirs. You'll also be able to meet a lot more people than you do today – stuck out in the middle of nowhere. Most of all, you'll feel much better fed than you're managing today."

> Issues and objections that the story dealt with:

Software Solution

> "We deliver this capability through a series of four clearly documented steps. We first send in two business consultants who carry out a three day study to scope the work needed to deliver

what you need and the cost of doing it. Because of the need to integrate with your mainframe, this will be broken down into core product and custom development.

In the next step, we install a core standard system, and use this to train your staff in using it over a period of two to three weeks. We'll also use this as a time to confirm the enhancements which you'd like to see reviewed by the actual end users. Our rapid prototyping system will allow us to actually confirm the changes with these end users.

There's then a short pause while we convert the prototypes into production quality code and then apply them to the already installed system – usually just an overnight job.

We then parallel run and carry out system and operator testing. It's then a joint decision to cut over – and only when both parties are in agreement."

Issues and objections that the story dealt with:

The 'Convincer Question'

The Delivery Narrative does many things to relax the buyer and give them permission to make the change in their belief that is needed to give you an order or decision. But for me, the most useful part of the Delivery Narrative is the ability to finish with that all important question:

"What (specifically) would it take to convince you that's all possible?"

It's my experience that, if you address all the concerns the buyer has raised, and your story is compelling and accurate, you'll have Built a Willing Buyer and get a very positive response. This might range from:

"I don't need to hear or see anything else. I can make the decision myself, let me explain how we issue a Purchase Order."

to

> *"That's all good to hear, but you'll need to demonstrate what you say to the engineering department, and go through the ROI with the finance director."*

The second might appear a little disappointing, but you should be pleased – you have created a well-motivated 'buying coach' who will help you build a Buying Plan.

A Little Help from your Friends…

Anything that involves preparing for complexity or exposure needs input from your subject matter experts. That's where you need to arrange a *Delivery Narrative Meeting*.

Who are these experts? Well (surprise, surprise), they're the people involved in real day-to-day delivery – the folk who actually do the work. They're your project managers and trainers, your developers, deliverers, and artisans – even the people in the finance back office. They're the support people who can tell you what goes wrong and what goes right in real life. They might also be your partners or subcontractors who supply part of the solution. The list is long – so make use of all their talent, stories, and experience.

If you're too small an operation, or on your own, then put on the different hats of these people and do a little role playing. The essential aim is to use *their safe professional words* rather than make them up yourself. Not only does this detail give your assertions more credibility, but, more importantly, it *limits the risk of you overcommitting* yourself or your company. It's not a script – it's sequences of untainted words that have the greatest chance of getting through your buyer's filters without deletion, distortion, or generalisation.

The best way to start a Delivery Narrative Meeting is to brainstorm the real life problems you solve and how your offering addresses them. Once you have the issues, let the team create the exact words needed to describe the delivery. When that's all been done, add the last piece to the puzzle – the *connection between the delivery sequence and the desired TakeAway(s)*. That final, key, connection to the TIRES may happen immediately or it might take a long time. Either way, the Delivery Narrative must be very explicit in making that last link between the features and functions your experts deliver and the actual TakeAways.

Do this for each Buyer/Offering combination you're going to encounter and agree on standard words for the Delivery Narrative for each of them. I've even had Delivery Narratives put into a smart document that I could give to the buyer.

The character of your Narrative, and the way you deliver it, will depend on your own personality, skills, and experience. There is no right way – except to be yourself. Some people have a dry delivery, some are theatrical – it absolutely doesn't matter where you are on the spectrum. As long as your experts have given you good information, everything in your story will be accurate – and compelling.

Delivery Narratives – a Health Warning

You've connected well with your buyer. You've smoothly guided the conversation around all the possible TakeAways you might deliver and determined which ones they truly need. You may even have elicited how much they're prepared to pay to get those TakeAways. You're feeling really confident and you ask whether that the list you've drawn out is correct. When they agree that's what they're really looking for, you can say confidently:

> **"Well that's great, because it's exactly what we do."**

At that point, you're a long way down the road to building a Willing Buyer. But this is one of your most exposed moments in any influence meeting. At that moment, *they* want to buy whatever it is you're offering and *you're* confident you can supply it. However, unlike an old-school spray and pray of features and functions, your buyer is probably feeling a bit short on detail.

So here's the problem – they're full of questions about the decision they're enthusiastic to make – but do you have all the information? If you don't have a well-crafted Delivery Narrative, two thing can happen. Option One is that you're forced to say:

> *"I'll get my installer/lawyer/trainer/techie to talk to you in detail."*

Option Two is that you know enough yourself to make it up as you go along.

So why are both options so hazardous?

The Risk from Option One

Waiting to talk to your expert risks a big reduction in intent in your buyer. The art of convincing is to make the buying decision stick. Most buyers need some sort of information as part of their Convincer Strategy – even the instant Convincer in chapter 3 needs a little meat on the bone – and they need it *now*. If you can deliver a strong, accurate, and compelling Delivery Narrative, this exposure is minimised. Follow that up with the Convincers the buyer needs and you're in really good shape.

The Risk from Option Two

Flying by the seat of your pants is exciting but even if you know your subject well, you're exposed to errors and guesses that can come back and haunt you many years later. The moment you start speaking, rather than asking questions about them, your buyer is likely to remember every word you say. Some will even see it as an early stage in the contractual process. This is risky if:

- The solution delivery is complex (e.g. analysis, configuration, training, etc.).
- It's hard to describe (e.g. a business solution behind complex technology).
- Significant services are needed (e.g. customisation or development).
- Partners are involved (e.g. needs third party components).

Delivery Narratives Tips

The Delivery Narrative is a classic example of 'Prepare Once, Use Many Times'. Put in some work up front (and use your colleagues) and you have yet another reason to relax and be creative – you know what to say, it's proven, and it's risk-free.

If you have a simple offering with a clean timeline and only a few events between getting the order and a complete delivery of TakeAways, you can create a delivery narrative for yourself. You can probably also shorten and lengthen it according to clues in the buyer's response.

There's no reason why your Delivery Narrative shouldn't include pictures, diagrams, datasheets, metaphors, case studies, and even quotes from users. The secret, as with any good story teller, is to react to your audience's reactions.

Use your visual acuity to spot when they're interested and want more, but be sure to spot when their Convincer strategy is full and *stop talking*. And, of course, always answer their questions – this will give you more access to their Model of the World and what their detailed concerns are.

The most important acuity you must have is how much capacity they have for the narrative. If they're an *immediate Convincer*, then their attention span may be short. If they need *chunked down* information to be convinced, you need some of this at hand.

Sometimes you'll do such a good job on their strategy that they don't want the detail you want to give them – so just shut up! Start discussing the Buying Plan with them.

COMMIT KEY FOUR – WHERE'S THE MONEY?

Someone who is a Willing Buyer but can't justify spending the money is a sad sight.

Whether the cost justification is for them, their partner, their board or their manager, *it's your job to help them create it*. Why should you expect them to have the skill to justify investing in your idea, product, service, or vision? *That's your job.*

The Return On Investment (ROI) Framework is one of the most convincing tools you can put in your commercial kit bag. But it's shocking how few sales people, entrepreneurs, or account managers can really master it. Put a little time and effort in beforehand and you'll replace fear and anxiety with much earlier, easier success. You'll also minimise the danger of making off the cuff pricing commitments that come back later to bite you and your profits.

Best of all, it can be introduced to your buyer *under your control* – and really *early in the process*. Introducing money early on will positively preframe all subsequent discussions of price. If, right from the beginning, you're discussing the *value of the investment* to them, not simply *telling them the cost*, the decision will always be seen in a more positive light, and building a Willing Buyer will be that much easier.

You need to prepare one ROI Framework associated for each Buyer/Offering pair. You must also make it your business to know precisely how the figures in the Frameworks change as you and the buyer move from discussing one offering to another.

An ROI Framework can be used casually, or as the basis for a highly structured workshop. It can be a complete document that your buyer can use, or some simple ideas you can discuss with them. If you're a natural numbers person who has no fear of dealing with these issues, it can add confidence to the team around you and add a strongly convincing power to your statements.

If you have Case Studies or Use Cases, the figures in them must be 100% built on those shown in your ROI Frameworks.

If there are gaps or assumptions in the Framework, that need not be a problem. State them explicitly and try to secure a management commitment from your own (selling) company to create or underwrite them for the buyer.

The tools in your ROI Framework

There are four simple tools with which you can create an ROI Framework. They are:

- The Use Case or Case Study.
- The Cartesian Challenge Quadrant.
- The Model Spreadsheet.
- An explicit list of variables and fixtures.

As with the Delivery Narrative, *use the great knowledge and experience of your experts*. They'll enjoy contributing and will automatically become a supportive resource you can use later.

Use Cases and Case Studies

I try to always have an ROI Framework attached to each of my Case Studies. But if you're a start-up, or moving into a new market, you'll be forced to create a Use Case with an ROI. Preparing the ROI Framework is another good occasion (as with the TakeAway Analysis in chapter 7) to bring in an industry expert, or someone in your company who's worked in that business. This will help you put credible flesh on to the story – words *and* numbers.

The main difference between a run-of-the-mill Case Study or Use Case and the one in the ROI Framework is that the case in the Framework goes into much greater detail about the business model. The whole purpose of the ROI Framework is to focus strongly on each the TIRES and how they each generate a financial advantage – not to tell the function and features of how the problem was solved.

The Cartesian Challenge

TakeAways only create a Desire to Buy. In most cases, this isn't enough – we need to add a financial justification to actually complete the transaction.

For example – I may be completely convinced that if I replaced my car, I would arrive sooner, my stress would be less, and I would be happier. These all pass the TIRES check – which is great. But they're not, on their own, going to make me take the final decision to buy a new car. It's *the financial benefits* of improved fuel consumption or reduced repair costs that will tip me into signing that contract.

The Cartesian Quadrant was invented by the French philosopher and mathematician René Descartes. He used it as a linguistic tool in debates – in TSB it becomes your principal tool for converting a buyer's TakeAways into financial benefits. It's extremely simple, but powerful.

Again, it becomes particularly powerful if you can bring in domain experts to extend your vision and drive out extra opportunities. You can do all this hard work *before* you connect with your buyer. This will allow you to concentrate on eliciting their TakeAways, and confidently presenting them with accurate numbers.

Cartesian Example
Let's say that you've engaged with your buyer, and they've agreed that *"saving time in loading our transport vans"* (which your offering delivers) would be a useful TakeAway. But they haven't mentioned what the precise financial benefits of *saving time in loading the delivery vans*

might be. Are there actually any benefits at all? Would the reduced time generate more money for them? Would the time that was saved *actually* reduce any costs?

Used properly, this can set the Frame for the conversation *right up front* to make the downstream discussion about price far easier to deal with. The basis for it is the *Cartesian Quadrant* in Figure 33.

Converse ~AB **What <u>wouldn't</u> happen if you <u>did</u>?** *....and what else?*	Theorem AB **What <u>would</u> happen if you <u>did</u>?** *....and what else?*
What <u>wouldn't</u> happen if you <u>didn't</u>? *....and what else?* ~A~B Non-Mirror Image Reverse	**What <u>would</u> happen if you <u>didn't</u>?** *....and what else?* A~B Inverse

With thanks to French philosopher, René Descartes 1596-1650

Figure 33

So let's use it on our *transport vans* example. These questions come directly from the scenario described in the use case or case study:

AB Case

"So what WOULD happen to your income or expense if you DID save time in loading your transport vans?" (Note the precise use of your buyer's words).

They might answer *"I could stop turning away business I can't handle and make more money"* ... or they might say *"Nothing really."*

A~B Case

"So what WOULD happen to your Income or expense if you DID NOT reduce the time taken?"

Their answer might be *"I'd have to pay for more loaders and more vans to deal with the growth of my business"* ... or they might say *"Nothing really"*.

~A~B Case

"So what WOULD NOT happen to your income or expense if you DID NOT reduce the time?"

They might answer *"I wouldn't be able to use the loaders for sorting, and have to pay for more sorters"* ... or they might say *"Nothing really"*.

~AB Case

"So what WOULD NOT happen to your income or expense if you DID reduce the time taken?"

They might answer *"I'd pay less overtime to clear the backlog on busy days"* ... or they might say *"Nothing really"*.

This complete conversation should take place (with a colleague) *before engaging* with a buyer – and the results put into whatever ROI Framework suits your offering best. But once you've mastered the technique, it can actually be used *with the buyer* – in fact, the ideal is to do both. This allows the industry figures you and your colleague used to be powerfully combined with the buyer's real numbers.

ROI Documents

The results of this analysis (minimum four challenges per TakeAway) then feed into the data collection spread sheet that is the core of the ROI Framework. This is available at *goo.gl/PX18g*.

Once you've captured the figures they can be crafted into a more 'buyer–friendly' document that reflects their Model of the World, not that of René Descartes!

The good thing about this way of generating an ROI is that you're unlikely to miss out any financial drivers because you've:

- Done an exhaustive SO WHAT TO TIRES analysis on all features and functions.

- Extended the TakeAways sideways and upwards with more challenges.
- Created a short but powerful list of Potential TakeAways.
- Run every TakeAway though the simple Cartesian Challenge Quadrant.
- Included both Income and Expenditure.

This all looks exhaustive and time-consuming. But it is actually not difficult if the process is followed. Not only that, *it only needs to be done once*, then reviewed only when the situation or numbers change.

> This approach will *always* generate the strongest possible financial case for buying whatever you offer.

One you've completed the Cartesian Challenge in your own office, you have two options. You can fill out the Framework using industry standard figures and create a use case for the expenditure. Alternatively, you can specifically leave some variables empty (e.g. hourly rates, frequency of occurrence, etc.) and leave your buyer to fill them in (preferably with you helping).

The first strategy is clean and can create a convincing case in itself. The second comes into its own if the buyer really wants to engage with you on the cost benefit. Because you've *supplied a spreadsheet Framework* for the discussion, you can often maintain a good degree of control over the process – even when you're not there. If your ROI Framework is easy to use and logical, your buyer is unlikely to make up their own from scratch. I've seldom seen a client ignore our sheet and use their own.

Permutations and Combinations

In the previous example, I've reduced the effort by combining income and expense. There's no reason why this couldn't be dealt with by *two separate* runs through the Cartesian Challenge Quadrant – the first challenging the income side four times, the second challenging the expense side four times.

This also needs to be done for each and every TakeAway. If you're preparing to engage with a buyer, you'll need to do it for every one of the potential TakeAways. If you're engaged with the buyer, then clearly you only need to run though the questioning for the TakeAways you've identified they need.

Assumptions and Exclusions List

One thing I've always found very powerful (and convincing) when creating an ROI Framework is the overt inclusion of a comprehensive list of assumptions and exclusions.

This can contain industry standard figures from your research; it can contain advice from any industry experts you've brought in to help with your preparation; it can, most powerfully of all, contain data from existing clients. If they're also referable, it's even more powerful.

Another great benefit of the assumption and exclusions list is that it's a powerful point of engagement with your buyer. Since you (or a close colleague) have created it, it's a great way of building credibility. During the conversation, why not ask them to review and comment on it? As they point out the differences their business has with norms, or the figures they use, it's all great information for you re-use.

NON-SALES VARIANTS

Personal

Most of what you need for personal (rather than commercial) influence is covered in a basic TakeAway or perhaps ABC Analysis. Once you've identified the TakeAways that are their personal Buying Drivers, the most useful 'extra' is the Delivery Narrative. People love stories and they can be a great short cut to you learning a lot.

In personal, rather than commercial influence, the financial side is significant less often to the stories more often.

Channels, Resellers, and Distributors

In channels and partnerships, the simplest idea to keep in mind is that you're looking at a two-headed monster in a distribution chain (which may be many steps between you and the actual end buyer).

The two heads need to look in two directions. Looking backwards (at you, the supplier), your partner has their own unique SWIIFM pressures. They're interested in stocking levels, support, training, finance terms, etc. This is one business model that you need to help them build.

The second head is looking at the buyer your distributor is feeding. They will be buying the distributor or reseller's offering – not yours – and you must take this into account when helping your partner with a TakeAway or Commit Analysis.

Investors, Partners and Angels

This, like the channel example, is another looking backwards situation. What is this investor going to TakeAway from investing money in your ideas? Are they getting the product, your offering, your management team's experience, your personal ability to self–manage? You must look back up the chain from *their side of the table* and understand what motivates them (hopefully after plenty of Buyer Discovery).

IN SUMMARY:
COMMIT KEYS TURN DESIRE TO BUY INTO A DECISION

We've covered a lot of detailed ground in this chapter. In the previous chapters we dealt mainly with creating and enriching TakeAways – they're the first of the four Commit Keys. In this chapter we've focussed on the final three.

We started by learning how your buyer becomes convinced that the TakeAways you claim to exist can actually be delivered. Becoming convinced is a complex and personal strategy that varies in individuals and in companies.

We then looked at mastering the three key elements that you'll be using to convince someone to take action:

- **Making the Decision Stick** – The material and activity you need to supply to maintain their Desire to Buy at a high level *even when you're not there*. It's sometimes hard to identify a person's desired Convincer Strategy and you'll need a good degree of preparation and determination. But when you get it right the decision will come so much more easily and it won't evaporate the next day.

- **The Delivery Narrative** – the detailed story of how your buyer will get to their TakeAways. Everyone *puts themselves inside a story* if they can identify their part in it. Make your story strong and believable and save yourself a lot of time, effort, and heartache later.

- **Where's the Money**? – Almost every commercial TakeAway leads to a cost benefit. Can you remember the last time you wanted to buy or do something but couldn't justify the cost to yourself? It's exactly the same on the buyer's side of the table. You need to *help them* to the greatest degree possible to maximize the justification for buying what you offer.

Together, the four Commit Keys will tip the scales of influence in your favour far more often, more easily, more predictably, and more quickly. Most importantly, you will have a massive amount of support for a 'fearless' approach to any buyer.

CHAPTER 9:
REVIEW QUESTIONS & SELF-DEVELOPMENT ASSIGNMENTS

Doing Your Commit Analysis – see Annex C for Answers

To print a copy of this section, download it directly from goo.gl/9B8EV or select it from the TSB Download Page at goo.gl/p0Ajn (password download999)

Self-Test Questions

1. What is the difference between a Commit Analysis and a TakeAway Analysis?
2. What is a Convincer Strategy? Who uses it, and when?
3. What are the three components of a Buyer's Convincer Strategy?
4. How do you detect a Buyer's Convincers? What do you do if you can't detect them?
5. What are the Four Commit Keys?
6. Where does a Case Study fit? What is it used for?
7. What is the Cartesian Challenge used for?
8. What data sources are there for any ROI?
9. What are the best data sources for *your* ROI Framework?

Self-Development Assignments

Ch 9 Assignment 1 – Your Own Convincer Strategy.

Over the next few weeks become aware of what *your* Convincer Strategy is and how it varies from situation to situation. How consistent are you when you buy clothes, make a decision at work, agree to someone else's proposal? If you can develop the acuity to observe your own strategy, that will help enormously with spotting other people's. Most important of all, become familiar with your own Convincer Channels, Modes, and Frames

Ch 9 Assignment 2 – Others' Convincer Strategies.

When you're in a meeting or going out shopping, find out about your colleague or partner's *own* buying strategy. Do they prefer to see, then ask, then experience? Or some other combination? Don't just observe (although that's the best place to start). Ask them how they made the decision, get them to run their normal strategy backwards, and see how they feel about that.

Ch 9 Assignment 3 – Where's The Money?

This assignment is in three stages. Firstly, as with the TakeAway Analysis, start with an existing offering – one that your team knows. What financial variables are already successfully used to justify a purchase? Where did those numbers come from? Are they industry standards? How provable or proven are they? This is a great basis for finding what's going to be needed for your new offering/Buyer combination.

Stage two is to invent a Buyer and document their situation and problem. You can then start making assumptions about their costs, productivity, risks, time savings, etc. This work is then a great basis for creating an imaginary Use Case around their situation. This will familiarize you with the type of spread sheet you'll need to use and the sources of data and how the calculations are made.

Stage three of the assignment is to take that Use Case, with all the figures around it, and turn it into an ROI Framework that you can use with a Buyer. Mark the solid, fixed figures (tax rates, etc.) in one colour, use another one for industry standards (with references to where they come from), use a third colour for figures where you've made assumptions (e.g. risk, productivity, etc.). Lastly come the gaps where your Willing Buyer can put *their own* real figures and confirm whether their Desire to Buy can be justified financially.

Of all the assignments in the book, this is the hardest. However, it's a critical step that only needs to be made once. As you use it in more and more situations, you'll add and subtract small variations, but you can now be confident you're not going to look foolish!

CHAPTER 10
The Best Elevator Pitch in the World

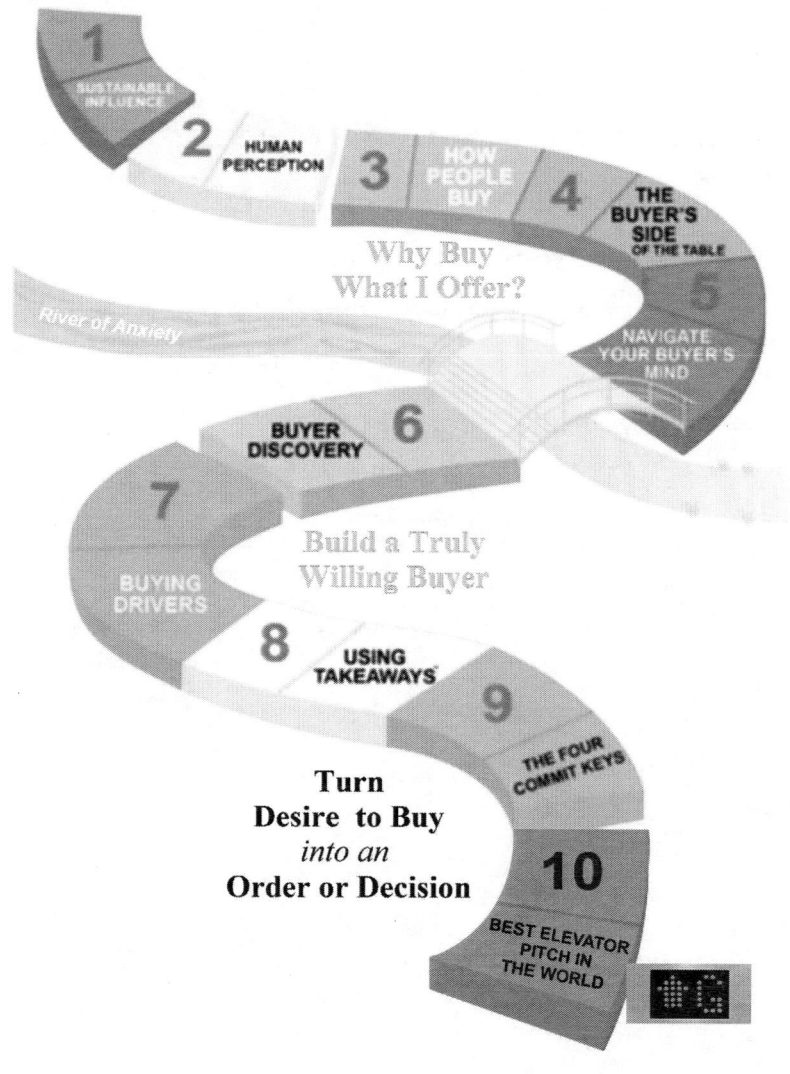

BY THE END OF THIS CHAPTER, YOU'LL UNDERSTAND ...

- The definition and only purpose of an Elevator Pitch
- How TSB supports you at a pitch meeting or Dragons' Den
- How your stories and 'The Vibe' can make such a difference
- The few different pitch structures you'll ever need
- Ways to make your pitch part of you

HOW WILL AN ELEVATOR PITCH HELP ME BUILD A WILLING BUYER?

Surely *Turning Selling into Buying* is about **NOT PITCHING** features and functions at your buyer…? So why is there a chapter with the word pitch in the title?

Well, real life is not always about nice, preframed, well-structured meetings where you have a degree of control. It's about chance encounters, delayed appointments, trade shows, and accidental networking. Sometimes it actually takes place in an elevator.

This chapter will prepare you to use that short opportunity *as profitably as possible* to:

> Qualify whether they might need what you offer.
> Arrange a follow up action by one or both of you.
>
> **– NOTHING ELSE! –**

So what's the best way to do this? Well, like everything else in TSB, it's down to a small amount of careful preparation – done once. Then when you meet *Warren Buffett* on the airport bus, you'll be able to focus on him, rather than working it out as you go along or, worse still, realising what you should have said – but fifteen minutes too late!

The final output from this chapter is really very simple – an easily remembered base for responding to chance or short-lived encounters with people you need to influence. Your offering may be an idea for a new charity, a web app for pregnant mothers, or an innovative payment system for banks. In every case your statements will now be short, accurate, and focussed on: *"What's in it for my listener to follow up later?"*

This chapter contains practical work. If you have an e-book or don't want to write in this book, download it from *goo.gl/tpGlV*

WHAT IS AN ELEVATOR PITCH?

An Elevator Pitch is:

A *short, simple* summary that
quickly and concisely *identifies your offering* to a listener so
they're attracted by the *Value Statement* in it and
can decide *What's In It For Them* ...
... and then agree on a *call to action*.

What most people forget is those four adjectives – short, simple, quick, and concise!

- **Short** = less than one minute
  – but with the skill to tune your pitch for the number of floors the elevator is taking!

- **Simple** = absolutely no account of how your product works
  – remember the 'Green Jelly' in chapter 2?

- **Quickly** = spoken clearly and confidently
  – not gushing out in a flood ... or thick with 'ums' and 'ers'.

- **Concisely** = not one extra, unnecessary word
  – that elevator will stop in moments. No Delivery Narrative!

To do this, you need to write it down, *practice it*, develop it, *practice it*, enrich it, *practice it* and integrate it into yourself – then *practice some more*. If you get this right, you won't just be collecting a business card, you'll start Building a Willing Buyer!

There are scores of web sites that can help you write Elevator Pitches. This section of TSB will take you to the next level – giving you a unique opportunity to:

- **Pr**eframe, your offering, your company and yourself really positively
  – so when you speak on the phone or meet them next, *they want to speak to you*.

- **Motivate** a desire for TIRES you can deliver – with concise Value Statements
  – possibly having also drawn out their primary Buying Driver.
- **Engage** with them and explore their needs *if they want to*
  – if they feel they have the time, need, and motivation from the first two points.
- **Agree** on your Call to Action with them
  – the *minimum* is a card and an agreement to act.

If you can completely integrate this approach into yourself, it will no longer be just a learned script – it'll be a secure base for unconsciously tuning exactly what you say according to a situation's variables:

- Did they approach you and ask you what you do? – they're open to information.
- Do you have an idea (dress, situation, manner) who they are or what they do? – CEO, techie, both?
- How many 'floors' do you have (do they seem in a hurry)? – start with the minimum and build on it.
- Is this a networking event? Are they actively seeking information – *be different*.
- What call to action do you want from this? Do you know yet?
- Do you have a 'prebuilt' Call To Action for them? Maybe you need some web/phone/email support?

Before we go further, let's clarify the difference between a 'pitch meeting' and an Elevator Pitch.

THE 'DRAGONS' DEN EFFECT'

The words Elevator Pitch used to only mean the brief encounters that I've described above. This does not seem to be true any more. The spread of TV shows such as Sony TV's Dragons' Den (see goo.gl/Vqee) that encourage and develop pitching has broadened the definition of the term. When I was pitching to investors, I always prepared for an interactive grilling from the people in front of me – unlike a brief encounter in an elevator. I call the grilling session a pitch meeting – but in many people's minds, the distinction has become blurred.

So let's be completely clear on this. If you're in a formal investor pitch meeting, base your *opening statements* on what you'll create in this chapter. Your real *Elevator Pitch* (or a variation of it) is a great start for a pitch meeting – particularly if 'The Vibe' and 'The Story' (which we'll discuss later) are strong.

But once you're past this introduction, you *must* start interacting with the investor panel or individual. Fortunately, TSB supplies *all the tools you need to do this:*

Four-See

This allows you to see *your business* clearly from the investors' side of the table. It allows you to understand the motivations and pressures on them and the stakeholders. It also helps you to see the effect that an investment would have on your customers and staff.

SWIIFM

When you do it well, the 'So What to TIRES' exercise (and the TakeAway Sequence it creates) will generate all of the TakeAways of your potential investors. This is so important to do. An investor's TIRES are going to be totally different from those of your buying customers. They may be asking detailed questions about your offering, but they're unlikely to be interested as buyers. They *will* want to see how buyable your offering is by (of course) seeing it from the buyer's side! They also need to know what the cost and risk of making it buyable might be – and thus the profit. Different from a regular buyer – but still TIRES.

Buyer Discovery

You'll get so much great information from your chapter 6 exercise. Gathering objective facts will make you fear-less and at ease with potential investors and their situation. 'Visiting their world' will give you the confidence that comes with familiarity.

Remember the Investor Newsletters that I subscribed to when we were looking for seed funding? Go and sign up for a few.

And don't forget the 'Day in the Life' exercise in chapter 6. Why not bring in some pals with investor experience to help and have a bit of fun? You may learn those few extra facts that will tilt the decision in your favour.

Cartesian Challenge

This is the most important preparation you can make for a Dragons' Den or pitch meeting. The judges (or a real investor panel) are not going to be excited by your features and functions (except perhaps as audience entertainment). Even strong TakeAways are not the end of the story.

Take every single TakeAway for your offering and carry out a full Cartesian Challenge (see Chapter 9) and I recommend doing it separately for income and expense. You'll then have the figures that they're bound to demand at your fingertips. And if you can hand them an ROI Framework sheet – that will really get their attention.

A Life in the Day of

In chapter 6, Buyer Discovery, we looked at doing a simple role play to reveal the pressures on your buyer. This is as true for a pitch meeting as for a sale.

What is each of them like? Think through a day in the lives of your panel. Check in the press or the web for an issue they're facing presently and work it through.

How did they get on the panel? What will they have been told about you and your pitch? Are they willing participants or under orders? Play out what drives them.

What keeps them up at night? – the classic question. Put your 'Life in the Day Of' players into the potential investors' shoes and see what fears or pains emerge.

Your Offering

You may be introduced as having a 'Revolutionary Paper Dispenser', but it's your full offering that the investor is interested in buying into. Look at the lists in chapter 3 and make sure you have described everything well – your products, services, partners, terms, situation, experience, etc.

There is one key difference in how your offering is seen differently by an investor and a buyer. *Your offering to an investor includes your ability to sell it.* If you're a student of TSB with practical experience in using it –

include that strongly in your description. Give them stories, case studies, and, *most importantly,* describe any sales you've already made.

Challenges

If you feel confident to answer their questions by responding with some precision questioning – then go ahead. *So What*, Chunking, the Cartesian Challenge – they all can have a place. You'll come over well, and you might just reveal some gem that only you can supply. Look in chapters 2, 3, and 9 for examples and details.

Turning Selling into Buying

When you're in front of your potential investors; when they're pitilessly grilling you, it'll always come back to sales at some point. So lean strongly on your TSB basics.

Too many potentially great businesses have run aground on the 'sales fear' – which you no longer suffer from! In fact, some entrepreneurs are scared of even saying the 'S' word. They spend far too much time on marketing plans, distribution strategies, product plans, management structures, etc., and far too little time on honest-to-goodness selling, sales activity, ROI creation, and Building Willing Buyers.

With what you've learned about *Turning Selling into Buying* (whether from this book, or in a TSB seminar or workshop), you have a crystal clear understanding of what makes people buy from you – and that attracts investors!

In summary

The Dragons' Den Effect is a great incentive for making sure you complete all the exercises in the previous chapter – and do them really well. Even if you never attend a Den event, become as well prepared for it as if it was going to happen tomorrow.

Why not even run your own Dragons' Den for practice? Get some friends and colleagues in and give it a go – you've nothing to lose and a whole lot to gain! Once you've equipped yourself to respond well to an investor grilling, your regular buyers and partners will be a lot easier to deal with!

Now let's get to what you'll use at the start of the show and in conferences, meetings, and in elevators.

THE CALL TO ACTION

It seems odd to start at the end, but this is the whole purpose of an Elevator Pitch. If you don't know precisely where you're going, you're unlikely to get there.

This is the bit that so many people get wrong. For many, a business card is enough of a trophy. Well, you're TSB trained and should expect better than that! Even if you only get a business card, you're going to process it well (see chapter 6) and follow up that same day or tomorrow. Note down everything you noticed – straight after you've met – on the card, your smartphone, or by sending a text or voicemail to yourself. You'll be grateful you did so in three days' time. Appearance, stories, location, attitude, incidents – everything.

A call to action is exactly what it says – a clear proposal to your listener to actually do something.

Sometimes it might be as simple as going to a website and registering for a webinar. Sometimes it might be an immediate appointment, or a call to an assistant. If they tell you to contact someone else in their company, then explicitly ask them to make the introduction. If they're an investor (or if it is a Den) be absolutely clear that there's an outline of a Buying Plan agreement.

The key thing is – it's *their action* you want and you need agreement on it. Your sending them some literature is not a call to action!

Your Call to Action is almost always in the form of a request. Here are some examples of reactions to an Elevator Pitch. Where there is text in [square brackets], it's optional and may change your answer – so write both. You'll know from the person, the circumstances, and their reaction, when to include it.

Read them carefully and write down what you think happened before the Call to Action was offered, who the listener is, and how you'd modify the words for your own use:

> "It sounds to me as if you could use what we deliver …
>
> … can I contact your secretary tomorrow to set up a meeting?"

> "You're clearly in a hurry at the moment…
>
> … [if you're interested in what we offer] may I phone you tomorrow?"

> "You're clearly actively looking for what we offer …
>
> … should we talk here and now, or arrange to meet for lunch?"

> "It sounds like this isn't your issue [department]…
>
> … could you put me in touch with the right person [and introduce us] please?"

> "You sound interested in being a part of this …
>
> … may I email you a membership form and information pack tomorrow?"

> *"It doesn't look like we offer anything that your company can use today...*
>
> *Option A: ... may I put you on our mailing list?*
>
> *Option B: ... could you put me in touch with anyone else who needs what we offer?"*

You should be happy with any of these results. Even the qualifying out in the final example is almost as useful as finding a need. At least it happened before you've wasted any of your (or their) time!

WHAT AN ELEVATOR PITCH IS NOT

In chapter 4 we looked in detail at how a decision looks from the buyer's side of the table. Now take that SECOND POSITION insight and recognise how the person you're talking to filters your pitch. One thing's for sure – that person has something on their mind besides you.

How would you like to hear yourself if you were them?

You've got perhaps 30-90 seconds in which to achieve:

- A memorable, positive image of yourself.
- A memorable imprint of what you sell/do.
- Their judgment whether it is of interest/use to them.
- A tangible connection (preferably a meeting time, usually contact details).

Rule 1: No Selling
It's not an opportunity to sell in the old school way of pitching feature, functions and benefits. They don't have the time – you'll just bore them. Think of their SWIIFM.

Rule 2: No Questioning

It's not an opportunity to engage the other person in Precision Questioning. If (as in the third example above) they're motivated to talk, then go for it – but that's the exception.

Rule 3: They're Not Interested (yet)

They're not interested in:

- You, your background, or genius – it's what you can offer to THEM.
- Your company details – it's what it can deliver to THEM.
- How clever your stuff is – it's what THEY can TakeAway from using it.
- Lists of features and functions – it's what makes THEM tune out.

Rule 4: Rejection is Not About You

If the response to a good Elevator Pitch (and it will be a good one) is them saying they're not interested, then that's OK. They probably *don't* need what you offer.

Being told "I'm not interested" does not mean you're a bad person.

Don't take dismissal of your title, experience, or qualifications to heart – they're not buying you, so don't take it personally. It actually frees you up to meet someone who does need what you offer.

When they say *'So What do you do?'*
they really mean:
'So What can you do for me?'

Rule 5: Keep It Simple

My rule is always *"Would my mum understand this?"* (she was smart but not technical). This warning is not just about jargon – also keep the story linear and simple. Whenever possible use accessible metaphors and similes e.g. *"In the same way as..."*; *"Just like...."*; *"Imagine ... but available to everyone"*.

STRUCTURE & INPUTS

The template that we use on our TSB Workshops and Seminars is shown in Figure 34. Let's look at its basic structure and then learn how you can extend and strengthen it. All the way through, your key should be to *use familiar language*. Don't use jargon, or new phrases you've carefully invented. You'll lose their attention the moment they don't understand what you're saying.

If there are cultural or language reasons to modify your Elevator Pitch, then do so. What may immediately grab the ear of a Canadian Bond Trader may not be so accessible to a South African Mining Engineer – even if, in reality, they have exactly the same need.

Go into 2nd position, become your Audience,
and use the words that you hear in their head.

So let's look, item by item, at the template for your Elevator Pitch in Figure 34:

Elevator Pitch Structure

Offering:	Audience:
[Preframe Story or Metaphor] For (*Target Buyer*) who (*Statement of Need or Opportunity*), our (*Offering Title*) is a (<u>Known</u> *product/service category*) that (*Differentiating adjective/phrase*)	
[Optional Story or Metaphor] (*Our customers*) take away (*Value Proposition List*) [optional ROI example]	
{Unlike (*Primary competitive alternative*), our offering (*Statement[s] of primary differentiation*)}.	

Figure 34

Offering

You may well have several different offerings. You might wear several different hats. I am a writer, a speaker, a trainer, and a management consultant. I have a different Elevator Pitch for each, as well as a consolidated (Chunked Up) version which pulls them all together. See chapter 3 for more on offerings.

Create, memorise, and practice all yours – and store them on your smartphone, too!

> List the offering for which you're going to build an Elevator Pitch:

Audience

Your audience is very important to your Elevator Pitch. You must tune in to your listener in the same way as any performer reacts to their audience.

The Elevator Pitch that you give to the person beside you at the salad bar at an investor event is going to have one style. The one you give to someone you meet at a dinner party will have another. If the person next to you at dinner turns out to be an investor, leave the table and either go into work mode for a time or (much better) arrange to meet for breakfast the next day.

More practically, if you're at an electronic engineering conference in Istanbul, your likelihood of meeting a 'heavy techie' is much greater than at an accounting conference in Berlin. It only takes moments to review your Elevator Pitch (which is now, of course, on your mobile device) to reap rewards when you enter a new situation.

Over time, you can build up your 'suite' of tested Elevator Pitches to dip into.

> List the possible Buyer audiences (including generic) for your Elevator Pitch:

The Setup Story

'The Setup Story' is ideally two or three sentences and it's a powerful preframe for the rest of your pitch. (See chapter 5 for more on Frames, reframes, and preframes).

Everyone listens to stories, even two or three sentence ones. Stories unfailingly create feelings in the listener as they plug in their own experiences. If they can see themselves in the situation you're describing, it's a human trait to step into the story. But if you can see they don't identify with it, it's an early indicator to you that they may not need your services – or maybe it's just a rubbish story!

To best create the State you want, you must introduce one of the Take-Aways that person might need into your story. A story about numbers that creates useful anxiety in an accountant may not produce the same powerful feelings in a professional athlete. A story about sales forecasting may cause a strong reaction in a sales director, but do nothing for an artist. That's why you need to learn to tune your setup story for different situations. In reality, you'll end up with a suite of different stories.

You should take every opportunity to practice your setup story and develop it well – it can become the most effective part of your Elevator Pitch. If you try to make it up as you go along, you're going to ramble and lose them. If you need expert help, get in touch with Steve Lowell at www.lowellworkshops.com – he's great at it.

Amongst much else, Steve has acted in some of my films (see goo.gl/cf7hd) and has taught me some simple verbal cues for Setup Stories that immediately grip people.

The first cue is '**You know how**....' and then the story. Here are some examples:

> "You know how doing – your taxes creeps up on you suddenly every year... ...well our unique accounting service removes that anxiety – forever."

> "You know how – your sales people sweat when you ask them for a forecast ... ...well my workshop replaces that anxiety with calm accuracy."

> *"You know how – frustrating it can be, waiting for accident damage repairs... ...well our coverage provides an identical vehicle – all through the work."*
>
> *"You know how – yummy, yet expensive, locally made birthday cakes are? Well now you can design a cake online, and get it the next day – at rock bottom prices."*

The second cue is '**Most people...**' and then the story. Here are some examples:

> *"Most people think riding a motorbike is dangerous, but could save them money... ... well our course teaches anyone to save money and enjoy riding safely."*
>
> *"Most people put sales into a box marked 'too difficult' and won't go near it... ...our seminars train anyone to sell, to sell well – and enjoy doing it."*
>
> *"Most people think that property development is expensive and difficult... ...our course doesn't just teach the skills – it connects you with real investors."*
>
> *"Most people think business data stored reliably in 'the Cloud' is expensive... ... our service is half the price of competitors and backed by global insurance."*

Write two opening statements for each of your offerings (focus on creating a strong State):

Target Buyer

If you've got a successful, established business, this will be your biggest buyer group. If you're just starting out, moving into a new geography or have a new offering, you have to make a clear decision. Saying *"everyone can benefit from our training"* is not a productive start. Examples of Buyer Groups might be:

'Working Mothers', 'Trainee Welders', 'Homeworkers', 'Equity Traders', 'Schoolgirls', 'Middle Managers'

Write the Target Buyers for your offering here:

Sort them by order of profitability; then by ease of sale:

Statement of Need or Opportunity

This is their Buying Driver, and *always contains* TIRES. It will be echoed (usually phrased differently) in the **TakeAway** section later in the Elevator Pitch. Examples are:

> *"taking too long to close deals", "an unprofitable distributor", "want to make more money", "are anxious about losing their data", "have stopped enjoying their job", "need to reduce their electricity bill"*

Write down the TIRES and TIRE Compounds in the story examples shown above: (e.g. End of Year Tax Anxiety = T/S)

> Now write down the Need or Opportunity that your offering satisfies:

Title of Your Offering

This is your label … your marker. If there is a product behind your offering, it may well not be the product name. This is your primary identifier – and when you get the business, maybe even what goes on the purchase order.

If you don't have one yet, you need to create it. It should have some sort of emotional impact on your audience and leave a lasting impression or emotional impact. It doesn't have to explain exactly what your offering does, just the State it creates.

'*My consultancy services*' is not a memorable offering.

'*My training software*' is only a little better.

Here are some examples that work at both a descriptive and an emotional level:

- 'Fearless Selling Workshop'
- 'Magical Kitchen Makeovers'
- 'Get-U-Home'
- 'Data Destructor'
- 'Coupon-Power'

> Put the Title(s) of your offering(s) here:

Known Product Category

It doesn't matter how cool and unique you believe your offering is – your listener must be able to classify it almost instantly. If they can't, it'll be hard for them to understand it. So don't be tempted to make up some zany category they've never heard of – your chance to differentiate will come in a moment. Here are some examples. *"We deliver a ...*

- *... four day sales influence class ..."*
- *... kitchen refurbishment team ..."*
- *... car breakdown service ..."*
- *... data security service ..."*
- *... smart discount card ... "*

Put your Product Category(s) here:

Why buy from me?

This is where you can show off to your listener. Your offering now has a name, they know where it fits – why should they buy it? Here are some examples:

... that focuses on building a Willing Buyer – not forcing a sale."

... that revamps your kitchen without your family having to move out."

... that takes you home first – then takes your car where you want it fixed."

... that cleans sensitive data from your computers – completely under your control."

... that gets you a discount in any and every major store in the country."

What can you say about your offering?

Optional Story or Metaphor

This is where you can hammer home your TakeAways. Here's an example of each – the second one also explicitly including an ROI statement:

> "In the same way as a failing athlete gets a new coach and restarts with a clean sheet of paper, a poorly performing sales rep can TakeAway a new, energised approach and a raft of profitable new skills."

> "A major corporation installed our middleware and eliminated a complete level of IT support. This reduced their annual cost by 20% and paid for itself within six months."

Create a TakeAway Metaphor and a ROI Metaphor pair
(for your best offering/Buyer pair):

Kick your competitor

This is your differentiator – where you can explicitly compare and contrast yourself with your competition – and remember that 'not doing anything' might be competition, so you need to counter that as well. Here are three very different examples, each built around the TIRES you deliver:

> "Unlike outsourcing operations that are completely offshore, our team share offices with yours, eliminating overhead and minimising the chance of expensive errors."

> "Where conventional sales training just teaches 'trick and tips', our workshops rebuild team profitability from the ground up, blending the experience of the veterans with the energy of new hires."

> "Consultants write reports – we actually finish the job and fix what's broken."

> Make a statement here about how you're unlike your competition (including your buyer's alternative of 'doing nothing'):

The Vibe

Anyone can deliver an Elevator Pitch just by reading it – and if your listener is listening, you'll get some sort of reaction. But in real life you're competing with everything else in their head. So give yourself a much better chance of displacing that other stuff with The Vibe.

The Vibe is the personal stamp that you put onto your Elevator Pitch. It doesn't have to be crazy, self-confident, wacky, or funny. We see those things on TV shows but many of us feel it's not really in us. It's a golden rule to be yourself in these situations.

But whatever it is that you're influencing other people to buy, you need to have, or build, a passionate belief in it. If it's your own idea – let it show. If it's a cause you feel strongly about – let them see it. If there's no passion or belief, maybe you're not doing the right thing.

If you believe, but find the passion hard to generate, hang around people who are enthusiastic about it – sales people, R&D, product managers, or even happy customers.

As long as it's underpinned by a strong Value Statement, your Vibe can have many characters. It might be crazy (for a new social media app), concerned (for a local charity), serious (for legal consultancy), brainy (for a new financial service), or sad (for a crisis charity).

As long as it's genuine, and if you have the confidence to do it, why not amplify your Vibe just a little by:

- Giving out an intriguing sample (with contact details on it).
- Include it as part of a powerful or amusing metaphor or story.

- Use the back of your business card as a prop – pictures, facts, etc.,
- Ask an unexpected, attention getting question.

   "So What colour are your socks?"
   "Have you ever exploded with happiness?"

…then use the response as a lead into *your* story.

What Vibe fits your character and your offering?

What are you now going to change to display it?

YOUR PITCH AND SOME EXAMPLES

Now you take the information you've collected, build yourself some Elevator Pitches, and then go out and practice them – every day for a month!

You can download a blank A4 Elevator Pitch from goo.gl/yif0G, or a Letter format one from goo.gl/ZA8Ps. Both are in blank or greyed out format. Or you can simply copy Figures 35 or 36.

Elevator Pitch Structure

Offering:	Audience:

[Preframe Story or Metaphor]

For (*Target Buyer*)

who (*Statement of Need or Opportunity*),

our (*Offering Title*)

is a (*Known product/service category*)

that (*Differentiating adjective/phrase*)

[Optional Story or Metaphor]
(*Our customers*) **take away** (*Value Proposition List*)
[optional ROI example]

{**Unlike** (*Primary competitive alternative*),

our offering (*Statement[s] of primary differentiation*)}.

Figure 35

My Elevator Pitch

Offering:	Audience:

Structure:

For

who

our

is a

that

Metaphor
Our customers take away
ROI example

Unlike
our offering

Figure 36

Example Elevator Pitches

Example 1

TSB Workshop Elevator Pitch

Offer: Fearless Selling® Workshop	**Audience:** Business Person

Example:

For <u>teams & individuals</u> who <u>need to sell complex solutions more effectively,</u>
our <u>Fearless Selling Workshop</u> is a <u>Sales Influence Training</u>
that <u>focusses on Creating a Willing Buyer, not pressuring a sale.</u>

In the same way that Tiger Woods had to rebuild his game from scratch, our students <u>gain brand new confidence & skills.....delivering **more profitable** business **sooner** - and more **easily** & **predictably**</u> - *some being 50% more productive*

Unlike <u>normal sales training,</u> that swamps students with detail,
we <u>build a new approach from the ground up – using a person's existing talent, [so the approach can be used by everyone - not just by sales]</u>

Figure 37

Figure 39 is a pitch for our sales training. It is more detailed as you progress down the sheet. The factual opening statement is enriched as time in the elevator progresses.

Example 2

Shaving Gel Elevator Pitch

Offer: Lady Shaving Gel	**Audience:** Retail Buyer
	(NOTE: Nick used a very different pitch on his Wholesale Distributor)

Compelling Opening Story Example:
"I'm sure you all agree shaving is one of those annoying things people have to do every day? What I've done has revolutionized that – by transforming 'shaving cream' into a soft 'gel bar' that makes shaving cleaner, quicker and easier than it is today...
Traditional shaving cream was designed for men to shave their face in front of a mirror. My product is designed for women to shave their bodies in or out of the shower – let me show you how it works..."

For <u>women</u> who <u>need to shave their legs in or out of the shower – and quickly,</u> our <u>Vanilla Shower Time</u> is an <u>environmental–friendly shave lube</u> that <u>combines a sensual experience with 100% hair removal.</u>

Unlike <u>costly lubricated blades,</u> that have been proven to be ineffective, Vanilla Ahower Time <u>is cheaper, reaches right to the roots and comes in a travel–friendly pack</u>

(Used by Nick May, CEO of <u>remay.com</u> to become Student Entrepreneur National Champion)

Figure 38

Figure 40 shows a female shaving product with a strong opening narrative.

WHY AN ELEVATOR PITCH 'SUITE'?

As I mentioned at the start, the term Elevator Pitch is now used by many more people than before. For this reason, you need to build a 'suite' of Elevator Pitches that will allow you to deliver a succinct, well-crafted answer in different situations.

You must use whichever suits the moment – sometimes you have the luxury of a 100 floor journey with a well identified buyer; at other times you have a few moments between floors talking to a complete stranger.

Engaging and asking questions is still the primary way in TSB, but sometimes you just have to be able to respond to *"Give me your pitch."*

Everyday Pitches

Start with the basics you've just learned – the simplest, best defined offering you have – to your most understood Buyer Group. Then vary it for different individuals in that same group – finance, techies, end users, administrators. Notice how their TakeAways – and thus the Elevator Pitch you'd give them – change.

Next, use different buyers with the same offering. These will move the TakeAways in a different direction – perhaps more driven by saving time than making money. This may need a different setup story or ROI. Finally, take another offering (or create one) and apply it to the first group and so on.

Really master your Everyday Elevator Pitches so you know you really could do it with Warren Buffet or a customer's receptionist (and everyone in between).

Dinner Parties

Try it in any social occasion where work and business are not the focus. Maybe at your canoe club or the local church – anywhere that someone might say *"So What do you do?"* This is not the time or place to embarrass your host by giving a full pitch, but you need to work up a short, but equally accurate version. It's polite and who knows, you might be sitting beside Warren Buffet's cousin (**HINT:** Exchange cards!).

Networking Events

The key difference here is that everyone, like you, is on the hunt. There's a different tone, and the "So what can you do for me?" is more open and two-way. The secret of success is to be *genuinely interested* in what everyone else does. Start by asking questions about them, drill down, learn new stuff – don't start by selling yourself.

This has another great advantage, since everyone at the event is motivated to ask you for your pitch. When they do, you can now pick the version that's most appropriate for what they've just told you about *their situation*. It's a great place to practice all the different versions in your suite.

Formal Pitches

These can be at a customer sales meeting, to potential investors or partners, or perhaps even in-house training for new employees. The content should be the same – after all, it's presumably as sharp as you can make it. You will probably have time to Chunk Down just a little, but no pitch should be complex.

As with any other presentation, you should tell stories. Only use *a few slides* to illustrate or summarise the message. Never put the slide up and simply read it out!

Investor Pitches are a particular subset of these. They're not strictly Elevator Pitches, but the same rules apply – see it from SECOND POSITION. Do they want a cool, fast selling product or an expert management team that's in it for the long haul? Do they want international channel experience or a great techie team – you need to find out.

Who should know and Use your Elevator Pitch Suite?

The Elevator Pitch Suite should be shared and used by every person in your team or company. If it's simple enough for my mum to understand *and* the CEO of your company gets it, then it must be a universal currency.

If customers, potential customers, partners, or industry analysts connect with anyone in your company, they should get broadly the same answer. If they question further, the person they're talking to (be they on the front desk or the head of finance) should be able to answer at the next level. If each person is left to make it up on their own, the results will be patchy at best and, at worst, damaging.

How you spread your suite of Elevator Pitches and keep them up to date is up to you. Here are some good places I've seen used:

- Posted on the wall in the canteen – *much more useful than* a mission statement!
- As the last page in the employee newsletter (different variants each month).
- In every new joiner welcome package.
- As a series of documents in the staff intranet.
- On the company website.

The Fisherman's Tale

Stefan had been travelling around Frankfurt for weeks. He'd been looking for investors for the start-up that he and his team had worked on so hard. But it was a tough market. Every meeting had gone well – they were good at their pitches. But no offers or investment term sheets had come their way yet. He was tired and looking forward to a weekend's fishing with his son.

As usual, they started with a very clear and concise presentation of what their company offered, their potential buyers, their marketing plan and some impressive cash flow projections. It was a pitch that he'd heard his colleagues do many times over the past few weeks and Stefan's weary mind drifted to the weekend and the relaxing time he'd have swapping fishing stories – an art form he and his son were masters of.

Then suddenly, it was his turn to talk – and his mind stayed in the same mode. Although he was supposed to focus on describing the management team and their distribution partnerships, he found himself weaving the team's story. He talked about how they had got together, he described how some of the battles they'd won in their existing business.

Most importantly of all, he told the story of when they'd been with a customer who had a need that couldn't be met and how, over a cup of tea afterwards, they'd realised what a great opportunity it was. He finished by transmitting the excitement of their existing customers when he'd later exposed them to this new idea.

The hard-nosed investors on the other side of the table were as gripped as Stefan's son by his well-told story. Before they knew it, they had put themselves into his story and travelled back to when they'd had their own businesses. They found themselves being convinced of the possibility of the story.

It wasn't a slam-dunk, and there were detailed plans and cash flow projections to be discussed, but Stefan and his team got their investment term sheet.

IN SUMMARY:
ELEVATOR PITCHES DON'T SELL – THEY ENGAGE

This chapter is easily summed up – remember to:

- Hear yourself from the buyer's side – what would you like to hear if you were them?
- Help them identify with your offering and know its TakeAways – not the details.
- Agree on a Call to Action (or qualify out) – but don't sell.
- In a Den or a pitch meeting– be totally fear-less! You have so many skills now.

So what should you do now?

First, download and print out the Elevator Pitch Sheets.

Then, using your imagination and your TakeAway Analysis, fill in the gaps.

The go out and practice, practice, practice – with friends, colleagues, business partners, and family (but warn them first!).

If you find some great metaphors or stories, share them on the TSB Community page.

BUT MOST OF ALL....

Never forget the power of a story –
it can connect you instantly with your buyer.

CHAPTER 10:
REVIEW QUESTIONS & SELF-DEVELOPMENT ASSIGNMENTS

The Best Elevator Pitch in the World – see Annex C for Answers

To print a copy of this section, download it directly from goo.gl/Fawg0 or select it from the TSB Download Page at goo.gl/p0Ajn.

Self-Test Questions

1   What are the two desired outcomes from an Elevator Pitch?
2   How does an Investor Panel or Dragon's Den differ from an Elevator Pitch?
3   List four productive calls to action you could use.
4   What might you *already* know about your Buyer before you open your mouth? How might you have you learned it?
5   Write yourself at least one 'setup story.' Do several if you're likely to come across *identifiably different* Buyers for whom you can tune your story.
6   What is the Known Category of your Offering? Is it immediately identifiable or do you need to explain it? Did you make it up or is it universally known?
7   Who are your competitors? Do they include Doing Nothing and/or Doing It Myself? List all the ways you're different from each of them:
8   What is 'The Vibe'? Do you have it? Can you create it? Does a colleague have it?
9   Why have an Elevator Pitch 'suite', not just one pitch? List four situations where *you* actually might need to use a variation.

Self-Development Assignments

Ch 10 Assignment 1 – Dry Runs

Ask your colleagues to imagine themselves as your target Buyer. Try your Elevator Pitch on them. Ask them for their reaction *as the Buyer* – not as themselves. Then repeat your pitch to their 'real' identities. Once you're fluent, take it outside, and try it on your friends and family. Explain that if *they* can understand your pitch – anyone can!

Ch 10 Assignment 2 – Real Life Pitches

Start small. Have one, maximum two pitches that you're comfortable with. But know where you may need to vary them. Then go out and try them at shows, conferences, business receptions, etc. Develop strong answers where people respond positively and want to engage. If they're determined to buy there and then, go for it. But in most cases, test the strength of your calls to action. Is your IT/assistant support adequate? What went wrong? Keep testing and developing it.

Ch 10 Assignment 3 – Dummy Investor Meeting

This is easier to prepare for than in the past. Most people have seen a Dragons' Den or equivalent – so use the best bits. Give colleagues and friends different roles and get them to ask you appropriate questions. The Marketer, the Techie, the Banker, the Pessimist. The aim is not to reduce you to tears – it's to practice your responses.

If you don't have the data to answer there and then, go and find it. Better to get it wrong now than in front of a real investor.

AFTERNOTE
Making the Change Stick

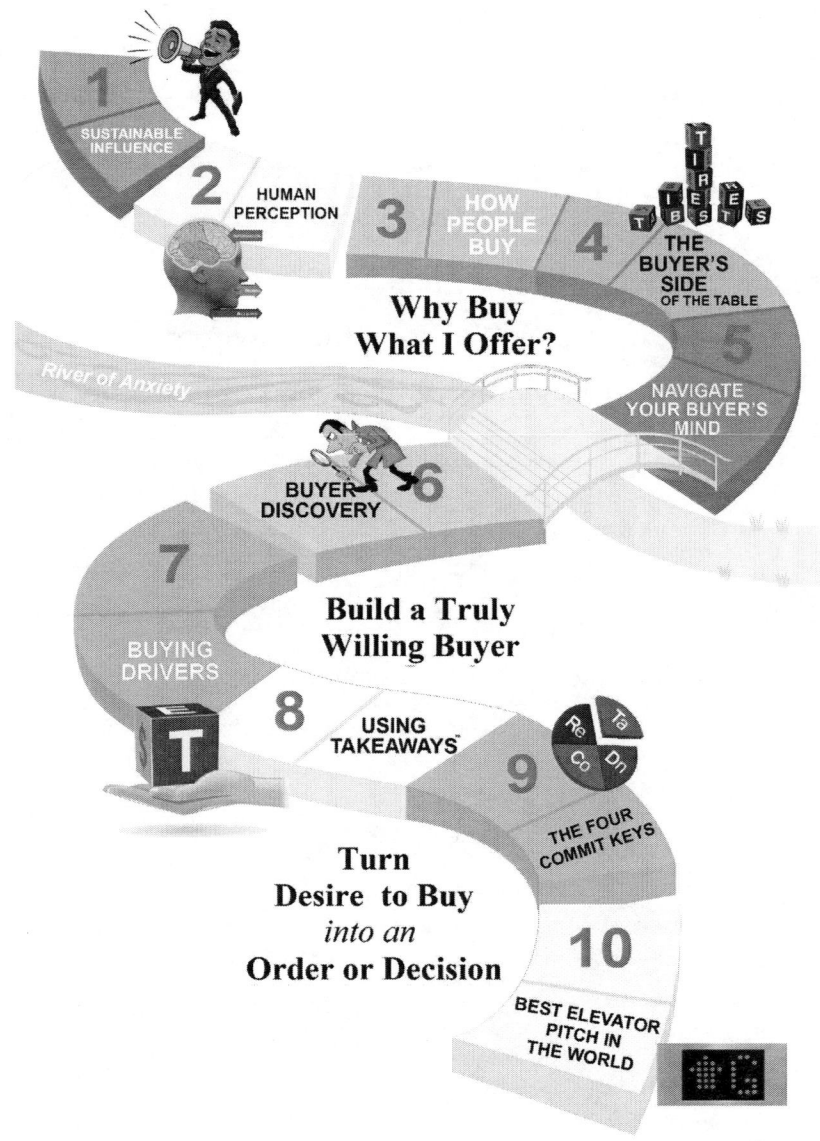

By the end of Making the Change Stick, You'll Understand ...

- The options open for further personal development
- How TSB can be delivered in corporate environment
- Our plans for development training using other media

ENSURE YOUR INVESTMENT IN THIS BOOK STAYS EFFECTIVE

You've made it to the last chapter – congratulations! I hope it's been as exciting and enlightening an adventure as it has been for me. All being well, you've had revelations and "Aha" moments along the way. I also hope you've discovered several things that you're *already* good at – boosting your confidence even more!

To reprise chapter one:

- There's no need to become stressed, tired, anxious or ill when you need to sell something.
- Tough, hard-nosed sales are old school – buyers are well-informed, smart, and won't put up with it.
- Sustainable sales are a win-win – the exchange is fair, there's repeat business, and the bond between you and your buyer remains strong.

You now have two choices.

Option 1 – Go with the flow

You can take what you've learned, integrate it naturally into your life and become a more effective and respected influencer. If you've done the exercises and assignments throughout the book, you'll discover yourself asking new questions and having fresh insights in your work and personal life – completely naturally.

When it happens, be aware of it and remember the Cycle of Competence in Figure 39 from How to Use this Book and below. Where are you in the cycle for that particular skill? How could you move further along the cycle? What else could you work on?

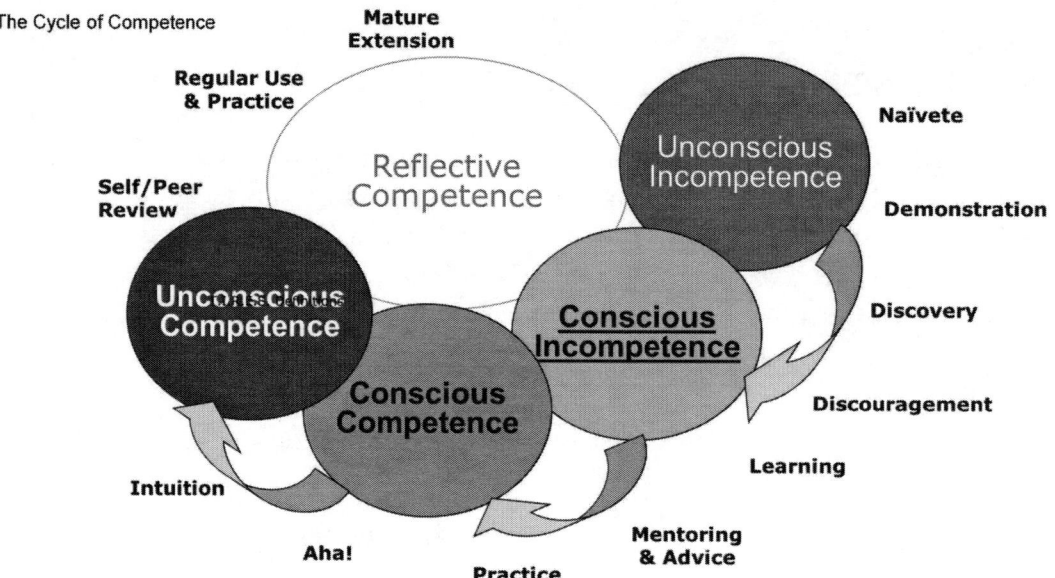

Figure 39

Option 2 – Foot on the Gas

Your second choice is to take your skills to the next level – particularly if your income depends on influencing others to buy your ideas, products, or services. This chapter covers some of the many ways you can make yourself a truly outstanding performer – as an entrepreneur, sales leader, 'intrapreneur', retail consultant, etc.

MOVING THE FURNITURE - A PERSONAL COMMITMENT

The most productive thing you can do is to make a *small but significant change* in your everyday life that will act as an anchor or prompt for the change you've acquired in reading this book. If you do this is in your office, you could even share it with your co-workers as a new business approach. If it's at home, maybe tell your family that you're changing how you do things.

What you're changing is the Frame of how you operate. Just knowing that *you* are changing the way you're approaching communication and influence often makes the people you work with change *their* approach and increase the likelihood of a successful interaction. Remember Willy Ross and his *So Whats* back in chapter 3? We all reacted to him by arriving with a solution, not a problem.

Literally Moving the Furniture

> The expression 'Moving the Furniture' comes from a technique used to help people to lose weight. It was discovered that eating the wrong things (cookies, sweets, etc.) was often not just a habit but actually *reinforced* by the physical layout of a room or building or the structure of a person's day.
>
> Moving a table or moving a cupboard so that the cookie jar or sweet box was no longer on the route to the front door or telephone had a significant effect on what people ate. Changing this habit had a dramatic effect on people's calorie consumption and most important of all, took much less further effort once the initial (easily-motivated) change had been made.

But it's not just the physical effect of the change that can help you. All of us unconsciously use anchors (i.e. fixed cues) to create a specific State – like feeling scared outside the headmaster's office, excited outside the cinema, energised when we put our sports gear on, etc. The same can apply *consciously* to many aspects of *Turning Selling into Buying*. Find the external cue or change that works best for helping you to see the decision from the other side of the table – then use it to the full.

We give out TIRES cubes (see Figure 40) to everyone at our trainings and I know that many people keep them on the other side of their desk as a permanent reminder that it's *the TIRES that drive a decision to buy TakeAways from them*. (You can download and print yourself a TIRES cube to make for yourself from goo.gl/yg5Ob. We also offer TIRES cubes for sale from the website as well – so go to the web shop if you're not handy with the scissors and glue!)

Figure 40

The same approach can be applied, both literally and metaphorically, in your work place. Simply changing the layout of your office or desk position can be an easy way to remember to reframe your approach. Repeated a few times, it quickly becomes a productive new habit.

A manager who completed one of our workshops turned her desk through 90 degrees and placed the visitor's chair beside rather than on the other side of the table. This gave her a permanent reminder that asking questions and being able to truly see the other side of the table is much more effective than just reciting features and benefits to a potential buyer.

Another change that I've seen used very effectively is to radically alter the format and timing of an existing (usually sales) meeting. There's no reason why the same couldn't be applied to a team or management meeting. A new time of day or a new day of the week, particularly a new format or running order – all can be used to remind all involved that "*we do things differently now*" – it even works with video and phone conference calls.

Sales Management

I always ensure that TakeAways are reviewed by each sales person at the start of an account update – it focusses our mind on SWIIFM – not just the sales process!

Probably the biggest furniture moving I've seen, and several times, was to radically alter a sales forecasting system. With TSB, the aim is fourfold:

- Qualify that the buyer needs our TakeAways.
- Build a Willing Buyer.
- Confirm the investment in delivering the TakeAways is worthwhile.
- Turn that Desire to Buy into an Order or Decision.

The change in the approach to sales management can be enormous – here is one example. The company determined that only the *confirmed documentation* of a buyer's TakeAways allowed the sales rep to actually move the opportunity to a 'prospect' status in their CRM system. Not only that, the rep had to confirm specifically which of the TakeAways was needed. Since they had determined from an ABC Analysis what they were, that really nailed down the TIRES they brought back to the office and how they elicited them!

What can *you* do to make sure your organisation becomes (and remains) one that's driven by your partners or your customers' *real* TakeAways – not the features and functions you'd like to sell?

Personal Change Sheet

It's all too easy to only practice and use a few of the techniques in *Turning Selling into Buying*. Start with the ones you find most fun – then move onto the more scary ones! One way I myself used to expand my own ability was to write down on a sheet the techniques that were most applicable in my situation (you can use the Book Index as a memory aid). Then every week, I'd make it my aim to use one particular technique – e.g. specific Chunking Up phrases, four-see, Cartesian challenge, etc. as often as possible.

I would print out the sheet, put the technique for the week on it (along with the words I should be using) and tape it right beside my computer screen – my unconscious soon learned its job for the week!

JOINING THE TSB COMMUNITY

The entry point to the growing online world of the TSB Community is http://turningsellingintobuying.com/the-tsb-community/. If you haven't already joined during the process of buying this book, please go there now and sign up. We promise not to sell your information to anyone. You can cancel your signup any time you want, and we won't spam you.

We will be bringing the following to everyone in the community:

- Webinars – introducing specific actions of the TSB Model.
- Local APEX Seminars with special pricing for community members.
- Our regular Blog – real life sightings of TSB in action – good and bad!
- Training videos – teaching specific TSB techniques.
- Community feedback – your ideas, your experience, your requests.
- Exercises and examples – extended versions of those in the book.

EXTENDING YOUR MODEL OF THE WORLD

There are many models of human behaviour. I have a completely pragmatic approach to the ones that I've used in TSB. The models I've looked at range from the complex and intellectually challenging to the crude and simplistic. One of the models in the 'center ground' has always been Neuro Linguistic Programming (NLP). This has many definitions, but the one I'm most comfortable using is:

> "The art and science of how people communicate – and the effect that communication has on their actions."

The NLP Model has been used all over the world for more than 30 years – in several forms – to improve outcomes in many, varied aspects of business and personal development. NLP was originally based on the careful observation and modelling of some amazingly effective people. It is now increasingly being ratified by the latest neuroscience studies.

This is beginning to deliver the laboratory-based *how?* that lies behind the observation-based *what?* upon which NLP was originally based. As a model that works it now has a solid reputation for delivering results –

which is why it's been used in almost every Fortune 500 Company and every country in the world.

I gained my certification as Master Practitioner of NLP in 2001, and started to use the techniques I'd learned as a sales coach. I worked with other practitioners and experimented with the full range of NLP techniques – using them in the 'school of hard knocks' that is real business. This allowed us to discover and confirm what works best and what's not so useful. As a result, I've only integrated NLP's most effective and easily-learned disciplines and techniques into TSB.

Once I'd decided what was effective, we then used our many years of experience to extend the use of each technique 'to the max'. We always focused on anything that helped with the two steps in TSB – *'Converting a Need to Sell into a Desire to Buy – then converting that Desire to Buy into an Order or Decision'*.

If you're already familiar with NLP, you'll have found much in this book that's familiar, but with innovative TSB extensions added. If NLP is new to you, and you've no desire to get into it, the techniques stand up perfectly well without the need for further study.

If however, you'd like to learn more about NLP techniques for personal development and team building, there are a number of sources I can recommend, some from my own use, some from recommendations. The web is full of NLP resources, but these are as good a place to start as any!

- NLP Basics: look through the articles at *renewal.ca/articles.htm*
- Advanced NLP Training: see *performancepartnership.com/*
- Business NLP Coaching: see *ppimk.com/sitemap.html*
- Skills resource: *businessballs.com/nlpneuro-linguisticprogramming.htm*

If you find your own resource that helps to extend TSB's use of NLP in your geography, sector or industry, do please share with us on the TSB Forum.

COMMERCIAL ACTIVITIES

TSB is based on a model that was tested and developed in real-life business, then used extensively for training seminars and workshops. That training continues today. If you or your organisation would like to make a change in your performance, or need help overcoming a specific obstacle, please contact me or your nearest Holis Associate (via the 'Delivery' link on the website).

The corporate delivery arm of *Turning Selling into Buying* is Holis (*'Whole-iss'*) Associates Inc. This growing network of successful, experienced specialists combines local knowledge with practical delivery of *Turning Selling into Buying*. They deliver APEX seminars and ABC Analyses in their own geography, sector, or industry. They more often deliver Fearless Selling workshops as part of a consulting assignment. Go to holisinc.com or goo.gl/9Nx5H for more information on the company.

The TSB syllabus, and more, can be delivered in several different ways:

APEX™ Seminars

These energetic seminars are delivered over 3 or 4 days. They cover the whole syllabus, and are delivered in two formats.

Public seminars are advertised or promoted with local entrepreneur groups, chamber of commerce, academic institutions, etc. and anyone can pay to come. The attendees cover a wide range – from shopkeepers, through sales teams and individual, to CEOs of major companies. Their varied background always ensures a stimulating session!

Closed seminars focus on a specialised user group with a common challenge. Real examples have included include pre-sales engineers, product managers, consultants, real estate agents, and student entrepreneurs.

Download details from goo.gl/srSjJ. See goo.gl/rDKEJ for event details in your area.

Fearless Selling Workshops

These are team development engagements that solve a specific problem or achieve a specific objective – one that's always agreed upon in advance. They are usually aimed at groups of sales, marketing, executive, or customer support staff within a specific company or group. They're usually delivered in close liaison with a local Holis Associate who works closely with the senior staff concerned to agree exactly what sales, product management, or channel problem needs to be solved.

The syllabus of each Fearless Selling Workshop is then tailored or extended to ensure a productive focus on the areas that need improvement. Any of our Associates can also contribute their own specialist skills (such as cold calling, web design, recruitment, etc.) to the content of the workshop. The local Associate is usually responsible for delivering the follow-on consulting and operational support to make sure that the change sticks. Click '*Delivery*' on the website for more.

If you're interested in a Fearless Selling Workshop for your organisation, please contact us at *sales@holisinc.com*. If you'd like to be considered as a Holis Associate, please email me personally at *sellingtobuying@gmail.com* and explain what you bring to the table and why you should be part of our team.

Holis Associates also deliver a wide range of other workshops including:

- Fearless Proposals
- Fearless Presenting
- Fearless Channels
- Fearless Negotiation
- Fearless Networking
- Fearless Leadership

Once again, please contact us at *fearless@holisinc.com*

ABC Analysis

Some companies are not ready to make the commitment to a full Fearless Selling Workshop, but need something more focussed than a seminar. For a start-up team that needs help in determining *"exactly what would drive anyone to buy what we offer"*, or for a business about to begin sales of a new offering or in a new market, we offer the ABC Analysis. This covers all of the practical work set out in chapters 7 and 8.

The standard ABC Analysis is available as an intensive one day Facilitation, or as a two day ABC Certification. The Certification also includes the teaching of sufficient extra skills for attendees to be able to carry out their own analysis completely independently.

See details at goo.gl/hIIuu. Email us at abc@holisinc.com to discuss booking one with your nearest associate.

Commit Analysis

The final step on from an ABC Analysis is to add the final 3 Commit Keys that are described in chapter 9. A Commit Analysis always follows an ABC Analysis, since the outputs from that feed into the ROI, Convincers, and Delivery Narratives it generates.

A Commit Analysis is very often part of a wider Fearless Selling workshop. Where it is a stand-alone deliverable, it is available as an intensive Facilitation, or as a Certification. The Certification again includes the teaching of sufficient extra skills for attendees to carry out their own analysis independently.

See details at goo.gl/hIIuu. Email us at abc@holisinc.com to discuss booking one.

Online Video and Practice Training

As we go to print, plans are under way for a comprehensive online training capability – either to consolidate the knowledge you've gained from this book or stand alone. Join the TSB Community or click '*Delivery*' on the website to discover what's available.

Keynote Speaking

The author, Trevor Græme Wilkins, is a member of the Global Speakers Federation (_GSF_), the National Speakers Association (_NSA_) and the Canadian Association of Professional Speakers (_CAPS_). He can deliver his robust and lively keynotes on a variety of subjects to suit any sales event, kick-off, conference, or product launch.

Some examples include:

- Anyone can sell, sell well, and enjoy doing it.
- The only five reasons anyone will buy – anything – from you.
- Stop selling and start telling stories.
- Entrepreneurs – turn your biggest worry into your biggest strength.
- Consultants - turn talking about you into talking about your buyer.

Go to _goo.gl/iP1pK_ for details.

OPPORTUNITIES FOR FURTHER DEVELOPMENT OF TSB

We're constantly rolling out new resources. If you think there's anything missing that would help you, _please tell us via the Forum_ – we can't always accurately sit on your side of the table!

We presently have plans to deliver the following:

- **TSB Coaching Guides** – worked examples for specific users – 'TSB for...
- ...channel managers, real estate agents, solution providers, retailers, consultants, lawyers, financial services, etc.'
- **Audio Books** – TSB – chapter by chapter – to listen to as you fly, drive, or walk.
- **Video Workshops** – the self-service equivalent of an APEX™ Seminar – without travel.
- **TSB Gems** – concise, focussed e-booklets that solve a specific problem using TSB.

What else would _you_ like to use to _Turn Selling into Buying_?

IF YOU FOUND THIS BOOK USEFUL...

Check out 'TSB *Part 3* – 'The art and science of engaging with any buyer'. Check for the publication date on the turningsellingintobuying.com website.

In Part 3, the TSB skills you've practiced and the powerful facts you've generated are taken to the next level. You'll learn how to use them most effectively in any meeting (be it face-to-face, video, telephone, messaging, etc.) – to even more effectively and predictably generate an order or a decision.

You'll learn how to prepare yourself, your team, your customer, and your offering to make the buying decision as straightforward as possible.

You'll discover and practice a simple five-step structure for any and every influence meeting – be it a planned sales call or project meeting, the immediate development of an elevator pitch, or a fully-fledged presentation as part of a formal process.

Most importantly of all, you'll discover a simple, foolproof way to construct a buying plan that completely eliminates the need to 'close the deal'. Your buyer will want to close it themselves – and be motivated to take the action required. Once again, the result could be a sale, a job offer, a partnership, or just an important decision. Oh, how I wish I'd known this stuff 30 years ago!

TSB *Part 3* contains techniques for use both at home and at work. The weight is a little more on the commercial side, but how many of us aren't selling *something*?

Your luck is the residue of your great preparation.

Trevor

ANNEX A

Index of Terms used in Turning Selling into Buying

I've done my best to avoid jargon, but, to be able to use one or two words instead of a couple of paragraphs, I've had to create some TSB shorthand – these are the main ones used throughout *Turning Selling into Buying*. Full definitions are in the CHAPTER SHOWN.

ABC Analysis (chapter 8)

A 'Step up' from a TakeAway Analysis that adds (for every Buyer/Offering combination):

- Towards/Away From & Personal/Corporate – in a TakeAway Quadrant.
- Value Statements for every TakeAway for each Buyer/Offering combination.

State (chapter 4.4)

We're all unconsciously in a specific State (happy, empowered, carefree, fatherly) and running a model of the world that makes sense of the information we're receiving. ALSO:

- *Breaking State*: changing us or another person to a more relevant or productive state.

Buyer (chapter 2)

Any person or group you're influencing to buy an idea, product or service from you.

Buyer Discovery (chapter 6)

Research you undertake on any aspects of a buyer's situation (personal, industry, company) that are likely to affect their decision making.

Buying Drivers (chapter 3)

The combination of a stated TakeAway, plus the TIRES it delivers.

Buying Plan (chapter 9)

The agreed actions, events, and influences needed to generate an order or decision.

Challenge (chapter 7)

Any Precision Question which causes your buyer to stop, to think *consciously* and to provide you with more, or different, or unfiltered, or justified information.

Chunking (chapter 5)

Questioning that reliably steers a buyer's thoughts and conversation using:

- *Chunk Up*: move a buyer up their hierarchy of ideas to a more abstract view.
- *Chunk Down*: move a buyer down into concrete detail and differences.
- *Chunk Sideways/Horizontal*: expand the options and potential at the same level.
- *Lateral Chunk*: increase choices by chunking up, then chunking down to a new option.

Commit Analysis (chapter 9)

Adds the final three Commit Keys to your ABC Analysis:

- *Convincers*: objective proof that something is true – which will sustain a desire to buy.
- *Delivery Narrative*: accurate, convincing story of a buyer's journey to their TakeAways.
- *ROI Framework*: financial background to a decision – that supports your price with industry data, buyer's figures, changed income or expense, etc.

Convincer Strategy (chapter 9)

The three components an individual consistently prefers to use – to become convinced:

- *Convincer Channel*: ... looks, feels, sounds right, etc.
- *Convincer Mode*: their 'Internal Schedule' ... automatic, repeats, never, etc.
- *Convincer Frame*: ... internal, external reference, SWIIFM, etc.

Frames (chapters 2.4 and 5.4)

Group of filters we all deploy in any particular situation or state to observe our world.

The reason the same information can be seen very differently by different people. ALSO:

- *Reframe*: changing another person's model of the world with a question or statement.
- *Preframe*: creating that positive change *before* your buyer actually engages with you.

Filters (Neurological) (chapter 2)

Fundamental ways we protect ourselves from the mass of information we receive:

- *Delete* – 'blinkers' that we all put onto situations and information.
- *Distort* – interpreting information in an incorrect way.
- *Generalise* – sweeping over-generalised interpretation of data.

Fulcrum of Influence (chapter 2.5)

The pivot point where influence moves from externally imposed to internally generated.

Influence Meeting (chapter 2.6)

Interactions that create a desire to buy, or that change a desire to buy into a decision or order. The word Influence is used instead of 'sales' because TSB helps you act in a way that builds a willing buyer. It can be a formally structured, quick and informal, by video, or even using text.

Intrapreneur (Introduction)

An employee who is given independent responsibility for directly turning an idea into a profitable offering – through assertive risk-taking and innovation.

Model of the World (chapter 2)

Neurological Filters we run and the Frames within which we run those filters. These include: beliefs & values; decisions; experiences; morals; attitudes; traits and character.

Objection (chapter 5)

A buyer's way of saying "*I don't like or don't completely understand your offer*". An objection is positive, as it means the buyer is interested and can often be reframed.

Offering (chapter 7.3)

Everything you offer that creates a desire to buy – not just the core product or service. Includes hidden extras such as stability, financing, training, partners, reputation, etc.

Precision Listening (chapter 2)

Combination of Precision Questioning and Active Listening that produces far better results than the unconscious processing we normally do. *Components*:

- *Precision Questions*: conscious use of verbal challenges such as *So What* or *Who says so* to engage more deeply with a buyer and drill down to their actual TakeAways.
- *Active Listening*: conscious recognition of the structure, content, and intent in another person's response to your question.

Qualify (chapter 7.1)

Objectively answer the question *"Is there sufficient cost and/or time benefit in expending my time, effort and resources in getting this order or decision?"*

Spray and Pray (chapter 1)

The barrage of facts and figures 'sprayed' at a buyer in the hope that some will stick long enough to make a sale. It involves no questioning or interaction.

SWIIFM (chapter 3.4)

So What's In It For Me? The basic human driver for any buying decision. Even an apparently altruistic decision will fulfil the beliefs and values of the buyer.

T.I.R.E.S. (chapter 3)

The tangible improvement in control or productivity of the five elements that are the only motivations to buy an idea, product or service. *The elements are*:

- **T**ime: something happens ... earlier; later; more predictably; more regularly.
- **In**come: is ... larger; better 'shaped'; more predictable; certain; delimited.
- **R**isk: the chance of an event is ... decreased; more understood; visible; reassigned.
- **Ex**pense: is ... reduced; better controlled; better shaped; re-assigned.
- **St**ate: someone ... smiles more; less stressed; more content; attractive; in a better light.
- *TIRE Compounds*: combinations of two or more TIRES e.g. **T/I**; **R/E**.

TakeAway (chapters 3, 7 and 8)

Long lasting effect that occurs a significant time after delivery of what's been bought.

- *TakeAway Analysis*: transforming Offering features into compelling Buying Drivers.
- *Potential TakeAways*: list of *all* TakeAways from a specific *So What?* analysis.
- *Confirmed TakeAways*: a subset of the *Potential TakeAways* list – that a buyer has confirmed they truly need.
- *TakeAway Chain*: linked sequence of responses to *So Whats?* that converge on TIRES.
- *TakeAway Quadrant*: simple field-use record of potential TakeAways for an Offering.
- *TakeAway Enrichment*: make TakeAways broader and stronger and thus more buyable.

Towards/Away From (chapter 8)

A buyer's tendency to either prevent something happening or to achieve a goal. Most buyers have a mix of both and vary the mix depending upon situation and State

Value Statement (chapter 8)

A combination of the statements made in the last few steps of the So What chain that, when combined with the appropriate TIRES, greatly increase the credibility of the TakeAway itself.

Willing Buyer (chapter 1)

Individual or group with whom you've agreed on the actual TakeAways they need. They have a desire to buy, but further work is required to turn it into an order or decision.

ANNEX B

Part One Answers

CHAPTER 1: ANSWERS TO REVIEW QUESTIONS

1 What's the most important lesson you took away from the story about my interview at the Stock Exchange? How many of the seven steps used to 'make me a Willing Buyer' can you list?

He did a SWIIFM for each interviewee/position combination.

He took a look at the Stock Exchange from our side of the table.

He was genuinely interested in each of us and our situation.

He gained permission to delve into our beliefs and values and discussed them.

When he saw a match for what he could offer, he drilled further.

When he saw he could deliver the TakeAways we sought, he stated it clearly.

He only presented us with Convincer information once he knew what was relevant.

2 What does Turning Selling into Buying do that's the total opposite of 'pitching'?

TSB involves engagement, questioning and discovering enough about a buyer's situation to discover whether and how you can help – rather than stating facts, figures and reasons they should buy from you.

3 Describe or define a 'Willing Buyer'?

A person who understands the long lasting, positive effect they would receive from what you offer. They would like to 'buy' but have not taken the final step of an order or decision.

4 What have the 'Best of the Best' in sales and influence always done?

They recognise what drives a buying decision from the Buyer's Side of the Table. With that knowledge they then determine whether it can be delivered, and what monetary value it has.

5 What is the big life saver for everyone – that could be for you too?

Doing all the objective and financial preparation well in advance of any influence call – freeing you from concerns about rejection, knowledge or aggression – and releasing your creativity.

6 Name 4 of the 8 keys problems TSB solves. Which are most relevant to you?

Results, timescales and revenue are more predictable

Less time and resources are wasted by replacing assumptions with objective facts

Achievable opportunities are spotted more easily and earlier

More successful outcomes through strong cost justification and greater buyer motivation

An open, facilitative approach – centred around your buyer is less stressful; more enjoyable

Timescales and plans are more easily managed when openly based on objective facts

Partnerships are based on what your partner needs – and supplying it

Teams are more productive if everyone contributes to influencing buyers to buy

CHAPTER 2: ANSWERS TO REVIEW QUESTIONS

1 What new skills make TSB so different from old-school approaches to influence?

The extra verbal skills of listening, questions and challenges that you learn to use.

2 What's the difference between a TSB Foundation and a TSB Mindset?

Foundations are the core skills and insights that you'll learn in Turning Selling into Buying. Mindsets are small changes in attitude that will make those skills easier to maintain and use.

3 List two of each (then go back and re-read the ones you couldn't list):

Foundations:

How we all react to the world of sensations around us.

How we make sense of this massive information assault.

How to change how the other person sees the world – and what you're offering them.

How to tip a buyer from dubious to convinced.

Mindsets:

"So What's In It For Me?"

"Assumption is the mother of all screw-ups."

The buyer is on the Other Side of the Table – seeing a different world from you.

Question Precisely – Listen Actively.

The Human Communication Model

4 List the 5 senses that are always delivering information to you – both unconsciously and consciously

Basic: *Sight, Sound, Touch, Smell and Taste.*

Advanced*: Proprioception (relative position of body parts).*

Exteroception (relative spatial position).

Interception (pain, hunger etc.).

5 How many parallel flows of information can your mind consciously process at the same time?

Between 3 and 7, depending upon the person and the circumstances.

Filters

6 Describe two types of people likely to have very different 'models of the world' and thus find it hard to communicate:

No 'right' answer. People from widely divergent backgrounds are most likely to have built different models, but they may also completely agree on certain aspects. But the chance of different models used by farmers, politicians, social workers, engineers etc. are high.

7 List the three types of filtration that our neurology carries out:

Deletion (usually selectively) of parts of the information.

Distortion is interpreting information so that it means something different.

Generalisation by making assumptions based on a limited number of inputs.

8 Give two examples of deleted information – each using a different sense:

"I can't hear any dissent from the audience."

"Our company has never had a dissatisfied customer."

9 Give two examples of a distortion filter in operation:

"No birthday card means they don't love me."

"The tunnelling operation has gone quiet – they must have problem.s"

10 Give two examples of a generalisation:

"Custom software is always badly supported after delivery."

"Employing graduates is a recipe for disaster."

11 What can you do to recover missing information when someone talks to you but it's clear to you that they're deleting, distorting or generalising?

Challenge the omission with a precision question to draw out the filtered information.

12 List three of the seven advanced filters and give one example of each:

Values & Beliefs – "Young people have no personal drive."

Attitudes – "Who cares anyway?"

Decisions – "I always ask my father for advice on cars."

Memories – "I've been swindled by so many cell phone suppliers that…"

Language – "Does 'customer care' mean selling us more?

Time & Space – "Lend us a fiver dad!" v. "I'm sorry to have to ask for a loan, but…"

Thinking Style – "I'm always driven by my vision. My executives only see what can go wrong."

13 List three examples of the influences on each of us that create the filters we use:

Our family and our close friends.

Schools and associations.

Our religion and community.

Books we read, films we watch, the media in general.

Significant emotional experiences we experience.

14 What does State mean?

State is 'how your mind makes you feel as a result of a situation or input.

Examples are:

Terror at seeing a tiger rushing towards you.

Excitement on hearing your team has scored.

Boredom at feeling yet another migraine.

Excitement at touching your lover's hand.

Hunger upon smelling your favourite dish.

Frames

15 What is a Frame?

The overall context within which we observe the world around us. It usually takes place after the more 'self–protection basic filters'.

16 What is a Reframe?

Using a question, statement or action (usually deliberately) to cause another person to use a different Frame to the one they had been using.

17 Give one example each of a reframing question, and a reframing statement:

"How would you feel if you could remove that problem immediately?"

"Unlike our competitors, we don't ask for payment until you go live."

18 Describe a recent experience that you can now recognise was you being reframed by someone else – or you reframing them:

No 'right answer'.

Influence

19 What is the Fulcrum of Influence?

A MODEL OF INCREASING EFFECTIVENESS IN WAYS TO INFLUENCE SOMEONE TO CHANGE OR TAKE ACTION.

20 Name as many of the steps on the Fulcrum of Influence as you can; from 'least effective change' to 'most effective change'.

Be told something.
See or hear it happen.
Identify with it.
Create an answer to a question about it.
Experience it.
Recognise it as correct.
Know it is correct (e.g. the moral thing to do, it will improve results, it will never happen).

TSB Mindsets

21 What are the 4 TSB Mindsets?

So What's In It For Me?

"Assumption is the mother of all screw-ups."

The buyer is on the Other Side of the Table – seeing a different world from you.

Question Precisely – Listen Actively.

22 What does SWIIFM stand for?

So What's In It For Me? – What TIRES improvements will I receive from doing this?

23 What is the Mother of all Screw-Ups?

Assumptions (and guesses) are the mother of all screw–ups.

24 In which situation is the ability to 'sit on the other side of the table' most useful?

Preparing for any influence call, analysing what would motivate a buyer of your Offering.

25 What are the two components of 'Precision Listening'?

Precision Questions.

Active Listening.

26 What must you be consciously aware of in Active Listening?

Consciously understand the contents and structure of a buyer's answer.

CHAPTER 3: ANSWERS TO REVIEW QUESTIONS

1 What is the fundamental motivation behind any decision a person or organisation takes to buy something or to 'buy into' an idea?

So What's In It For Me? (even if it's just the Satisfaction of seeing someone else happy).

2 Name as many of the six 'classic' mistakes people make when they sell to or influence anyone else:

Selling to yourself.

No personal connection.

Selling Features and Functions.

Selling on price.

Selling what's asked for, not what's needed.

Only selling to the person in front of you.

3 Which of the six mistakes above do you *personally* make least? Which is the one do you do most?

4 Are you a bulldog or a sheepdog? When is each best employed?

Sheepdogs are best employed to deliver predictability and great relationships. Bulldogs deliver important sales results when the 'chips are down'.

5 What are the three main causes of fear, doubt or anxiety in sales or influence?

6 Which one affects you most? Which one affects you least?

Anxiety about being caught out by a lack of knowledge.

Discomfort at being seen to be too 'pushy' or assertive.

Fear of rejection by a buyer.

Buying Drivers

7 What (in full) are the only 5 reasons that anyone is 'motivated to buy'?

Time – reduced, controlled, earlier, regularity.

Income – increased, better shaped, more predictable.

Risk – reduced, increased as required, visible, mitigated, re-assigned.

Expense – reduced, controlled, shaped, re-assigned.

State – smile more, less stress, content, look better.

8 Give one good example of each type and then check that what you've written 'passes the test'

T: You spend less time travelling.

I: Income is increased with no extra effort.

R: The risk of something occurring reduces.

9 What phrase was Ted Levitt famous at the Harvard Business School?

"People don't go to buy a ½ inch drill – they actually go to buy a ½ inch hole."

10 What is the (full) definition of a TakeAway?

A TakeAway is a desired effect or change which will be in place a significant time after delivery is complete or the work finished. It should be Specific, Measurable, Realistic and Achievable!

11 Is each of these a TakeAway? If not why not? What changes would make it a TakeAway?

"Training costs reduced by 25%."

Yes – clear and measured.

"Supported by live call centre staff 98% of the time."

No – It looks objective but "So What do you get from live call centre staff?"

Needs TIRES drawn out from "…live call centre staff 98% of the time".

"A low void ratio and high aspect ratio that reduce fuel consumption by 20%."

Yes – clear and measured.

"Your consultant will have an MBA and 20 years' experience"

No – So What TIRES do I get from an MBA and 20 years' experience?

Needs drill down to what a buyer might take away from MBAs and experience.

12 What are TIRE Compounds? Give 3 examples (with letters and description)

I/T: You get paid before the job, not at the end.

R/I: Your income becomes more predictable.

S/R/E: You're a more relaxed, capable driver – so less likely to have an expensive accident.

Your Offering

13 What is 'an Offering'?

Everything that is included in whatever you want someone to buy or 'buy into'. At the heart there is a core of product or service, but it also includes many less obvious things such as reputation, partners, funding, stability etc.

14 Develop your Offering by using the Offering Worksheet downloadable from *goo.gl/i0oaX* or at:
http://turningsellingintobuying.com/tsb-book-links/

15 Create a metaphor similar to 'Green Jelly' – but for your Offering. Make it easy for your Buyer to see the TakeAways separately from the features and functions.

CHAPTER 4: ANSWERS TO REVIEW QUESTIONS

1 What is the main benefit of using Four-See?

It delivers insights into the decision making process of your buyer and the influencers that act upon them as they move from willing buyer to an order or decision.

2 When and where can it be carried out?

Pretty much anywhere you can shout off external stimuli. When done well in advance, it can be a quite office; just before a call, it can be a taxi, an airport lunch, a waiting room.

3 Name the Four-See Positions – numbers and titles!
First Position – the Influencer.
Second Position – the Buyer.
Third Position – the Impartial Adviser.
Fourth Position – the Stakeholder or Affected Party.

4 How many chairs, what should be distinctive about them – and why?

Two chairs with different characteristics to emphasis strong state change between them.

5 What (honestly) is the greatest benefit that you personally are likely to gain from being in First Position?

6 Why always 'Break State' between positions? What ways are there to do this?

It's easier to go from a strong 'induced' state (such as the buyer) to another induced state (such as the Adviser) via a neutral state created by the Break State.

7 What should you try to complete before you go to Second Position?

Buyer Discovery.

8 What must you always leave behind when you move to Second Position?

Yourself, your beliefs, your values, your decision and experience.

9 What is the key quality of the individual in Third Position?

They have a strong and well-intentioned desire for success for all parties.

10 What 'magical capability' does Third Position have? How can they use it?

They can see all the filters used by First and Second Positions.
They use this power to give useful advice to First and Second Positions.

11 What communication attributes, faults and successes should Third Position look for as they watch First and Second position?

Balance and control of talking? Information versus enthusiasm? Balance of hearing and listening? Language patterns used? Balance of telling, questioning and discussing?

12 How many people in Fourth Position? List characteristics each might have. List typical Fourth Position people that might be useful in your situation.

No limit but usually 2 or 3. All would affected by or have an important opinion on the outcome.

13 Apart from an Influence Meeting, when else is Four-See effective?

As preparation for an ABC Analysis.
Before a negotiation.
To prevent or resolve a dispute.

CHAPTER 5: ANSWERS TO REVIEW QUESTIONS

1 What are the two skills covered in this chapter? What makes each of them so very productive commercially and how?

Chunking and Frames including:

Chunking Up, Down, Sideways and Laterally to expand a buyer vision.

Reframes and Preframes that help a buyer to recognise their TakeAways

2 What is the Hierarchy of Ideas and how many levels does it have?

The way we mentally 'classify' a fact or idea. It ranges from information that's Abstract or Big Picture down to information that focusses on Concrete Detail – and everything between. The number of levels is not fixed, but depends upon preferred 'chunk size' – a 'big chunker' has fewer levels than a 'small chunker'.

Chunking

3 Give an example of two generic Chunking Up questions.

For what purpose are you…?

What is … a part of?

4 Create two Chunking Up questions that will be of use in your situation.

5 Give an example of two generic Chunking Down questions.

What is the root cause of…?

Please give me some examples….

6 Create two Chunking Down questions that will be of use in your situation.

7 Give an example of two generic Chunking Sideways questions.

What's another example like that?

Anything else?

8 What can you do if your Buyer's answers are going 'down the wrong vector'?

Chunk them up, then sideways to a better position, then down.

9 Describe how Lateral Chunking works and what it can be used for.

Chunk up one, two or three levels, then sideways in any direction, then same number down.

10 What three attribute of a Buyer's Model of the World can Chunking reveal?

Chunk size.
Preferred level in hierarchy.
Mobility between levels.

11 What is the most important verbal key to successful chunking?

Listen fully to the answer, then place their words directly back into your next question.

12 How else can you use the new-found skills to help another person?

Coping with an overwhelming or complex situation.
Negotiating.
Project Management.
Creating Rapport.

Reframes

13 What is a Frame? What is a Reframe? Are they statements or questions?

A Frame is Frame of Reference within which we deploy and prioritise our filters.

A reframe is a statement or a question that helps your buyer to 'see things differently'.

14 There are the three places in any path of thought or communication where we all apply our own frames (of reference). What are they?

On the way in to our brains via our 5 senses.
As we process them in our brains.
As our brains create words and actions as a result.

15 List and describe three of the six most common reframes.

Change Position – *looking at the situation from a different location to where they are.*

Change Frame Size – *understanding things from a larger perspective of time or group.*

Counter Example – *a factual statement that moves or displaces the buyer's beliefs.*

Change Hierarchy – *consider situation in a more chunked up or down perspective.*

Basis Challenge – *challenges the basis for your buyer's belief.*

Intent v. Consequence – *proposes a new, positive intention for an event.*

ANNEX C

Part Two Answers

CHAPTER 6: ANSWERS TO REVIEW QUESTIONS

1. What are the three most common causes of sales fear?

   Anxiety about being caught out by a lack of knowledge.

   Discomfort at being seen to be too 'pushy' or assertive.

   Fear of rejection by the buyer.

2. What is the 'key success factor' in researching your Buyer?

   Becoming genuinely interested in the buyer and their situation.

3. Give one example of a Google Advanced Search and describe how you would use it to help you Build a Willing Buyer

   Do a SITE: search for the buyer on their company website, discover a public document they're responsible for and then ask for information on that subject.

4. Describe 3 useful LinkedIn searches and what you can achieve from them.

   Own Twitter account? What else are they interested in outside of work?

   Length of time in once job? Ambitious? Conservative? Committed?

   Whom are they connected to? Competitors? Your colleagues? Your existing clients?

5. Describe three other productive sources of Buyer research data.

   Your own contacts.

   YouTube.

   Libraries.

6 Why is acquiring a picture of their Buyer so useful for some people?

If they're visual it can increase rapport, confidence and creativity.

7 Describe two ways to tap into the expertise or knowledge of friends and colleagues.

A Life in the Day Of exercise.

Circular email requesting assistance or information.

8 What should you do with your new contacts at the end of every day – no matter how late you get back? Do you? What will you change so you do it tomorrow?

Record their details, respond to them, add subjective information, classify them, add date.

9 Devise and describe one new 'off the wall' way you might research your Buyers.

CHAPTER 7: ANSWERS TO REVIEW QUESTIONS

1 What are the Five Buying Drivers? Why aren't features and benefits enough?

Time, Income, Risk, Expense and State.

It's the TIRES that the Feature and Benefits finally deliver – and which drive people to buy.

2 What is qualifying an opportunity? It might be an opportunity for a partnership, for a sale, for an investment, or even a job.

Confirming whether or not there is a need for a TakeAway you can supply.

Then determining whether there is a budget, timescale or external event that will turn that desire to buy into an order or decision.

3 Why don't you just pitch your TakeAways? After all, they're so much stronger than features and benefits...

TakeAways are only an unproven statement of the final delivery of TIRES. They can even sound less interesting than Features and Benefits. They are best elicited, then proven.

4 Describe Steps One and Two in a TakeAway analysis. Why are they so important?

Confirm your Offering.

Confirm your buyer or buyer group.

Both are equally important because the tighter they are defined, the smaller the number of potential TakeAways – thus the more easily they can be drawn out from a buyer.

5 What do you do if your feature list is very long? (Perhaps several hundred.)

Group and reclassify them. Then create a smaller number of 'composite' features.

e.g. a long list of every single way in which brakes can be applied in an emergency could be given a composite description of 'brakes apply automatically in every safety–critical situation'.

6 When do you stop saying S*O* W*HAT* in response to the answer?

When the reply contains a TakeAway that passes the TIRES test.

7 Name and describe as many of the Success Hints as you can. Go back and re-read the ones you can't remember

Little, Dumb Steps *– don't try to reach TakeAways too quickly.*

State *– do the analysis in the same State as your buyer.*

Don't Overthink *– don't be afraid of random, 'wacky' answers.*

Bring in the Buyer *– someone similar to or who knows your buyer.*

Enter the Buyer's Room *– create the same environment as your buyer.*

Enrichment *–go wider and deeper than the competition and alternatives.*

8 What form can you download and use to make this job much easier?

TakeAway Generator Form.

9 Describe each of the four Enrichment steps once you've uncovered your initial set of TakeAways.

So What Else? – other TIRES from that TakeAway .

Reverse Back – other TakeAways from previous questions.

Challenge TakeAways – chunk up and down on what you've created.

Combining TakeAways – understand relative strengths and values.

10 What are the three types of Buyer you can encounter?

Away From – driven to prevent something happening.

Towards – driven to achieve an outcome.

Cautious – a balance of Away From and Towards.

CHAPTER 8: ANSWERS TO REVIEW QUESTIONS

1 What is a TakeAway Quadrant used for?

Recording, adding value and easy access of TakeAways.

2 What are the four classifications of TakeAway in a Quadrant?

Towards, Away From, Corporate, Personal.

3 How many Quadrant Sheets for each Buyer/Offering combination?

One sheet for each unless TakeAways and classifications are identical.

4 How does a Value Statement differ from a TakeAway?

A Value Statement delivers factual support to the mechanism that created the TakeAway. e.g. "Our web access tool allows engineers to order parts instantly online, to fix the job quicker and return your factory to profitability sooner."

5 When would you use a Value Statement?

Once you have drawn out the TakeAways confirmed by your buyer, to immediately support the statement "Well that's great, that's exactly what we do."

CHAPTER 9: ANSWERS TO REVIEW QUESTIONS

1 What is the difference between and Commit Analysis and a TakeAway Analysis?

A TakeAway analysis produces the data that will help to Build a Willing Buyer.

The Commit Analysis adds the three pieces of information that will help to turn that desire to buy into an order or decision.

2 What is a Convincer Strategy? Who uses it, and when?

Everyone uses Convincer Strategies to become convinced of a new truth.

3 What are the three components of a Buyer's Convincer Strategy?

Convincer Channel *– their preferred way of receiving convincing information.*

Convincer Mode *– their 'internal schedule' for actions needed to convince them.*

Convincer Frame *– internal/external confirmation; towards/away; personal/external TIRES.*

4 How do you detect a Buyer's convincers? What do you do if you can't detect them?

Listen to the words they use and things they do for the clues they may give.

If nothing detected, offer alternatives and see which they select first.

As a last resort (or with good rapport) ask how they made the decision another time.

5 What are the Four Commit Keys?

TakeAways; Convincers; Delivery Narratives; ROI Frameworks.

6 Where does a Case Study fit? What is it used for?

A Case Study can contain all of the above and can be a very fast Immediate Convincer.

7 What is the Cartesian Challenge used for?

To drive out every single permutation and combination of income/expense increase/reduction.

8 What data sources are there for any ROI?

Industry figures, sector reports, your own proven benchmarks, the buyer's figures

9 What are the best data sources for *your* ROI Framework?

CHAPTER 10: ANSWERS TO REVIEW QUESTIONS

1. What are the two desired outcomes from an Elevator Pitch?
   Qualify they may be interested in the TakeAways you supply.
   Make agreement for next action.

2. How does an Investor Panel or Dragon's Den differ from an Elevator Pitch?
   It will start with an Elevator Pitch but then develop into a much more robust, interactive discussion.

3. List four productive calls to action you could use.
   Register on a website (and give them a card with the url).
   Agree how you will make an appointment to meet.
   Make an appointment to meet – and do it there and then.
   An explicit introduction to someone else.
   Schedule a phone call.

4. What might you already know about your Buyer before you open your mouth? How might you have you learned it?
   The location, event, their demeanour, overheard conversation, their earlier presentation, name tag, dress etc. may allow you to deliver a more 'accurately tuned' elevator pitch.

5. Write yourself at least one 'setup story.' Do several if you're likely to come across identifiably different Buyers for whom you can tune your story.

6. What is the Known Category of your Offering? Is it immediately identifiable or do you need to explain it? Did you make it up or is it universally known?

7. Who are your competitors? Do they include Doing Nothing and/or Doing It Myself? List all the ways you're different from each of them:

8. What is 'The Vibe'? Do you have it? Can you create it? Does a colleague have it?
   The Vibe is the creation in the buyer of the same motivation to buy from you that you have in you to influence them to buy.

9 Why have an Elevator Pitch 'suite', not just one pitch? List four situations where you actually might need to use a variation.

A raw 'catch all' elevator pitch may not immediately generate an interest in every potential buyer. By tuning the introductory story, the TakeAways you choose to mention, and the 'unlike' statements to their direct needs, you're more likely to agree a call to action.

Notes

Notes

About the Author

Trevor's career started as a British Army captain with an honours engineering degree from Cranfield University. He served in the REME - in Northern Ireland, Germany, the Falklands War and the Commando Brigade. He then joined the London Stock Exchange and worked his way up the City of London sales ladder. He started as a quota carrying sales rep, then sales manager and managing director. Along way, he influenced clients in Finance, Telco, and Transport to buy complex technology solutions, software products and business services.

He ran worldwide channels and enjoyed great success partnering with IBM's global software business. He jointly started - in his home office - the European operation of what became a thriving NASDAQ company and led his team over three years to a turnover of $32m. Before that, he set up a successful new business unit at Logica International selling complex banking solutions. His technology career started with designing, coding and selling real-time navigation software for racing yachts.

He now runs the management consultancy, Holis Associates Inc., is a visiting lecturer at the University of Ottawa, and loves travelling worldwide – training and speaking to companies, sales teams, entrepreneur groups and individuals about Turning Selling into Buying.

Originally from a Scottish family, but raised in London UK, Trevor has now made Ottawa, Canada his home. The four amazing women in his life inspire him every day, but when he has time and energy left, he loves motorcycle racing and touring, kayaking and canoeing, sailing and cycling.

He tweets on matters worth tweeting about @sellingtobuying and can be found at *ca.linkedin.com/in/sellingtobuying/*